A LATIN AMERICAN SPEAKS

THE MACMILLAN COMPANY
NEW YORK · BOSTON · CHICAGO
DALLAS · ATLANTA · SAN FRANCISCO

MACMILLAN AND CO., LIMITED
LONDON · BOMBAY · CALCUTTA
MADRAS · MELBOURNE

**THE MACMILLAN COMPANY
OF CANADA, LIMITED**
TORONTO

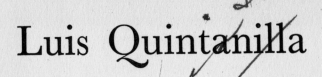

Luis Quintanilla

A
LATIN AMERICAN
SPEAKS

1943

NEW YORK

THE MACMILLAN COMPANY

To the men, women, and children of Republican Spain

with pride in a common ancestry
and faith in a common victory

I humbly dedicate this book

Foreword

THIS is not a book written by one American on *the other* America. It is a book on America, by an American.

Heretofore, the problems of the Western Hemisphere have been examined from the limited angle of North, Central, or South. These distinctions—however useful in the past—are now obsolete. The America of today must be viewed as a unit.

Columbus discovered America in *1492*. Americans waited until *1942*. Many factors account for the delay. But, paradoxically, it took the crimes and blunders of a Hitler to hasten America's discovery of America. Little wonder that a Latin American diplomat humorously proposed the erection of the Führer's statue, in full military regalia—with swastika, mustaches, and all—in the patio of the Pan American Union, amidst the languid palms and screaming parrots.

If it is true that a common threat awakened us to the existence of America, it is also true that only a common belief in the goodness of a certain way of life, which we call democratic, holds us together. Threat begets fear; and fear alone creates a negative attitude. It merely compels one to stand against something. On the other hand, faith in democracy—America's lasting bond—is a positive force. It impels us to go forward. Where? That is precisely what the following chapters endeavor to answer.

The book is divided into three parts: the first deals with national conditions, the second with inter-American relations, and the third with America's international role.

Of course, the feelings and views expressed in these pages are those of a Latin American, a citizen of Mexico caught in the stream of world events. Yet the outlook is genuinely *all*-American. Because of this, it may at times displease incorrigible chauvinists. But the hour is much too serious for anyone to worry about trivialities or nasty people. Today in every continent of the world men are fighting and dying. While we can, we must endeavor to understand.

In our Hemisphere, we share vital problems. Tomorrow will bring us even closer together. Tomorrow may well be America's day. We must prepare ourselves for it.

Finally, throughout these pages I have tried to remain resolutely fair and sincere. This and the nature of my topic compose perhaps the only merit of the book.

Contents

Part One: INTRA-*America*

CHAPTER I

America: What?

To the question "What is America?" a valid answer may be given only if we assume that America *is;* that there is one America.

Following roughly geographical lines we speak of two Americas, North and South; more exactly, an *Anglo-Saxon* America confined to the United States and Canada, and a *Latin* America embracing the twenty other republics of the Hemisphere. This broad generalization has acquired such popularity that seldom, if ever, does one stop to consider whether it is valid or sound. To most people, the existence of two Americas is plain axiomatic truth. However, if we begin differentiating Americas, there is no reason why we should stop at *two*. Why leave out English- or French-speaking America, Spanish or Portuguese America, Indian or Negro America, Catholic or Protestant America? Not to mention the hybrid Americas, Mestizo, Mulatto, and Zambo. All these are valid distinctions indeed. But, however useful they might prove in a description of America, they do not help us to understand it. And today, more than ever, we must understand America. No international fog, however dense, should hide it from us.

Of course, there is one America! To feel it, we do not have to reject arbitrarily the originality of national features. It simply requires a broad interpretation of our continent. Knowledge implies analysis, differentiation; but there is no complete knowledge without a synthesis.

The narrow, elementary Americas are so well known that they require no explanation here. They are authentic, but none of them may claim *per se* a monopoly in the constitution of America. Moreover, most of them are brought forth not to explain Greater America but rather to deny it. For instance, *Spanish* America gives birth to Hispanism; *Indian* America, to Indianism; *Latin* America, to Latin Americanism; *Portuguese* and *Spanish* America, to Ibero-Americanism. Only *America* provides a ground for inter-Americanism. Individual Americas are so narrow that they exclude one another. For instance, Hispanism is irreconcilable with Indianism. Each is narrower than and therefore incompatible with Ibero-Americanism or Latin Americanism. Only inter-Americanism, affecting *Pan* America, is broad enough to include all the Americas.

Moreover, there is no limit to the theoretical disintegration of America. Recently, analytical scholars have discovered two brand-new Americas. I refer to the erudite distinction, not between North and South America, but this time between *Eastern* and *Western* America; an *Atlantic* and a *Pacific* America. This newest of all differentiations is certainly as valid as the others. It rests essentially upon the contention that Eastern America, facing the Atlantic and Europe, is different from Western America, facing the Pacific and Asia. To the first, "the Atlantic is for them a pool, an English Channel, a strait, which each day becomes easier to cross." And for this reason "the Argentine, like the Brazilian, the Cuban, the Uruguayan, or the New Yorker looks much more readily to Europe than to what is behind him: Western America." What is then Western America? "An America where the Spanish tradition has become most concrete. An America that has turned toward itself. The very circumstance of facing a sea as vast as the Pacific, the impossibility of establishing relations with Asia, has caused

these countries to have a very different cultural formation." [1]
Those are the words of a subtle Colombian essayist. According to him, the cities most typical of Eastern America—
New York, Habana, Rio de Janeiro, Montevideo, Buenos
Aires—are of European cut because they have always faced
toward Europe and have established easy and permanent
contacts with that continent. Whereas San Francisco, Bogotá,
Lima, and La Paz, in Western America, have been unable
to keep in touch with Europe or to contact Asia and the
Orient, because of the immensity of the Pacific Ocean. These
cities had to look into themselves, that is to say into the
past, the tradition of the Spanish Colony. Arciniegas claims:
"Moreover, one feels deeper within this [Spanish] tradition
in California, speaking English, than in Buenos Aires,
speaking Spanish." And as to the United States, where the
difference between Eastern and Western America can also
be felt, "there is as profound a difference between New York
and San Francisco as there is between New York and the
rest of the Pacific cities [of Latin America]." [2] Pedro Hen-
ríquez Ureña, the eminent Dominican scholar, agrees completely with Arciniegas. Says he: "The distinction which he
has established between the America which faces the Atlantic
—and therefore Europe—and the America which faces the
Pacific, and therefore emptiness, because the Orient is too
far away—is a very real distinction which I have keenly felt.
. . . What the Spaniards brought to America still exists un-
affected by the great changes wrought on the Atlantic coast by
constant communication with Europe. Indeed, even in California—where changes have naturally been greater because a
change of language has taken place—there exist those Spanish
roots which can be perceived, if not in the language, at least

[1] "Is America a Continent?—A Round Table Discussion," *Points of View,*
No. 2, Oct., 1941 (Division of Intellectual Cooperation, Pan American
Union, Washington, D.C.), p. 4.
[2] *Ibid.*

in taste. There is something Spanish in the taste of many people of California, and there is a Californian way of life which is so different from the Bostonian or the New York way, or in general from that of the East or the Middle West, that one feels it to be a totally different milieu. . . . And so it is of paramount importance for Latin America that the inhabitants of the Atlantic coast become acquainted with those of the Pacific coast, and vice versa. . . . The Atlantic America ends abruptly. One has only to cross the Andes to find oneself in Hispano-Indian America." [3]

But of all the partitions of our Hemisphere, none is more generally accepted than that between *Anglo-Saxon* America and *Latin* America. This distinction, resting superficially on linguistic grounds, remained, at least until the collapse of France, the Hemisphere antinomy *par excellence*. With incredible simplicity, it divided the continent into: (a) an *Anglo-Saxon* America, materialistic, money-minded, and brutal; and (b) a *Latin* America, idealistic, generous, and gentle. In the drama of our Hemisphere, the United States played Sancho Panza to Latin America's Don Quixote. The things of the spirit belonged to the Latins, those of matter, to the Saxons. Thus, for many years, subsisted this continental dualism of Good and Evil. The past record of United States imperialism, with its ruthless disregard of the sovereignty of many Latin American republics, contributed powerfully to widening the gulf.

Admitted that the twenty non-English-speaking Hemisphere republics speak Latin languages, and that two other outstanding Latin features of those republics are the Catholic Church and Roman Law, let us see how Latin are the populations and therefore the temperament of Latin America.

Roughly speaking, there are substantially fewer than twenty-five million Whites in Latin America out of a total population, for the twenty republics, of one hundred

[3] *Ibid.*, pp. 6-7.

twenty-five million. In other words, Latin America is only *one-fifth* White. From 50 to 75 per cent of the populations of Paraguay, Bolivia, Ecuador, Guatemala, and Nicaragua is of pure *Indian* blood. Honduras, Venezuela, Peru, Colombia, Mexico, Panama, and El Salvador are anywhere from 50 to 75 per cent *Mestizo.* Haiti is almost completely *Negro,* and the Dominican Republic practically all *Mulatto.* Only Chile, Costa Rica, Argentina, and Uruguay—four "Latin" republics out of the twenty—are predominantly *White.*

In the light of these statistics, it becomes apparent that the contention for a *Latin* America finds no demographic ground. I do not have before me the percentages of people of Latin extraction among the populations of the United States and Canada, but important sections of these two countries are, demographically speaking, more Latin than many of our republics.

The well-known Peruvian scholar and author, Luis Alberto Sánchez, denies that there is such a thing as a Spanish, a Catholic, or a Latin tradition in our America. Writes he:

"One of the most common errors made in the United States in estimating our spiritual and cultural background is to confuse the Hispanic with the colonial, and the colonial with the South American. This line of thought will lead us to another amazing conclusion: that one can hardly speak of a unified Spanish tradition because in the Spain of that time a struggle was going on between various conflicting elements: Arabs, Goths, Latins. An attempt has also been made, under the shade of a supposedly Hispanic tradition, to identify Latin America with the orthodox Catholic tradition; but while basically our countries are Catholic, espe- cially in form, we must not forget that our religious belief includes factors at variance with orthodoxy, and it is pre- cisely from these that the tradition of our independence stems.

"Our Liberators were freethinkers, liberals, and many of

them heterodox. Neither Bolívar nor San Martín nor O'Higgins were fervent Catholics; rather they were Masons, like Miranda, the precursor. Later, among the greatest intellectual leaders who gave character to our culture, neither González Prada, nor Montalvo, nor Lastarria, nor Bilbao shone particularly for their orthodoxy. They were freethinkers, like Sarmiento. We have a freethinking tradition inspired in Voltaire and, during the nineteenth century, in Renan. Whence, therefore, originated the claim of an orthodox tradition in South America? And when I say South America I include in the term Mexico and Central America, since the natural boundary between the two Americas is the Río Grande. . . .

"As far as I know, neither the Indians nor the Negroes came from Rome. So that the supposedly Latin tradition is another of the many fictions or one-sided interpretations utilized to smuggle in intellectual contraband." [4]

The truth is that *Latin* America is a French creation—a brilliant name given by Paris to a vast cultural province over which the genius of France claimed, for many years, an undisputed and well-deserved sovereignty.

During the colonial period, the Ibero-American populations were kept under the exclusive intellectual rule of Spain and Portugal. Territorial independence did not bring intellectual emancipation. However, after independence, the former Spanish and Portuguese colonies were open to other foreign influences. They did not wish to continue under the spiritual hegemony of the Mother Countries. They were eager to find a means of expression genuinely theirs. Naturally, the first step in that direction was a systematic rejection of outworn colonial patterns; but to reject Spanish or Portuguese culture was not equivalent to creating a new culture. For many

---

[4] "The Presence of Tradition," by Luis Alberto Sánchez, transl. Angel Flores, *Points of View*, No. 4 (Division of Intellectual Cooperation, Pan American Union, Washington, D.C.), pp. 2-3.

years we were at a loss: we had detached ourselves from the Old World, but had found no time to create a New. "We have abandoned the Old World, and we have not yet found the New," said the Brazilian, Afranio Peixoto, in a most enlightening discussion on the cultural ties between Europe and Latin America.[5]

Once freed from Spanish and Portuguese influence we were gradually drawn into the dazzling orbit of French culture. Paris—*Ville Lumière*—became the intellectual capital of a *Latin* America. French *esprit* succeeded where the massive lances of the Conquistadores had failed: it conquered the soul of Ibero-America. So irresistible was the spell that for generations we actually lived with our feet in the Western Hemisphere but our heads in France. For nearly a century, the highest ambition of a cultured, well-to-do Latin American was to visit Paris and stay there as long as he could.

At home we read and spoke French, ate and dressed French, lived and thought French. Never in history had a foreign capital so completely fascinated the minds of peoples from twenty republics of a Hemisphere thousands of miles away. Without Paris, life was not worth living . . . Yet it cannot be said that we were happy. We understood France. We loved it, as we still do. But we knew that, not being French, we were left without a culture. As Leopoldo Zea writes: "This is the core of our problem: we do not feel the heirs of an autochthonous culture, the latter lacks meaning to us; and the one which, like Europe, means something to us, we do not feel is ours." [6] We had lost contact with Spain and discovered France, but we had yet to find ourselves. To that wandering stage, characterized by melancholy, corresponds the artificial existence of a Latin America; melan-

[5] Held under the auspices of the International Institute of Intellectual Cooperation at Buenos Aires in 1937.

[6] "En torno a una filosofía americana," in *Cuadernos americanos*, May-June, 1942, p. 67.

choly, because we knew that Paris was only a stop and not a terminus in our quest for culture. After its emancipation from England, the United States went through a somewhat similar trial, a painful gestation.

Nothing seems more anachronistic than fascist Hispanism, a movement which attempts to revive the ghost of the Colony and to drive countries like Mexico back into the old Spanish background. Such retrogression is impossible because today there is America. As F. Carmona Nenclares states,[7] Franco's Hispanism is nothing more than Spanish fascism adapted to Latin American consumption. It is creole nazism.

In a timely address given in July, 1939, before the Institute of Public Affairs at the University of Virginia, Professor David Efrón, now Latin American adviser to the National Planning Association, threw full light upon the direct connection between Hispanism and nazism, through Franco's falangists. From that address I take the following quotations:

"José Pemartin, National Chief of University and Secondary Education of the Franco regime, in a book called *What Is the New Spirit?* [8] in praising 'the magnificence of the German National Socialist Movement,' declares that one of the imperatives of Spanish existence is:

" 'To extend and expand . . . our political jurisdiction, above all, over the South American countries, of Hispanic soul and language.'

"Julián Mario Rubio, President of the University of Valladolid, in an article 'National Spain and the South American Countries,' appearing in the March, 1939, issue of the Franco magazine, *Spain,* published in the United States, says the following:

" 'Nationalist Spain is bound to Latin America by a triple

[7] See "Hispanismo e Hispanidad," in *Cuadernos americanos,* May-June, 1942.
[8] Burgos, 1932, p. 137.

bond—the past, the present, and the future. It is immortal Hispanicism. It is Spain of the past, once again placed on the route to mission in Latin America. Nationalist Spain does not take a single step without considering the motherland and Latin America simultaneously: because we want to triumph and conquer in our war, in order to share the victory with our brothers across the Atlantic, and if necessary, to give it to them so that they may be saved. . . . Spain maintains unharmed . . . her imperial enthusiasm, her desire for universality. . . . This tradition, whether we will it or not, is as Spanish as it is Peruvian, or Chilean, or Argentinian, or Colombian.'

"Compare all this with what Marshal Goering said in his *Nationale Zeitung* of Essen:

" 'Spain is the key question for the two continents. The victory of Franco decides between chaos and reconstruction in the two hemispheres. His final victory alone can preserve for Ibero-American countries their true Spanish culture and tradition. If these are lost, then the American continent is more or less surrendered to the influences of the Yankees and the Muscovites, who march arm in arm, especially in the New World.' [9]

"At the victory procession of May 19, 1939, in Madrid, General Franco, at the head of 250,000 Italian, German, and Spanish soldiers, appeared surrounded by the banners of the Spanish Conquistadores of America."

If that were not enough, I might call your attention to a most significant dispatch sent by the Associated Press correspondent directly from Madrid on April 21, 1942. That dispatch was headlined by the Latin American press, and yet, as far as I know, it passed unnoticed by the North American press and public opinion. In this extraordinary document, whose authenticity was never questioned or denied by any

[9] Quoted by Wallace R. Deuel in a special cable to the Chicago *Daily News,* Feb. 18, 1939.

of Franco's agents anywhere, Serrano Suñer (Spanish Goebbels and then Franco's Secretary of State) invited Latin Americans to turn against the United States and sabotage Pan Americanism, in order to help Hitler save the world from bolshevik domination. Not satisfied with "congratulating" Argentina and Chile for their "aloofness," this official spokesman of the self-styled *caudillo* (whose agents enjoyed diplomatic immunity in all the nations of the Hemisphere, with the exception of Mexico) tried to bribe Latin American republics by specifically promising them trade rewards if they showed a willingness to play ball with Hitler. Here is Serrano Suñer's statement, as it widely appeared in the Latin American press:

"We are extraordinarily pleased to see that Argentina and Chile demonstrate with absolute certainty and energy that they understand the significance of the present conflict by withholding themselves outside the circle of countries controlled by Russia. * . . . The blood, fervor, and lives of many of our comrades remain in the frozen steppes of Russia.

"It is most urgent that we save the world from bolshevism. General Franco said in Seville that in spite of the difficulties through which we are passing, if the great German masses are unable to stop the tremendous Russian danger, *Spain will help, not with a mere fifteen thousand men, but with a million.* For this reason we are saddened to see that Hispano-American countries, which possess the same blood and spirit as Spain, find themselves willing to take positions that deny the high ideals of the Hispanic world. . . .

"I am convinced that *at the end of the war a great future will be opened for those countries that understand how or are able to remain aloof* from the margin of the struggle. During the civil war we were more badly treated by France than by any other country, but since the defeat of France, our relations have improved. The Spaniards know how to respect misfortune. The great figure of Marshal Pétain is

* All the italics in quoted passages are the author's.

sincerely dear to us. I believe that *it was a wise move on his part to give over the power to M. Laval.* Although on former occasions he was called a traitor, I believe that history will demonstrate that *Laval is right,* and instead of treating him as a traitor, he will be proven a good Frenchman.

"If I were French, this intelligent solution would interest me very much, now that France realizes finally that she spent a whole winter hoping day after day that the Russians would destroy the German army.

"As Europeans, *we cannot remain indifferent to the incorporation of France*—which is such an important part of the continent—*into the New European Order,* or to its contribution in the war." [10]

If ideological affinities and the historic fact of Nazi-Franco collaboration throughout the war against the Spanish Republic did not count, what more would we need to be convinced that some day the democracies will regret their policy of appeasement with Franco?

Of course we feel Spanish, by blood, tradition, and language! But the Spain we have in our minds and in our hearts is the one that Franco's Moorish troops, Mussolini's legionnaires and Hitler's bombers tried vainly to wipe out of existence. Natural affinities with Spain? Yes! With Loyalist Spain, the Republican Spain whose triumph will become inevitable after Hitler's collapse.

Nazism wears no swastika among Spanish-speaking Americans. Undisguised, it would get nowhere . . . It needs a mask: that is where Spanish fascism comes in. Thanks to it, nazism may move about unmolested in this Hemisphere. But as long as the United Nations tolerate fascist usurpation of power in Spain, World War II will not have been won for the cause of democracy, at least in the minds of Spanish American democrats.

Even from our Latin American point of view, this Hispan-

[10] Translated from *Novedades*, Mexico City, Apr. 22, 1942, where it appeared under the headline, "España se define al lado del eje."

ism is shameful. In order to clear the ground for the later military moves of Hitler, it is intent upon the execrable task of deflating the national values of Latin America. In articles, pamphlets, books, and lectures, foreign propagandists and a handful of native fascists have been actively engaged in dislodging national heroes from their pedestals. These adventurers dare to put their nazi-branded fingers on such giants as Hidalgo, Bolívar, Morelos, Juárez, Sarmiento, and Martí. And whom do they want to enthrone? Cortés, Pizarro, Valdivia, and other ghosts of the Spanish Conquest. They vilify America, Freedom and Democracy; while they glorify the long dead and buried Spanish "Empire," the counterfeit glamour of Nippo-Nazi-Fascism and the heavy gloom of theocracy. In our countries, where the very mention of these words arouses indignation, the stooges of Gestapo-Hispanism even dare to exalt such "spiritual" achievements as the Spanish Inquisition or the dreadful *Encomiendas*. But there is America . . .

America is a continent. So conspicuous a fact has been disputed by sophisticated minds. Still, America is a continent. In comparison, Asia, Africa, Europe, and Australia are mere geographical fictions. America is the only continent totally one and distinct. The other four are crowded in the Eastern Hemisphere. America occupies, in solitary grandeur, the entire Western Hemisphere. It is free, horizontally and vertically, east and west, north and south, from ocean to ocean, and from pole to pole.

America is well formed, symmetrical, and graceful: powerful chest of Canada and the United States, tapering waist of Mexico and Central America, well rounded Amazonian hips, slender legs of Argentina and Chile. Its topography is simple, logical. An almost uninterrupted range of lofty mountains, stretching from Alaska to Tierra del Fuego: Rocky Mountains, Sierra Madre, Cordillera—three Americas linked together; a gigantic palisade standing out against the Pacific.

Eastward, the land gradually slopes down until it reaches
the shores of the Atlantic; unfolding fertile plains: North
American prairies, Middle American llanos, South American
pampas. And spreading over those twelve million square
miles, the world's largest lake and river systems: Great Lakes
and Titicaca, the Mississippi and the Amazon, the Orinoco
and the Plata; and two thunderous curtains of rushing water
—Niagara, Iguazú—falling on the wide-open stages of America North and America South.

There are all kinds of climates in the Western Hemisphere. Quite frequently altitude corrects latitude. Between
snowcapped volcanoes and the inferno of the tropical jungle
lie diaphanous plateaus combining tropical sunlight and
thin mountain coolness.

Stately, powerful, unique: such is physical America, dis-
covered by accident, named by mistake. Columbus discovered it because it stood in his way to India. A careless pro-
fessor of cosmography is responsible for naming it after
Amerigo Vespucci, boastful, unreliable sixteenth century
Florentine explorer. Originally, the name was restricted to
Brazil; later to South America. For a long time, the Western
Hemisphere was referred to as "Terra Incognita," "Novo
Mundo"; finally, America. But remember, it was only dis-
covered, not invented. America was already very much there;
only, Europe had not noticed it. Neither had aboriginal
America noticed Europe.

America is a history. Again, that simple assertion has been
disputed by subtle intellectuals. Following Hegel, some have
repeated that America has yet *no* history; for it is still in a
state of Nature, that anteroom of History.[11] I know that
America is a continent because I stand on its soil. I know
that it is a history, because I am living one of its moments.

[11] See "Do the Americas Have a Common History?" by Edmundo O'Gor-
man, transl. Angel Flores, *Points of View*, No. 3, Dec. 1941. (Division of
Intellectual Cooperation, Pan American Union, Washington, D.C.).

Many centuries before Columbus—in fact, before Christ—
Aztecs and Mayas had built empires comparable to those of
Asia Minor or Egypt. Still flourishing at the time of the con-
queror Pizarro, the Incas had built highways and bridges,
in a well-organized empire not unlike Rome. Today our
Hemisphere has the privilege of being both a monument to
the past and a cradle of the future: inscrutable past indeed,
and unpredictable future. Centuries before Discovery, there
stood Mexico's Place of the Gods, Teotihuacán, glory of the
Toltec Age. In Middle America, the Mayas of Southern
Mexico, Guatemala, and Honduras had built Chichen Itza,
Holy City of Feathered Serpent Kukulcán; Uxmal and Pa-
lenque; Quiriguá and Copán. To the South, pre-Inca civilizations had erected Machu Picchu; and there was Cuzco, imperial capital of the Incas, with its Temple of the Sun.

Following the discoverers, came English settlers and Spanish Conquistadores. The Pilgrims found scattered nomads.
The Conquerors had to subdue sedentary populations. The
Pilgrims had left Europe for good, determined never to go
back, eager to find a new life in a New World. The Conquistadores left Europe temporarily, intent upon going back.
The Settlers came to America in search of freedom and security. They and the Pioneers built a new world with their
own hands; they created a new life. The Conquistadores remained loyal to Europe, King, and Church. They were more
interested in transplanting an Old World than in creating
a New. Their motives were different indeed, but they both
made America. Anglo-Saxons brought invention; Spaniards,
tradition. They do not compete with, but supplement each
other. An altogether New World would be as inconceivable
as a tree without roots. In this Hemisphere, two worlds
found a common ground.

Pilgrims and Puritans were representative men; not like
Cortés or Pizarro, makers of history. They worked patiently,
anonymously. The Spanish Colony created men like Bishop

Bartolomé de las Casas, women like Sor Juana Inés de la Cruz; it also produced Liberators. From Conquistador to *Libertador,* from Master to Emancipator of men: there is one of America's miracles. . . . What is it, in this Hemisphere, which so radically transforms man?

Liberty seems to be America's natural climate. The highest title bestowed by Spanish Americans upon one single individual is that of Liberator. Up to this day Bolívar remains, in our minds, the outstanding American, because he won the title of Liberator. Europe admired Conquerors, America honors Liberators and Emancipators.

America's next historical moment, Independence, saw us fighting together against a common foe: Europe. The simultaneity of our struggles for independence was more than coincidence in space and time; it was coincidence in feeling and purpose. First, we wanted freedom from Europe: then, Freedom!

Washington, Hidalgo, Bolívar, and San Martín had been builders of nations. Builders—this is another essential feature of America: freedom in order to build. Under Bolívar and San Martín, practically all of Spanish America won its emancipation from the Mother Country. North, Central, and South, it was practically *one* battle in which we shared one another's misfortunes and triumphs. We did imbibe much of the revolutionary impulse from Anglo-Saxon Americans, but on the other hand, as Professor Bolton has pointed out, the United States owes to its Latin American forefathers the independence of much of its territory. He says:

"We [the United States] have been taught that the American Revolution was fought and won by Washington and his comrades in arms. Now we know that Washington liberated only a very small fraction of America. Territorially considered, the Greater American Revolution was in Latin America. Washington freed from Europe only the eastern third of the United States, as far west as the Mississippi River.

. . . The rest of the United States and all of America from Oregon to Patagonia were freed by our Latin American fore-fathers—by Pedro I of Brazil, by Bolívar and San Martín of Spanish South America, and by Hidalgo, Morelos. . . . Independence was first celebrated in California, for example, not in 1776, but in 1822. California, like all our Southwest and Mexico, has two Liberty Bells—one in Philadelphia, which we westerners revere, but possess only through our adoption; and one in Mexico City, the one which was rung for our freedom by Hidalgo in 1810. In a large portion of our country we have two independence days, one on the Fourth of July, through adoption, and one on the sixteenth of September in our own right. For we in all the Southwest owe our independence from Europe to our Mexican fore-fathers." [12]

In that gigantic struggle for the emancipation of some twenty new countries, we in the Americas helped one another. We may consider ourselves as veterans of a continental war. But our territorial freedom did not suffice. The next step was a struggle for Democracy. Washington, Hidalgo, Bolívar, Sucre, and San Martín had won territorial independence and nationality. Men like Jefferson, Morelos, Lincoln, Juárez, Martí, or Sarmiento gave us political freedom and democracy. Thanks to them, our Hemisphere is entirely Republican. The continent of Freedom became also that of Democracy. Bolívar had presaged an America which would be "Mother of Republics." The dream of the Liberator came true. America is more and more what Bolívar wanted it to be.

Not all Americans have been Liberators. In fact there have been, on our continental stage, too many villains.

---

[12] "We Owe Latin America," address delivered Nov. 9, 1939, by Herbert E. Bolton, head of the Department of History, University of California, to the Conference on Inter-American Relations in the Field of Education, Washington, D.C. Quoted in *American Neighbors* (American Red Cross, Washington, D.C., 1940), p. 10.

Powerful countries have, at times, disregarded the rights and even the integrity of their weaker neighbors. Mexico, for instance, lost more than half of its territory to the United States of America. But the fact remains that, in America, even those who had conquered by force were not proud of their record. No one denounced more energetically than Representative Abraham Lincoln, of Illinois, the injustice of the Mexican War. Americans are human, not angels; but it should be noted that they are reluctant to glorify their sins. That is a hopeful sign. The entire Hemisphere has not produced a militaristic hero. And that, again, speaks well of America.

Not all Americans have been democratic emancipators, either. In fact, we have had so many dictators and tyrants that occasional or systematic pessimists do their best to undermine our faith in America by bringing out the fact that in our Hemisphere, I should say in Latin America, Democracy has been a mere legend or is now a failure. We know our deficiencies; but we want to correct them because we believe in Democracy. We share, at least, a common belief in the essential quality and the ultimate triumph of that Democracy. And a community of ideals is as fundamental and far-reaching as a community of experiences. The dreams of yesterday have become present history; those of today will be the facts of tomorrow. This common faith is so deeply American that even our non-democratic forces—and they are many and powerful—have to wear the mask of democracy when they dare to fight it. And that is symptomatic.

Freedom, democracy, America: the three words are synonyms. Not one of them is conceivable without the others. A blow to freedom is a blow to democracy; a blow to democracy is a blow to America. Because of that, World War II is America's war, *all* America's war. Thomas Paine, immortal citizen of the world and pioneer of American freedom, had been hardly a year in America when he wrote, in *Common Sense:* "The sun never shone on a cause of greater worth. 'Tis not the affair of a city, a county, a province, or a kingdom; but of a continent. . . . Now is the seed-time of continental union, faith and honor. The least fracture now will be like a name engraved with the point of a pin on the tender rind of a young oak; the wound would enlarge with the tree." [13] These words, written more than a century and a half ago, have a meaning today. This war against militaristic imperialism, against physical and mental oppression, is the affair of our continent. There must be no names engraved with the point of a pin on the tender rind of our America. The wound would enlarge with the tree. We must keep intact that mighty and generous tree—because it purifies the air we breathe; because we have often rested in its shade; and because we want our children and our children's children to enjoy its protection. It shall be marked by no wound.

America is a culture. Two hundred sixty million people are still building it; men of all races and creeds, Indians, White men, and Negroes. America was a challenge to the absurd myth of racial superiority. To those who still preach national, racial, or religious supremacy, one may point to this Hemisphere and say: Look at America!

Our culture is not exclusive but inclusive. It is richer than any other on earth, because it incorporates mankind. They all made it; there lies its originality. It is inaccurate to say that our culture is that of Europe. America is Europe and the world; not an addition, but a multiplication; not a sterile juxtaposition of disconnected cultures, but more and more a synthesis in which individual ingredients spontaneously blend their identities for the benefit of the final product. Eliminate, through prejudice, any one of the ingredients and you will automatically impoverish that product.

[13] Quoted in *The Living Thoughts of Tom Paine,* presented by John Dos Passos (Longmans, Green & Co., New York, 1940), p. 65.

To divide America is to weaken it, not only in the political but in the cultural field as well. Our essential originality lies in the limitless amplitude of our culture. It is, if any, a universal culture. That is one more reason for our unshakable conviction in its ultimate triumph. Never has mankind witnessed so portentous an enterprise.

Culture is like a symphony: the more instruments, the more powerful the orchestra; and the more powerful the orchestra, the richer can be the symphony. Also, America's culture is a dialogue. Never was it meant to be a soliloquy. It claims no infallibility. We like to keep wide open the windows of our continent, so that light may come in, and the breeze from any direction. Finally, we wish to hear other peoples' voices and we want our own to be heard by them. American culture is real, universal: human.

We are truly human when we share universal feelings. In fact only then are we certain that we exist. The more we find in others, the more we know ourselves. America is rich in human material, that is why it is so authentic. We despise conventionalism, superficiality. We dislike automatism as well as useless complexity. We refuse to lose contact with life. To sophisticated minds we may at times appear candid. Some Europeans have even called us childish. Let us be proud of our American candor. Far from childishness, it is maturity. Only Mickey Rooney seems to us in the right age for sophistication.

Dreiser's *An American Tragedy,* Dos Passos' *42nd Parallel,* Sinclair Lewis' *Main Street,* and Steinbeck's *The Grapes of Wrath* are voices of the Hemisphere because they satisfy this American longing for authenticity. Even when United States writers of such talent as Pearl Buck or Ernest Hemingway write on foreign lands, they remain true to the American naturalist tradition, by writing *The Good Earth,* or *For Whom the Bell Tolls.* Latin America's outstanding novels are equally authentic: for example, Ricardo Güiraldes' *Don*

Segundo Sombra, Euclydes da Cunha's *Os Sertões,* José
Eustacio Rivera's *La Vorágine,* Gregorio López y Fuentes'
El Indio, Rómulo Gallegos' *Doña Bárbara,* to mention only
a few. And the same could be said of our painters, our sculp-
tors, our musicians, our architects, our dancers, and last but
not least our many great poets.

The culture of America is wholesome. If I may employ
here a well-known Bergsonian terminology, I will say that
America's culture is both horizontal and vertical. It *ex*tends
and it *in*tends. It is horizontal in that, through sympathy, it
spreads to all men the world over. And it is vertical in that,
within each man, it involves his entire personality. On this
side of the world, we mean to live generously, authentically.
For that end, America's continent, history, and culture are
well suited. In fact, so well suited that they have made it
possible for a dream of mankind to materialize. In spite of
the multiple national differences, America has a coherent
personality; and when it speaks the world can hear one
majestic voice.

America is a voice. In the confusion of world voices, that
of America can be identified by two characteristics: strength
and purity. A strength that emanates from an immense and
wealthy continent; a purity that flows from the lips of decent
and free people. The world feels America's material weight.
History has recorded America's moral value.

In times of struggle and despair, our forefathers heard
the voices of America lash tyranny and proclaim liberty.
Today, millions listen to these same challenging voices,
speaking again for the rights of man. Uttered by people of
all races, countries, and creeds, America's voices—whether of
Paine, Washington, Jefferson, Lincoln, Morelos, Juárez,
Martí, Morazán, Bolívar, San Martín, O'Higgins, Del Valle,
or Sarmiento, or more recently, Woodrow Wilson, Franklin
D. Roosevelt, Henry A. Wallace, Lázaro Cárdenas, Manuel
Ávila Camacho, Ezequiel Padilla, or Vicente Lombardo

Toledano—form but one portentous voice: a continental appeal for democracy.

Listen to PAINE, speaking on the eve of American Independence: "O, ye that love mankind! Ye that dare oppose not only the tyranny but the tyrant, stand forth! Every spot of the old world is overrun with oppression. Freedom hath been hunted around the globe. . . . O! Receive the fugitive, and prepare in time an asylum for mankind."

JEFFERSON: "The last hope for human liberty in this world rests on us. . . . Let us consecrate a sanctuary for those whom the misrule of Europe may compel to seek happiness in other climes."

DEL VALLE: "America spreads through all zones, but it forms one single continent; Americans are scattered through all climes, but they should form one single family."

MORELOS: "Indian, mulatto, and mestizo are designations that must be abolished. . . . There should be only one name for all of us: American! . . . The townspeople are the owners of the land. . . . Land must be turned over to the people so that it can be tilled and never be rented." (These words came from the Mexican leader who, in the early nineteenth century, had proclaimed that equality, security, prosperity, and liberty were the essential rights of the American man.)

LINCOLN: "This country, with its institutions, belongs to the people who inhabit it. . . . Labor is prior to, and independent of, capital. Capital is only the fruit of labor, and could never have existed if labor had not first existed. Workingmen are the basis of all governments. . . . The strongest bond of human sympathy, outside the family relation, should be one uniting all working people of all nations and tongues and kindreds. . . . Thank God we live in a country where workingmen have the right to strike!"

SARMIENTO: "He sins against mankind who foments and propagates racial conflict and hatred."

JUÁREZ: "Peace is respect for the rights of others."

WOODROW WILSON: "The nations of the world must in some way band themselves together to see that the right prevails as against any sort of selfish aggression."

FRANKLIN D. ROOSEVELT: "In the field of world policy, I would dedicate this nation to the policy of the Good Neighbor . . . The neighbor who resolutely respects himself and, because he does so, respects the rights of others."

LÁZARO CÁRDENAS: "As long as there exist great masses of human beings dispossessed of the lands of their ancestors, of their rights as men and as citizens, and treated like beasts or machines, it can never be said that equality and justice prevail in America."

MANUEL ÁVILA CAMACHO: "The moral condemnation of aggressors is not enough. Our continent cannot stay out. . . . So precious is the enjoyment of independence that we cannot remain still and let others do the fighting for us. . . . If we wish to remain free, we must begin by making ourselves worthy of that freedom."

HENRY A. WALLACE: "The march of freedom of the past one hundred fifty years has been a long-drawn-out people's revolution. . . . I say that the century on which we are entering—the century which will come out of this war—can be and must be the century of the common man. . . . The people's revolution is on the march, and the devil and all his angels cannot prevail against it. They cannot prevail, for on the side of the people is the Lord. . . . We who fight in the people's cause will never stop until that cause is won."

SUMNER WELLES: "Our victory must bring in its train the liberation of all peoples. Discrimination between peoples because of their race, creed, or color must be abolished. The age of imperialism is ended."

And EZEQUIEL PADILLA: "The men who gloriously fell on Wake Island and in the Philippines have not fallen in the defense of the honor and sovereignty of the United States alone. They have also met their death in the defense of human liberties and the free destinies of these Americas."

Or VICENTE LOMBARDO TOLEDANO: "We must join the United States; join the other peoples fighting in the Orient and in Europe against Hitler and his allies and accomplices. There can be only two attitudes: against Hitler and his allies, or in favor of Hitler and his allies. It is absurd to speak of neutrality, because the neutral is but an ambushed fascist, cynical and cowardly."

There are countless other American voices. These are only a few of the more forceful. None of them is marred by ambition or hatred. All are vibrant, optimistic. They forecast the world of tomorrow. They will outlive the infernal roar of battle.

They reflect the amplitude of America's open spaces, the clarity of America's rivers, the exhilaration of America's mountains. All of them are faithful to the history of our continent. They reverberate our united cry for individual, national, and universal decency. Finally, all are true to America's culture, based on integral humanism, embracing in *each* man the qualities of *all* men.

CHAPTER II

South of the Border

"THERE are some things which any American knows about all Mexicans: Mexicans are bandits, they carry guns, they make love by moonlight, they eat food which is too hot, and drink drink which is too strong, they are lazy, they are communists, they are atheists, they live in mud houses and play the guitar all day. And there is one more thing which every American knows: that he is superior to every Mexican. Aside from these items the atmosphere between Mexico and the United States is mild and friendly." This quotation from one of Hubert Herring's excellent books [1] strikingly sums up the common prejudices in the United States not only against Mexico but all Latin America.

It is difficult to ascertain which false ideas are the more preposterous: those common among Latin Americans with respect to United States citizens and their way of life, or those common among United States citizens with respect to Latin Americans and their way of life. However, one thing is true: these prejudices stand in the way of continental rapprochement. We have discussed in Chapter I some of the gravest misconceptions that stand in the way of inter-Americanism; but countless minor ones, in spite of their triviality, are in the end just as harmful.

They say that "ignorance is bliss"; and that is a good example of groundless thought. But even ignorance is less harmful than prejudice. It is negative, whereas prejudice

[1] *Good Neighbors* (New Haven: Yale University Press, 1941).

does positive harm. Ignorance is emptiness, naked virgin soil; whereas prejudice is a tangle of cumbersome weeds. In order to know the truth, an ignorant mind has merely to learn; whereas a prejudiced one must first uproot.

Also, not being rational, and requiring no intellectual effort, prejudices are dangerously easy to acquire. Finally, being hasty as well as nasty generalizations, they apply to all cases without exception. Thus, people will go on repeating, "*All* Latins are lazy," "*All* gringos are silly," and so on.

But before going any further, let us reassure the English-speaking reader about the meaning of the word "gringo." It means simply, in most Latin American countries, a citizen of the United States. (In Argentina, it applies to all foreigners.) The feminine of "gringo" is "gringa." In spite of characterizations to the contrary, given in current English dictionaries, neither term is contemptuous. When referring to Latin Americans, especially to my own countrymen, some bad gringos use not inoffensive nicknames but deliberate insults. This indicates that the user is witless, or that he is mean.

Gringo is an old Spanish word antedating the Mexican War. Frank H. Vizetelly traced the word back to *1787* and found it explained as follows, in a Spanish dictionary published in Madrid that year: "*Gringos*—the name given in Málaga to those foreigners who have a certain accent which prevents them from speaking Spanish fluently and naturally; and in Madrid the same term is used for the same reason, especially with reference to the Irish." [2] From the same source we learn that the word may be also found in a Spanish-French dictionary published in Paris as late as 1845: "*Gringo,—ga* (figuratively and colloquially). Greek, Hebrew. It is said of a thing that is not intelligible." [3] Mr. William

[2] James B. Stewart, "Who's a Gringo," *American Foreign Service Journal,* Sept., 1940, p. 491.
[3] *Ibid.*

C. Wells reminds us that *gringo* appears in the latest edition (the fourteenth) of the Dictionary of the Spanish Royal Academy and appeared in the ninth and twelfth and probably other prior editions: "It is a corruption of the word *griego* (Greek). Correctly used, as stated in the Academy's dictionary, it occurs only in the phrase *'hablar en griego.' Hablar en griego* is to speak unintelligibly, or in gibberish; so one who speaks gibberish, e.g. a foreign language, is a *gringo.*"

At this time, when we are all doing our best to clear the ground for an intelligent Hemisphere policy, it would be highly desirable to wipe out all biases, big and small. But the job would require the patience of a saint and the spare time of a playboy. Lacking both, I will merely try to throw light upon some of the oddest ideas entertained.

To begin with, many North Americans have only a vague idea as to the whereabouts of Latin America. It is simply "south of the border." Yet several republics of our Hemisphere are islands, and all these are located *east* rather than south of the border. But this is unimportant compared with the extravagant ideas on the people themselves.

People in the United States are referred to as "men" or "women." Not people in Latin America! There, all men are *caballeros* and all women are *señoritas.*

Caballeros must have a well-groomed, jet-black mustache, sweeping sideburns, smoldering eyes, and dark complexion. A caballero is inconceivable without his Hollywood outfit: ball-fringed sombrero, embroidered jacket, brilliant satin sash and skin-tight *charro* pants, coquettishly slit and laced from the knee down.

As to the señoritas, they are all beautiful. They have dark eyes, ink-black hair, magnolia-white complexions, and long eyelashes shadowing their angelic faces. But a señorita is inconceivable without a huge Spanish comb, a lace mantilla, a fluttering fan, a gardenia nestled in her curls, and a red

rose between her gleaming Spanish teeth. Of course, by definition she is terrific; but when a señorita dances, *rumba* or
conga, she becomes irresistible.

Caballeros conceal daggers in their sashes. Only a few
señoritas, of the Carmen type, store knives in their stockings.
The milder type—not Lupe Vélez but Dolores del Río—
simply wear black crucifixes, rising and falling on their
dove-white bosoms.

Both Hollywood caballeros and señoritas live continuously
in a world of musical comedy: extravagant costumes, laugh-
ter, flirtations and guitars.

A Latin American setting is, of course, incomplete without a *patio.* This is to Latin Americans what an aquarium is
to fishes. Only, in the aquarium fishes still behave like
fishes; whereas in Hollywood patios, Latins cease behaving
like human beings.

A patio is the setting for the highly fantastic musical
extravaganza known in the U.S.A. as *fiesta.* Palm trees, a
fountain with night-club tables all around, crowded with
noisy, boisterous people who never stop smoking, puff incessantly, and dance wildly to the clicking of castanets—such
is the colossal surrounding created by Hollywood for a fiesta
anywhere in Latin America. And we almost forgot the conspicuous, the inevitable serape—in Spanish, *sarape*—draped
on the Spanish balcony. Were it not there, dashing Pedro
could never meet beautiful María, because, without a serape
there would be no balcony, and without a balcony there
would be no María.

Then, at the climax of the fiesta, enters the villain. Ah,
the villain! An honest-to-goodness North American gangster
would just walk in, pull his gun, shout, "Stick 'em up," and
then quietly carry on his routine job of raiding the place.
Not Pancho, the Latin American bandit: he is always suave
and affected, in fact quite a man of the world. Then, whereas
a Yankee gangster goes for the safe and money, Pancho—

God bless his soul—goes for señoritas. With the unerring instinct of a true connoisseur he singles out the most glamorous specimen and immediately starts wooing her, preferably with a song or a dance or both. Small wonder Main Street movie goers are convinced that "south of the border" everything is fun and is crazy; that life down there is just a blissful succession of siestas and fiestas—today, *mañana* and again after *mañana*.

Another United States fixation is that Latin Americans are never at peace, that they *always* have revolutions. The truth is that, partly because of our impulsiveness but mainly because of serious deficiencies in the political life of many of our countries, we do lack electoral "landslides" and abound in revolutions. But remember, not to be unfair, that violent solutions are not the invention nor the monopoly of Latin America. Orientals, Europeans, and North Americans are equally fond of them when there is no other way out. Remember that such American leaders as Thomas Paine, Jefferson, and Lincoln were outspoken advocates of revolutions. Paine wrote: "If universal peace, civilization, and commerce, are ever to be the happy lot of man, it cannot be accomplished but by a revolution in the system of governments." Jefferson was more explicit: "Let them [the people] take arms. . . . The tree of liberty must be refreshed from time to time with the blood of patriots and tyrants. *It is its natural manure.*" And if that were not enough, listen again to Jefferson: "I hold it, that a little rebellion, now and then, is a good thing; and as necessary in the political world as storms in the physical . . . *It is a medicine necessary for the sound health of government.*" To that I take off my sombrero—trinkets and all!

As a matter of fact, the United States of America is the only nation in the world—and that includes Russia—which consecrates revolutions by acknowledging in so formal a charter as the Declaration of Independence that "when a long train of abuses and usurpations, pursuing invariably the same object, evinces a design to reduce them [the people] under absolute despotism, *it is their [the people's] right, it is their duty, to throw off such government,* and to provide new guards for their future security."

Abraham Lincoln, an American if there has ever been one, said, in his memorable "Mexican War speech": "Any people anywhere being inclined and having the power have the right *to rise up and shake off the existing government,* and form a new one that suits them better. *This is a most valuable, a most sacred right—a right which we hope* and believe is to liberate the world."

Yes, Rumba, Revolution, and Romance: these three *R*'s of Latin America seem to be, in the minds of many, the equivalents of the other famed three *R*'s of Europe—Renaissance, Revolution, and Reformation.

But perhaps there is something deeper in these as in other prejudices; they may be symptoms of frustration. . . . The average American tourist, for instance, is a kind and lively person eager to escape the monotonous routine of his well organized existence. The tourist who stands in awe before a wall of towering mountains, in the breath-taking road lift from Tamazunchale to Mexico City, frequently comes from the flat plains of the Middle West. He crosses the border because he needs excitement. He cherishes the company of romantic and wild neighbors. He would be terribly disappointed not to find "down there" what he does not find at home. His visit to Mexico is a catharsis, an escape. He comes back to South Bend, Indiana, or Wichita, Kansas, a more peaceful and more balanced person—not so much because of what he actually saw "down there," as because of what he thinks he saw.

Latin America and Romance are as commonly connected as United States and Liberty. The U.S.A. is the land of freedom; Latin America, that of romance.

Here we find ourselves confronted with another current prejudice. *"So, so romantic"* is usually followed by a wistful sigh straight from the heart of an otherwise normal, undemonstrative schoolteacher. One prejudice is as bad as the other. The U.S.A. has no more a monopoly on freedom than we have on romance. Of course, we love romance. But be careful with the word "romantic." Latin Americans are passionate, not romantic people. To be romantic implies a certain spirituality. To a great extent, romanticism is an interpretation of life. And we temperamental Latin Americans prefer action to interpretation, any time. To be romantic, one must not be too impulsive. Romanticism—which as a philosophy originated in Germany, as lyricism became articulate in England, and as an intellectual movement found expression in France—seems more at home among milder northern Europeans than among fiery Spaniards or Slavs. Besides, our romantic hero is Don Quixote rather than Don Juan. In the U.S.A., the nearest thing to Don Quixote is Don Charlie Chaplin. Yet, I wonder how many people would accept the extraordinary type created by Chaplin as *romantic.* I am afraid that the confusion and the abuse of this magic word are explained by the fact that people here, especially women, think of passion when they use the word "romantic." When high-school girls say that Latins are romantic, probably this confusion exists in their minds.

We have to mention the myth of Latin American romanticism because, to a large extent, it is responsible for another prevalent misconception—our supposed *laziness.* Considering us as romantic (not to say oversexed), people naturally think we can have little time to engage in practical activities such as industry, mechanics, or business. Latin Americans must be totally incapable of constructive work. . . . "They cannot exploit their own countries because they have neither the capacity nor the physical strength to do it." Anyhow, "they would not know what to do with modern machinery"; and of course, "they" could never efficiently run any kind of business enterprise. These and a few more absurd ideas are the price that we Latin Americans have to pay Anglo-Saxon public opinion for the dubious privilege of being considered "romantic."

A romantic aureole may make one popular with the ladies, but it does not help any with men. When a Latin American enters a United States home, he becomes immediately the object of concentrated attention on the part of all the ladies in the house; but, to say the least, he remains a perplexing curiosity to the men: a puzzle they are reluctant to tackle. The result is that neither sex receives the right impression. We are not crooners or gigolos. Latin Americans enjoy immensely talking to, and associating with, men. They do so at home, and they like to keep on doing it in other countries. We are perfectly capable of discussing subjects of usual masculine interest, from the chances of the Brooklyn Dodgers to the cleaning of a pipe. . . . There should be more personal friendship between the *men* of North and those of Latin America. To consider us "ladies' men" is as silly as to think that, in contrast, gringos do not know what to do with a girl. If you look around, you will discover in Latin America as many active, efficient, and practical people as you may find in the United States. They love serious work. No enterprise seems to them too difficult. They are descendants of hard-working races: Spaniards, Portuguese, and Indians.

A friend, manager of a large dairy farm in the eastern United States, raised his hands to the sky, when speaking of Mexico, and said: "My God! What you could do with that country!" His sense of efficiency and split-minute timing was outraged by what he termed the slipshod organization he had seen *"down there."* He himself, coming from a region of temperate climate and abundant water, could not imagine the problems that opposite conditions entail. But this friend may rest assured that anything which can be done with "that country" will be done as quickly and efficiently as possible, by Mexicans themselves. What we cannot make of our country, no foreigner can. This friend, like so many other United States businessmen, held to the outmoded myth of untold Latin American riches waiting for some Yankee with initiative to exploit.

Latin Americans lazy? Look at them tilling the soil, erecting capitals such as Buenos Aires, Mexico City, or Rio de Janeiro, to mention only three; see their highways—like that from Laredo to Mexico City, built entirely by Mexican labor and Mexican engineers; look at their bridges, their dams, and a thousand other things, built mostly under physical handicaps such as climate, mountains, unsanitary conditions, the like of which even the American pioneers never knew. Look at them also when they work in foreign lands: the Mexicans in the fields of Texas and California. It would be impossible to find more industrious people. The descendants of Spanish conquerors and Pyramid builders cannot be thought of as lackadaisical good-for-nothings. They are tough, hard-working people. I should even say that members of the economically active population of Latin America work harder and longer than their more fortunate fellow workers in the United States. No, Latin Americans do not just sit in the sun and eat bananas.

Finally, the Latin American republics are not lands of mañana. They are lands of yesterday, today, and tomorrow. We are impatient people. In fact, so impatient and enthusiastic about things that too often we jump straight to conclusions, and consider things completed, when we are really only beginning to achieve them. The mañana legend is simply wishful thinking on our part. Where a calmer North American, after a careful analysis of the difficulties involved, would reasonably say "Next year," we impetuously say "Tomorrow," mañana. And, of course, often mañana comes too soon. We must learn to be more careful, that is all. Because of our nervous temperament, we like to see things done quickly. In reality, we achieved many important things before the United States had a chance to start them—as acknowledged by Samuel Guy Inman:

"The first printing press in America was set up in Mexico about 1539, a hundred years before the beginning of printing in the English colonies. The first university was founded in Santo Domingo about 1538. In 1551 two more universities were founded, one in Mexico City and one in Lima. When the first college was started in the English colonies (Harvard, 1636), Latin America already had six universities. In 1585 a literary contest was held in Mexico City in which some 300 poets took part. When the Dutch were trading trinkets to the Indians for Manhattan Island, the city of Asunción in the heart of South America was a well-organized community with schools, churches, and literary clubs." [4]

My good friend could have added that the first *school* in the Americas was established in Mexico, as early as 1536; that one year later, Mexico opened the College of Santiago—perhaps the first college for women in the world. In Santa Fe de Bogotá, in 1563, the first school of Latin grammar was established. The Dominican Republic had a hospital before 1503. Puerto Rico's first was established about 1511: Panama's about 1521. As reported by the Pan American Sanitary Bureau, the oldest hospital in the Americas still functioning is that founded in Mexico City by Cortés in the early sixteenth century.

Latin America boasts of world-famous scientific institutes such as the Butantan and Oswaldo Cruz in Brazil, the Bac-

[4] "Latin America: A New View of Our Neighbors to the South," in *Compton's Pictured Encyclopedia* (Chicago: F. E. Compton & Company, 1941), Vol. VIII, p. 67b.

To be more exact, it should be said here that the University of Santo Domingo was *chartered* in 1538. In 1551 royal edicts authorized the establishment of universities in Lima and Mexico, respectively. Mexico's university was inaugurated in 1553.—Author.

teriological Institute of Argentina, the Institute of Hygiene in Mexico. The first Chair of Medicine in the Americas was established in Mexico in 1580.

In the field of art, Latin America's contribution stands out prominently. Centuries before the Spaniards came to our shores, native populations had built architectural wonders such as the Pyramids of Teotihuacán near Mexico City —the then stately Tenochtitlán, proud capital of the Aztecs; and there were other wonders in Yucatán, in the jungles of Guatemala and Honduras, on the high plateaus of Bolivia and Peru. After the Spanish conquest, creoles and mestizos produced thousands of churches and other buildings in original Spanish American baroque style. In this Hemisphere, only Radio City or the Empire State Building can be compared with the Mexican pyramids or the Spanish American cathedrals.

The paintings of Rivera, Orozco, and Siqueiros, to mention only the best known contemporary masters of Mexico, rank in the world's art with works by the famous Italian Renaissance painters. United States critics have enthusiastically praised Mexican painting. And there are also Quirós of Argentina and Portinari of Brazil.

In the field of literature, Latin America's fame is surpassed by none. Heredia, Bello, Alberdi, Sarmiento, Mitre, Villalobos, Machado de Assis, da Cunha, Toribio Medina, Isaacs, Asunción Silva, Eustacio Rivera, Martí, Batres y Montúfar, Inés de la Cruz, Díaz Mirón, Gutiérrez Nájera, Nervo, Santos Chocano, Mariátegui, Rodó, Herrera y Reissig, and Rubén Darío, one of the greatest poets the world has known: those names would suffice to give any country a solid literary reputation. But in that list I have mentioned only a few of the outstanding and none of the living.

However, it is in the field of music that we take the cake. Cuba's "Peanut Vender" precipitated the avalanche. The United States has been simply swept off its feet by the tempo and melody of our popular music. *Rumbas, congas,* and *sambas* have tended to displace the long popular American jazz. From *tango* through rumba to conga, Latin America has conquered the United States. The delicate Mexican songs have completed this subtle annexation of our powerful industrial neighbor. Mexican songs have been so warmly received that they are in danger of becoming naturalized. Not only sentimental old-timers like "La Golondrina," "La Paloma," "Cielito Lindo," "Borrachita," "Estrellita," and "Sobre las Olas" (Over the Waves), but also the more spirited "Cucaracha," "Rancho Grande," "Perfidia," "Frenesí," "Cuatro Vidas," and a dozen other popular "hits" can be heard at almost any hour in the U.S.A. at the turn of a radio dial.

Gringos knew they had hands and legs and brains. They were quite efficient at expressing their feelings with their feet—e.g., tap dancing—but there was one thing they ignored until the devilish *maracas* and *sonajas* started beating their jungle rhythm: and that was the flexibility of the hips and their magic power of expression. And all this fundamental change in the "American way of moving" has occurred only after dancing tangos, congas, and rumbas. *Amigos gringos!* Wait until you become acquainted with the *pericón* of Argentina and Uruguay, the Chilean *cuecas,* the *marinera* of Peru, the *bambuco* of Colombia.

CHAPTER III

"*Amigos Gringos*"

LET it be said that Latin American prejudices concerning the United States and its way of living are as numerous and absurd as those prevailing in the United States about its southern neighbors.

The most outstanding of these misconceptions is: "All gringos are businessmen." The U.S.A. is Wall Street in the "good old days." This generality is as deeply imbedded in the minds of most Latin Americans as the one held by the majority of American women: "Latin men are *so* romantic!" Not only is every American a businessman, but he *must* be a millionaire. Therefore, as a welcome tourist he should pay more for what he buys. Even if actually penniless, he will have difficulty convincing a Latin American that he is broke.

Physically, an American *must* be big, strong, light-haired, blue-eyed, and close-shaven. Mustaches and beards, attributes of the Spanish male, simply would not grow on American faces.

The gringo dresses simply: he wears ready-made suits of good material but without a touch of "personality." He has immense feet encased in "horrible" square-toed shoes, *all* rubber-heeled; immense feet, stubby fingers, and square hands.

He is always in a hurry, pushing people around, for no reason at all. He does not carry a cane because, not being a Latin, he would not know what to do with it. His tastes are very simple: baseball, automobiles, and cocktails. When he is not chewing gum, smoking cigars, or gulping Coca-Colas, he is eating ice cream.

Intellectually, this creature, so successful in business, is rather slow and limited. Not so heavy as a German, but something like that.

All Americans are mechanics. In that field they are undisputed masters. If your automobile breaks down on the road and an American tourist passes by, you are saved. He *should* know how to fix it.

Sexually, it goes without saying, a gringo is completely indifferent and cold. *All* Americans are amateurs in matters of love: that is definite. (One cannot be a successful business-man and a good lover at the same time.) To a gringo, business and even golf are more important than women. He no more knows how to handle the latter than he knows what to do with a cane. He is aware of it. That is why he feels uncomfortable in the company of women; and it explains why there are so many men's clubs in the United States.

The business office is the natural habitat of a gringo. When he works—and the poor devil must work incessantly because "his wife spends all the money"—he always does so in shirt sleeves, propped back in a swivel chair, with feet on the desk. He seldom takes off his hat, and once seated never gets up, even to greet callers. Also, he never shakes hands; but instead calls you by your first name almost on sight.

In the light of such prejudices, it would be inconceivable to imagine a gringo taking a walk in a park at sunset, for the sake of beauty.

American women are different. They *all* have beautiful legs, just as *all* gringos are businessmen. They *all* are blondes, with blue eyes and curly hair; anything coming from the U.S.A. must have light hair and blue eyes. . . . They are completely untamed. See how they walk in the streets, in slacks! They *all* have baby-doll complexions. In short, physically they make the grade. But morally! They are dangerous specimens. They are cold-blooded. If you are not careful, they will take you to a hotel room and blackmail you later. Of course, they are never at home—except to sleep, very late at night. All of them henpeck their husbands, for which they are not entirely to blame. Their men stand for it. Finally gringas love to divorce. It is a habit with them.

Being so beautiful and reckless, they are of course dangerously provocative. When you take one out, she will get you into trouble, unless you can talk her into behaving with Latin circumspection. She should be taught to refrain from crossing her legs so carelessly; and to wear restraining garments, such as stockings, girdles, brassieres, and even jackets when necessary. But (we think deep in our hearts) there is one thing in favor of gringas: they are crazy about us. They *all* crave a Latin sooner or later in their lives; the sooner the better. They are temperamental. Why, with proper Latin training, they could become even passionate! That, logically, explains why American women love to travel. . . . When they go to Latin America, they are in quest of romance and adventure. That is why, also, hotels and public places popular among American tourists are crowded with prospective Latin lovers ready to gratify their beautiful admirers. . . .

So far I have been faithfully pointing out specific and trivial prejudices; but the time has come when it is urgent seriously to denounce some general concepts pertaining to the North American mentality. In Europe, as well as America, a widespread legend prevails that the United States is a *big* country, but "without tradition," "without art," "without soul." As if the spiritual could exist totally independent of the material! The United States is even reproached for being "young." As if youth could be a reproach. And as if the culture of the United States were not, in part, the *sum total* of those aged cultures transplanted by the millions of immigrants who made this great nation.

However, those who have contributed to this absurd belief abroad are not entirely to blame. North Americans themselves, so often underestimating the noncommercial values of their national life, are equally guilty. Because my words are those of a foreigner who knows the United States well and admires it sincerely, I feel assured that they will not be misinterpreted.

Most Americans with whom I have come in contact are victims of an intellectual complex. They have been so successful in their scientific control of material things that they seem to think they can afford to be modest in other fields. How many times have American friends told me: "Oh, Mexico! How beautiful, how romantic! You are lucky. *Here* there is no beauty."

I have also found among many of my American friends a certain fear—I will even say a certain shame—of being called intellectuals. Among pragmatic people, one might as well be called a "sissy." I was recently discussing aesthetics with a most intelligent Washington doctor. In the heat of discussion he came out forcibly several times with the statement, "And I am *not* an intellectual." This emphasis perplexed me, because from the very expression of the doctor's thought it was altogether evident that he was an intellectual. In schools and universities, I have found a similar atmosphere. American students are afraid to be labeled intellectuals. In contrast, muscular activity is always something to brag about. Football men, basketball men, advertise their status in big letters spread all over their powerful chests.

But the most severe critics of American culture, and also the most unfair, are Americans themselves.

Some time ago I was fortunate enough to visit in the city of Washington a modest exposition of paintings by Negro artists, organized under the auspices of the Works Progress

Administration. I discovered among the exhibits some of truly extraordinary artistic value. Hanging on those walls were three or four paintings worthy to figure by the side of masterpieces signed Rivera, Orozco, or Picasso. And yet—except for the European consecration of Whistler—few people here or abroad seem to be aware that in the United States painters of genius can be found.

The same may be said of American music. In Paris nine years ago, I witnessed the sensational success of the American composer, Duke Ellington. His success was sensational in that he was acclaimed not as a band leader but as a great composer; and not in the frivolous environment of a night club but in the solemn atmosphere of a concert hall. Outstanding critics of Paris enthusiastically praised, in scholarly fashion, the novelty of this music which contains melodic and technical elements capable of bringing about revolutionary changes in universal music. And Duke Ellington is not alone! Jazz—as Gershwin might have proved had he not died so prematurely—has elements of composition and technique capable of giving birth to a new epoch in the history of music. The day is not far away when the United States will find its Debussy or its Stravinsky. Modern music would be inconceivable without jazz, or to say the least, incomplete.

The same can be said of the amazing modern American architecture. The skyscraper is *the* outstanding contribution of man to the architecture of our times. The latest type of skyscraper, totally emancipated from European influence, has at last become 100 per cent American. The American architect has surmounted traditional prejudices. He has eliminated the profusion of detail so typical of some ancient, most Renaissance, and all Gothic buildings. He has found beauty in extreme simplicity of line and smooth geometric surface. Skyscrapers are not only aesthetic masterpieces; their functional beauty makes them impressive symbols of our modern way of living, comparable to the prehistoric Pyramids, or the Greek temples, or the cathedrals of the Middle Ages, or the palaces of the Renaissance. We can rightfully say that these colossal office buildings have become classic architectural monuments.

I heard a charming lady, with a fine college background, say of Rockefeller Center: "How can you admire those buildings? They look *so new!*" I had a hard time explaining to the good lady that when the Pyramids of Egypt, the Greek temples, the Gothic cathedrals, and the palaces of the Renaissance were built, they also were *new,* and they looked that way. Architects always build *new* buildings! Young, yes, thank Heaven! New, certainly! That is precisely why the art of America is important.

The plain truth is that the people of the United States are essentially artistic. It is time that Latin Americans became aware of it. I believe that nothing has been more detrimental to mutual understanding in the Americas than the continental prejudice according to which all spiritual culture belongs to Latin America and all material civilization to the United States. When that prejudice is erased, a great step will have been taken to weld North and South.

Americans love music and literature. It would be difficult to find a country where more music is offered to the public, and where more people crowd to hear it. There are in the United States approximately one hundred fifty semiprofessional orchestras; over two hundred university and college orchestras; and, last but not least, about twenty major symphony orchestras, most of them world-famous, such as the New York Philharmonic, the Philadelphia, Boston, Chicago, and San Francisco symphony orchestras. Outstanding conductors lead these American orchestras: Toscanini, Stokowski, Barbirolli, Koussevitzky, and Bruno Walter.

Americans love to read. One finds them reading at home, in restaurants, in streetcars, in busses. Illiteracy in the

United States is today only about 4 per cent. Around twenty-three million pupils from five to seventeen years of age attend the *public* schools, and nearly eight hundred thousand men and five hundred thousand women are registered in American universities and colleges. In 1936 the libraries of some fourteen hundred schools and universities contained over sixty-three million bound volumes. On books, it may be pertinent to note that in 1939 over nine thousand new books and nearly two thousand new editions of previously published works were issued in the United States. Because these figures may be considered as one index of American culture, I should add that of the total books published in that year, some twelve hundred were devoted to fiction, and the rest, listed in descending rank according to the number of items in each field, were: children's books, sociology and economics, history, religion, *poetry* and drama, biography, general *literature,* science, technical books, medicine and hygiene, geography and travel, business, education, and fine arts; then sports, and a few other classifications. Nearly six hundred books of *poetry* and drama and six hundred of general *literature* were published in that year, whereas only a little over four hundred were dedicated to *science* and less than three hundred to *business.*

Finally, few people know that the total of books in United States public libraries is today over one hundred seven million. The public libraries of the State of New York alone possess more than thirteen million books. In 1940 the Library of Congress reported more than six million books and pamphlets, around one and one-half million maps and charts, about as many volumes and pieces of music, and over half a million prints! Editions of popular books run into the hundreds of thousands. Nearly half a million copies of John Steinbeck's *Grapes of Wrath* were sold in a little over a year. H. G. Wells's *Outline of History* and Will Durant's *The Story of Philosophy,* both nonfiction, broke records as popular best sellers. That in itself speaks very highly of the intellectual level of the American reader.

At the end of 1939 there were in the United States more than two thousand daily newspapers with a circulation of nearly forty million. The combined total of dailies and weeklies was at that time well over thirteen thousand.

Americans unintelligent? Radio City, the Lincoln Tunnel, the San Francisco Bay Bridge, Boulder Dam, and scores of other such marvels—would they be the product of unintelligent people? If so, then the Pyramids of Mexico and Egypt, the temples of Greece, the Gothic cathedrals, are also the miraculous products of unintelligence.

Americans unintelligent? The Nobel prizes accorded each year, through careful selection by an international body of undisputed celebrities, may be considered as another safe index of cultural achievement. The first Nobel prizes were awarded in 1901. Since then, up to 1939 when the war broke out, Americans received Nobel prizes as follows: Physics, in 1907, 1923, 1927, 1936, 1937, and 1939; Chemistry, 1914, 1932, and 1934; Medicine and Physiology, 1912, 1930, 1933, and 1934; Literature, 1930, 1936, and 1938; and Politics (Peace), 1906, 1912, 1919, 1925, 1929, and 1931. In order that we Latin Americans may understand the significance of these statistics, let me recall that *not a single* Nobel prize in science or literature has ever been awarded to a Latin American; and that of the total of 170 such prizes bestowed in all fields since their establishment, only *one,* in politics, has been given to a Latin American, Saavedra Lamas, of Argentina. In this respect, may I add that also with one single exception—Ramón y Cajal, who in 1906 won the prize in Medicine and Physiology—we do not find another Spanish name in the Nobel prize list.

Americans are not only as intelligent and as artistically inclined as the people of any other nation, but they are generous and kind. They not only have brains; they also have a heart, and a very big one at that. There is no country in the world in which private individuals spontaneously give more of their money to charity and social needs. In spite of the depression, Americans in 1930 gave more than six million dollars a day "for the benefit of humanity." Six million dollars a day! According to reliable sources, total gifts are estimated "in excess of two billion dollars a year." [1]

The total capital of foundations dedicated to collective welfare in the United States, as reported also by reliable investigators, amounted to more than nine hundred fifty-five million dollars in 1939—nearly a billion dollars. Those foundations granted in the same year nearly thirty-nine million dollars, distributed as follows: [2]

	Percentage
Medicine and public health	35.1
Education	23.8
Social welfare	12.2
Physical and biological sciences	5.9
Government and public administration	4.5
Economics	3.5
Social science	2.5
International relations	2.3
Art	2.2
Humanities	2.1
Child welfare	2.0
Engineering	1.4
Religion	0.7
Heroism	0.5
Race relations	0.3
Agriculture and forestry	0.2
Unclassified	0.8

These figures speak eloquently. Some people say Americans give millions because they are wealthy. But the amazing

[1] David Quick Hammond, *Fund Raising Procedure*, New York, 1931.

[2] *American Foundations and Their Fields* (study made by Raymond Rich Associates), compiled by Geneva Seybold, New York, 1939.

fact about these statistics is not the amount of money given for such charitable purposes, but its proportion to individual incomes. Where Americans give millions, people of other nations could give thousands for their charities. American generosity knows no frontiers. An earthquake in Japan, Mexico, Chile, a flood in China, a famine in Europe, move the citizens of this country to immediate response through the American Red Cross.

Americans like money—who does not?—but certainly not for itself alone. In Europe I have seen people hoarding money for the sake of money. That attitude is entirely un-American. Americans are born *gamblers*. They gamble in business and in fun. They need money to keep things moving. To them money is rather a means than an end in itself. The attitude of the French peasant who hoards his money in a woolen sock, hides it under the mattress, and keeps on living in poverty, so as to have the satisfaction of actually touching the pieces of this precious metal, seems simply maniacal to most Americans.

In the light of these reflections, it is easier to understand why no saying has been more harmful to the prestige of the United States than the famous and infamous "Time is money." As I pointed out in the preceding chapter, such a principle seems monstrous to us of Latin America, for whom, if anything, life is beauty and time is feeling. "Time is money" may be an ideal device for efficiency in business, but it certainly does not represent the general attitude of the American people toward life.

I am sure that any unbiased citizen of a Latin American country who is personally acquainted with the United States has to reach these conclusions. Unfortunately, because of the expense involved, only an insignificant percentage of Latin Americans can afford to visit the United States. In forming their opinion the majority of Latin Americans have to rely entirely on what they hear and see at home. Their sources of information thus are limited to American tourists and salesmen, or American movies.

American tourists are "all right." Mexicans have found that out, because the tourists flock there. But, unfortunately for the rest of Latin America, those 'tourists very seldom go south of Mexico. Few people in the United States even know the names of South American countries, except Brazil, Argentina, and perhaps Chile and Peru. After all, there are *twenty* Latin American republics, each with its native color and personality.

As for traveling businessmen, they are neither better nor worse than businessmen of other countries. They are not concerned, of course, with anything that does not affect the specific purpose of their trip. To them Latin America is a market and we are customers. As a rule, they travel in a hurry and they don't know the language—much less the customs, the history, or the art of foreign people with whom they come in contact. Their business is profit, not international friendship or hemispheric solidarity. The latter is the government's business. They are not diplomats or apostles. This is easy enough to understand, but it does not make things any better. The fact remains that Latin Americans form hasty conclusions, one-sided and superficial, from accidental contact with these men.

The third source of information on the U.S.A. is Hollywood. At times, I believe it is the most harmful. In defense of the American moving picture industry, let me say that truly Hollywood is not an annex of the State Department. It is a business, and a major one in the United States. It is concerned with the sale of films rather than with missions of international or continental understanding.

Hollywood films are superficial. They seem to be made for a prosperous, happy-go-lucky people who attend the movies simply to relax and be amused. The ordinary plot is concerned with a handsome boy who meets a stunning girl.

They fall for each other on sight. The boy shows his love immediately; the girl cleverly conceals hers until about the middle of the film, when she thinks that she has made him wait long enough. Then comes the inevitable *happy ending*.

Such things happen everywhere, but Hollywood might follow the example of some European and even Latin American films, and present a more realistic aspect of life. Everything is not so conveniently simple as Hollywood would like us to believe. We are not so prosperous in Latin America. Economic conditions are harder. We spend more time struggling and fighting. In most of our countries social issues have become more important than trifling personal episodes. Most people with whom we come in daily contact have neither Greek profiles nor Hollywood glamour. In the world of American films, even when a millionaire debutante falls in love with her chauffeur, her butler, or a tramp, she *has* to discover, before the end of the film, that her hero is a legitimate scion of a wealthy family, and preferably a Harvard or Yale man. . . .

Foreigners who see one after another of these trivial films end by consciously or unconsciously forming the opinion that Americans never go deep into life; that they are a tedious although at times amusing people, incapable of strong emotion; in a word, that Americans are good-looking and good-natured, but childish and silly. This emphasis on physical glamour and happy endings should be modified. As you have successfully done in some of your great films, show us more real and less conventional aspects of your everyday life. We are sick of melodrama, baby talk, and "million dollar" super-productions. We know that life is not always smooth or beautiful; but we know also that we can always discover beauty in it. And you know it too. There is not a natural feeling which you could not share with us.

I remember having seen on the face of a little Indian girl

—one of the many flower venders in Mexico—a smile, the quality of which I shall never forget. It was almost the smile of someone confronted with a miracle. In a group of tourists a young American college girl, carried away by her passion for flowers, found that she had not enough centavos left to buy the bunches of orchids, gardenias, and carnations she had selected. The little flower seller, understanding the situation, smiled at the tourist and cheerfully said, *"Si le gustan, guárdelas, niña."* "If you like them, keep them, little one." Although obviously penniless, that child of Mexico spoke those words with genuine delight. She was glad to discover that a tourist, a gringa, had a heart like hers, that she loved *her* flowers, the flowers of Mexico. Not only did she make the offering with a radiant smile, but she arranged her flowers with maternal tenderness. The young gringa was so touched that her eyes moistened and, not knowing what else to do, she untied the bright scarf from around her neck and offered it to the little Indian. The latter graciously refused to accept the scarf. *"No, no, niña, es un regalo,"* she said, with emphasis on the last word. "No, no, my little one, it is a *gift.*"

I understood what went on. I have seen many street venders smile when they sell their products, but their mercenary satisfaction does not resemble that smile. . . . My *paisanita* had just discovered that gringos have souls; that they are human beings; that nothing stands between them and us.

CHAPTER IV

Living and Dying: United States Way

MANY United States authors have analyzed and criticized Latin American democracies. But few Latin Americans have shown similar interest in United States democracy. The reason is simple: Such Latin Americans as have written at all on the United States had mainly one purpose—to denounce "Yankee Imperialism." The national policy of the U.S.A. was only of academic interest to them, whereas its foreign conduct affected directly the life of their republics. Thus, for years North Americans specialized in scrutinizing our domestic affairs, while we specialized in criticizing their foreign affairs.

It should be added that most books written by United States citizens have shown but one side of the picture: the dark side of Latin American democracy. That is regrettable because it has added new prejudices, new divisions; e.g., the fictitious distinction between an opulent and an indigent America, an efficient and a helpless America, a happy and a distressed America—a cleavage which almost corresponds to a "class" distinction among the republics of this continent. It is also to be lamented, because most United States critics failed to acknowledge that their respective national conditions were not beyond reproach. They dealt with conditions to the South as though they were exotic, distant products. A unilateral criticism is irritating to any people who have inherited a deeply rooted national pride. Besides, even when made with tact, a one-sided criticism of our material conditions is harmful because it leaves the disturbing impression that, in the family of American nations, the U.S.A. is a wealthy and distant uncle, who wishes to have nothing in common with his poor relations to the South.

In reality (although generally speaking the shortcomings of United States democracy seem less shocking than those of less industrialized Latin America), even a superficial survey of general conditions throughout the Hemisphere will show that our masses have definitely one thing in common: the plight caused by a ruthless exploitation of man by man. In all our countries, democracy is still more a promise than a tangible reality; and, proportionately, it can be said that there is as much exploitation and misery in the United States as in the rest of the continent. The trouble is that, because of the vastness of their territory and the complexity of their daily life, United States citizens are apt to ignore national conditions. My many years in North America have convinced me that few people in the world are blinder to their own shortcomings than the average happy-go-lucky citizens of the United States. That accounts, to a great extent, for the popularity of the much vaunted "American way of life." We hear so much about it that it would notably help Hemisphere policy to consider, with equal concern, the American *way of dying*. People living in comfort—thank Heaven, there are millions in the United States—speak of the "American standards," as if they were shared by all their fellow citizens. They forget that conditions a few miles away, if not a few blocks, are entirely different; that there is poverty and starvation for millions of other United States citizens.

In Latin America, we have a tendency to exaggerate our shortcomings. That may be honest, but it creates a disheartening pessimism. The task of improvement looms so large that to many timid souls it seems discouraging and even hopeless.

I have no doubt as to the fairmindedness of my United

States friends, their unquestioned love of truth, whatever it be. Therefore, I do not fear throwing light upon some of the darkest corners of their democracy. It will serve a two-fold purpose: first, to let Latin Americans know that the United States is as subject to suffering as we are; and second, to remind North Americans that they have misery and injustice at home, and that the problems of Latin American democracy are no different from theirs.

To begin with, in a genuine democracy, the weapon of the oppressed should be the ballot. Yet, although it is a well known fact, one often forgets that in the United States too many people in dire need of votes are practically disfranchised. Seven states (Alabama, Arkansas, Florida, Mississippi, Tennessee, Texas, Virginia) require payment of *poll tax* to vote. Three states (Alabama, Oregon, South Carolina) require a property qualification. In Georgia and Mississippi delinquent taxpayers are disfranchised. Thirteen states disfranchise recipients of state relief. Thirty-seven states require a year's residence, thereby affecting migratory workers. Thus the poor are not only economically exploited but legally penalized. They are made politically speechless. I ask: Are there any limits for the wealthy to vote? Has anyone ever heard of federal or state laws fixing wealth *maxima* for the right to vote?

In a democracy—by definition a government of, by, and for the people—we should find at least a fair, if not perfect, *distribution of wealth and income.* It certainly cannot be seen in the United States. Robert Doane, in *The Measurement of American Wealth,* estimates that 1 per cent of the people owned 40 per cent of the nation's total wealth in 1929. Representative Amlie—in his speech of August 26, 1935 (see the *Congressional Record*)—gave the following explanation of how the wealth of the U.S.A. is actually divided:

"If we let $100 represent the total wealth and 100 people represent the total population, the wealth of the country would be divided as follows: 1 man would own $59; 2 men would each own $9; 22 men would each own $1.22; and 75 men would each own less than 7 cents."

That is based upon a survey conducted by the Federal Trade Commission in 1926, which in turn was based upon the distribution of wealth as disclosed by the probate records for 1921 and 1922. Whatever the cause, is this a democratic distribution of wealth?

The distribution of *income* has colors as somber. Representative Amlie reminded us that in 1929, supposedly a very prosperous year, "144,000 persons got $10,000,000,000, and 47,000,000 persons got $10,000,000,000. . . . One-tenth of 1 per cent of the families at the top received as much income as 42 per cent of the families at the bottom." I repeat, one-tenth of 1 per cent receiving as much income as the total income earned by 42 per cent of United States families. In that same year, 513 wealthy people alone received as much income as the total earned by 8,000,000 poor people. Five hundred thirteen men receiving as much as was earned by *eight million* of their fellow citizens.

There is no such thing as an "American standard of living." Rather, there are *several* standards. Average figures are always fictitious. Even so, according to the latest (1940) census, the average wage and salary income of males and females, in the United States, was $800 a year [1]—$800 in a country where $1,400 a year is generally regarded as the amount needed for most necessities and a few comforts.

In reality, income received by real people and not by the nonexistent "average worker" is distributed as follows: 26 per cent (that is, 8,156,400) of the 31,409,520 workers who were dependent entirely on wages or salaries received under $400 a year. Those receiving between $400 and $999 numbered 10,117,380 (32.2 per cent of the entire group). Those

[1] "Average Income Still at Low Level," article by Raymond P. Brandt, in the Washington *Sunday Star*, July 19, 1942.

receiving from $1,000 to $1,999 numbered 9,870,760 (31.4 per cent). Those receiving from $2,000 to $4,999 numbered 3,066,500 (9.8 per cent). Those receiving $5,000 or more numbered 198,480 (0.6 per cent).

Concentration of *control* is another alarming symptom of North American economic democracy. As clearly stated by Professor Leighton, among others, it results from the increasing separation of ownership from management and control; and of both, from the productive workers. Under unrestricted capitalism, the process of ever increasing mass production makes this separation unavoidable. The owner no longer has to be a worker or technician or even manager: the owner may merely be a speculator. Nothing, under the present system of capitalist democracy, can prevent it. According to a study by the present Assistant Secretary of State A. A. Berle, Jr., and G. C. Means, pertinently quoted by Professor Leighton, the situation is so alarming that, "if the mergence of small corporations in the large ones were to be kept up, by 1950 all the corporate wealth of the United States would be vested in about fifty corporations." [2]

Again from the important book by the same professor at Ohio State University, well known author and scholar of unquestioned loyalty to democracy, I take this additional information:

Through interlocking directorates of speculative capitalists, enterprises, and investment bankers, about two thousand men control the two hundred large United States corporations. "At the present time in the United States it is said that ten institutions control about 80 per cent of the banking facilities; 5 per cent of the population own and control 85 per cent of the material wealth . . . Eight leading banks in New York City . . . had 287 directorships in insurance companies, 301 directorships in other banks, 521 directorships in public

[2] Joseph A. Leighton, *Social Philosophies in Conflict* (New York: D. Appleton-Century Company, 1937).

utility companies, 587 directorships in railroad, steamship, and aëroplane transportation companies: 846 directorships in manufacturing companies. These eight banks had a total of 1,201 directorships in various other corporations, making a grand total of 3,741 directorships held by the eight banks in various corporations." Writes Professor Leighton, "The eight banks above-named controlled most of the capital investment in these United States." [3]

I am no hot-headed demagogue. The only reason for bringing out these figures is my unflinching faith in democracy. But, precisely because I consider myself a 100 per cent orthodox democrat, I see no reason why we should hide the wrongs of our economic system and thus contribute to its disintegration, rather than help to strengthen it by throwing light upon its obvious defects. The only way to correct the evils of a system is to examine them patiently and methodically, but relentlessly, until we find a remedy.

The American dream of the past century was to develop a nation of independent farmers and businessmen. The Homestead Act of 1862 looked to the family farm system of agriculture as the foundation of democracy. Independent homesteads, displacing feudal possessions, "to keep the plow in the hands of the owner"—such was the hope of the founders of America. For a while it looked as though it would become a reality. But the Industrial Revolution introduced a new technique of production which, in turn, required a new technique of financial control. Thus, in the field of agriculture as well as in that of business or industry, the small independent man has been displaced by the more efficient and powerful corporation.

The plight of the farmer is most serious. According to other official sources, almost 60 per cent of American farmers in 1890 owned their farms, whereas forty years later this ratio had declined to 42 per cent. Each decade showed an in-

[3] *Ibid.*, pp. 148, 149.

crease in tenancy; from 25 per cent in 1880 to 35 per cent in 1900; from 38 per cent in 1920 to 42 per cent in 1930 and 1935. In other words, the situation in the field of agricultural democracy was steadily getting worse. Of the South's white farmers, 46 per cent are tenants; and 77 per cent of the Negro farmers are tenants. The situation of the Negro has always remained deplorable: 75 per cent were tenants in 1900. But, since 1900, tenancy for white farmers increased 10 per cent in the South. Tenant families of a southern plantation—a form of agricultural exploitation not unlike the hacienda of Mexico's Díaz—earn average net incomes of $309, or $73 *per person,* for a year's work. Wage hands have a net income of only $180 *per family.* The average for croppers ranges from $38 to $87 per person. An annual income of $38 per person is equal to slightly more than *10 cents a day.*[4]

The voluminous report of the United States Senate Committee on Education and Labor, recently published by the Government Printing Office and signed by Senators Robert M. La Follette, Jr., and Elbert D. Thomas, clearly shows what the growing industrialization of agriculture by finance corporations is doing to the small independent American farmer. "The census figures do indicate an impressive concentration of control of California's agricultural production on large farms. Most prominent of the large-scale owners and operators are corporations." [5]

"The economic and social plight of California's agricultural labor," the report indicates, "is miserable beyond belief. Average annual earnings for agricultural laborers are far below the minimum standard necessary even for the

[4] See *Farmers Without Land* (Public Affairs Pamphlets, No. 12 Revised, 1940), by Rupert B. Vance of the Institute for Research in Social Science, University of North Carolina.

[5] U.S. Senate (77th Cong., 2nd Sess.) Committee on Education and Labor, *Report on Employers' Associations and Collective Bargaining in California* (Washington: Government Printing Office, 1942), Pt. I, p. 36.

maintenance of an existence on proper levels of health and
decency. Agricultural laborers are ill-fed, ill-clothed, poorly
housed, and almost completely lacking in many other things
commonly considered necessary for civilized life. They have
no job security, and except in rare instances no job preference
or seniority.

"The California agricultural laborer is underemployed and
frequently meets the unfair competition of child and relief
labor. He has no control over wage rates and no voice in
fixing them. He must be housed for the most part in private
labor camps dominated by the employer. He lacks adequate
medical attention. His children are unable to secure satisfactory continuous education. He has no adequate protection from industrial accidents and no workmen's compensa-
tion. State minimum-wage and maximum-hour laws do not
give him any protection. Residence requirements often bar
him from relief. Organized protests on his part have been met
with the blacklist, the denial of free speech and assemblage
through the application of illegal ordinances of various kinds
and through acts of outright vigilantism. His right to organize and bargain collectively is unprotected." [6]

And, as stressed by the Senators who drafted the report,
"the California agricultural labor problem cannot be dismissed as peculiar to that State. There are aspects of the
California situation which are prevalent in other parts of the
Nation. . . .

"Today . . . the 'family farm system,' which has never
prevailed in the cotton-and-tobacco producing areas in the
South, and long ago lost its dominance in California, seems
on the wane throughout the Nation. Large-scale operations,
specialization of functions, mechanization, multiple or chain
farming are the predominant characteristics of our changing
agriculture. Drought, depression, dust storms, and a con-

[6] *Senate Report,* pp. 37-38.

centration of ownership and control slowly but inexorably are separating the farmer from the ownership of the land he tills. The course of the industrial revolution is becoming clearly visible on the land. In the wake of expanding cash crop and commercial farming, industrialized or semi-industrialized agriculture is translating the lessons of the industrial revolution from the urban shop to the factory farm. Even in the regions where this system has not been established, the security and prosperity of the independent farm operator, who with his family and an occasional hired man works his own land, is passing. His future is dark and, except for the few who may become large commercial farm operators depending upon hired wage labor, the path of the farmer is likely to lead to the role of landless farm laborer or share tenant, with a precarious footing on the land. . . . The unchecked force of finance capitalism and the efficiency of large-scale and mechanistic operation are rapidly eliminating the prosperous 'family farm,' the institution around which our rural democracy has functioned." [7]

No wonder, again, that according to the Housing Division of the P.W.A. "three-fourths of all farm families live in homes unfit for human habitation—a striking condition in a modern country. Ninety-two per cent of farm homes have *no* bathtubs, 80 per cent have *no* running water, and 89 per cent have *no* electricity." But to those of us accustomed to the bright aspects of American life these figures seem incredible. On glittering State Street at night, it is difficult to imagine that 89 per cent of American farm homes have no electricity.

And there are thousands of migratory workers, a human river of native Americans whose Calvary, masterfully depicted in John Steinbeck's *The Grapes of Wrath,* is another blot on Hemisphere democracy. Between the middle of 1935 and the end of 1939, about 340,000 persons of this type were

[7] *Senate Report,* pp. 60-61.

counted entering California.[8] Every year from one to two million hungry and homeless men, women, and children rove about the country seeking farm jobs. They follow the crops and harvests from one section of the country to another. They are not human beings but mere commodities. Wheat Belt, Western Cotton, Berry Crop, Sugar Beet Migration: these are heads of chapters telling heartbreaking stories not only of undemocratic but of unchristian, inhuman conditions of life. A study by the Resettlement Administration of migratory laborers at work in 1935 found average *annual* earnings of about $250 per worker. In the same year a study of 753 migratory labor cases of the California Emergency Relief Administration showed average family earnings of only $289 a year. No wonder that an official of the United States Department of Agriculture made this pressing appeal in 1940: "It has been conservatively estimated that the conditions of holding land in this country are such that one-third of all farm families of the nation are now living under such disadvantageous conditions of land occupancy as to reduce their level of living below any acceptable standards of decency. What will be the aspects of the picture fifty years hence, if appropriate remedial measures are not soon instituted?" [9] And the same author, Mr. Anderson, reminds us that 58 per cent of the equity of farm real estate is in the hands of *non-farm* operators.

Many superficial people have a tendency to believe that *peonage*—which is fast being wiped out in Mexico since the 1910 Revolution—is a Latin American institution. Peonage is a system of forced labor performed by a debtor who remains bonded until he has worked out his debt. This form of exploitation is in reality no different from slavery. And it exists

[8] See *Adrift on the Land* (Public Affairs Pamphlet No. 42), by Paul S. Taylor, Professor of Economics, University of California.

[9] Wilhelm Anderson, "Land Ownership and the Nation's Life," *Land Policy Review*, Vol. III, No. 7, pp. 32-33 (Nov., 1940).

today in the United States, in regions where indebtedness entails various forms of forced labor.

It is true that all forms of involuntary labor, except as punishment for a crime, are prohibited by the Thirteenth Amendment to the American Constitution. It is also true that, in 1867, Congress expressly prohibited peonage; and the United States Supreme Court, in 1911, declared state laws which tolerated peonage unconstitutional.[10] But it is equally true that, despite these prohibitions, a number of states of the Union today have on their statute books one or more laws which have encouraged the practice of peonage and indeed given it legal sanction. These are not my words but those of a high United States official who, after a thorough survey of the situation, kindly communicated to me the results of his inquiry.

The parole system, vagrancy and enticement laws, lynching or threats of lynching, the Rainey amendment to the Emergency Immigration Act, the Georgia and Florida naval stores industry, and, last but not least, the share-cropper system of agricultural work, are some of the disguised forms of peonage still in practice in the United States today.

It was reported that members of a penitentiary commission were administering the *parole system* in such a way that parolees were placed in custody of members of the commission, members of the state legislature, other state officials, and their close friends and relatives, and were compelled to work on their private plantations for wages below the prevailing rates.

Vagrancy statutes, which are frequently used to fit peonage into the legal framework of a state, are found everywhere in the Union. When vagrancy laws are enforced, employers may invoke their use in order to obtain a supply of labor. Other vagrancy laws have permitted employers to secure indigent workers who have been arrested merely by "buying"

[10] *Bailey v. Alabama,* 219 U.S. 219.

them out; that is, by paying their fines and court costs. Planters have forced such persons to work without wages, employing them to work out their debt on the plantation.

Enticement laws have operated to advance conditions of peonage. In Arkansas the enticement of any contract laborer —or renter—subjects the accused on conviction to a fine of $25 to $100 and liabilities to the original employer or landlord for all advances made to the worker. Similar laws exist in Florida, Georgia, Kentucky, Louisiana, Mississippi, North Carolina, South Carolina, Tennessee, and West Virginia.

Trespass laws contain the germs of peonage, in so far as they make it a misdemeanor to go out on the premises of any citizen without his permission between sunset and sunrise, to help a laborer or a tenant remove his property.

Lynching or threat of lynching has been used as an instrument of economic exploitation bordering on peonage. Mobs drive out labor recruiters who enter their county from an adjoining county where, for instance, cotton picking rates are higher. This occurred in September, 1937, in Warren County, Georgia.

Under the so-called *"Rainey amendment"* Mexican workers were not permitted to seek other employment or to leave the employment of their importer. It was passed during the First World War, and resulted in a modified form of peonage for Mexican workers who were imported by Arizona cotton growers and other planters.

The approximately 30,000 *wood workers* employed in Georgia and Florida in the naval stores industry are known to live practically under *peonage,* growing out of their helplessness as Negroes. The large majority of these workers are permanently and even hereditarily in debt and cannot leave the turpentine camps where they live. Debts incurred at the camp store or commissary are rarely paid in full, and are often passed on from father to son. That is exactly what happened in the old-time hacienda—itself a survival of the

Spanish *encomienda*—before the Mexican Revolution of 1910.

Finally, most everyone can see why a *share cropper* is the United States version of the Latin American peon. Indebtedness to the landlord, either manipulated or real, serves to tie the share-cropper family to the land and to almost continuous dependency on the plantation operator. The meager "furnish" of the cropper's family consists of goods supplied by the landlord, his agent, a local merchant acting on his behalf, or the plantation commissary. Meal, molasses, and sowbelly represent the major items of diet for share croppers. Excessive commissary charges, usurious interest rates, deductions for seed, tools, mule, pick sacks, hired labor, etc., appear in the settlement amounts at the end of the crop year. Even when croppers and share tenants clear anything on the year's operations, they usually exhaust their resources within a few months and invariably are destitute again at the beginning of a new crop year. In so far as the economic status of the share cropper is that of a chattel, it comes nearest to a genuine condition of peonage. The system places at the disposal of plantation operators an ever ready supply of labor at no more cost than that absolutely necessary to maintain it physically, and to enable it to reproduce itself. The dependence of these workers on their landlords is in many cases complete. The latter often control not only the work lives of their croppers but also their social existence.

Once more, may I say that my purpose in bringing up these facts is to stimulate the endeavors of all fellow democrats in a country which, like the United States of America, is one of the world's best hopes for social decency. However, even at the risk of being misinterpreted by people afraid of the socialist implications of any true democracy, I should still insist on mentioning them because if we, who have the time and the education necessary to deal with the situation, selfishly and cynically keep our mouths shut, then who will speak for these helpless victims? Most of them are illiterate, underfed, overworked. How could they state their own case? And if they did, who would listen to them? These human beings may have been rendered temporarily inarticulate, but that cannot rub them out of existence! If they cannot speak, someone must speak for them. The more voices are heard for the people, the safer will democracy be.

A similar situation may be found in industry. There, too, the middle class has been squeezed to the wall. Professor Leighton, whom we have already quoted, devotes a brief but eloquent chapter to "The Decline of the Middle Class." In it, he briefly refers to the fact that "political democracy marched on and proved fairly effective until mass production assumed great proportions. The growth of mass production brought increasing concentration of control, through the development of the business corporation and its control through finance-capitalism. *This development spelled the decline of the middle class.*" [11] All the United States critics of outmoded laissez-faire economy have seen it. But the figures brought forth by Professor Leighton are particularly significant. According to them, by 1927 over two-thirds of the "middle class" (i.e., people not farmers, wage workers, big bourgeois, or members of wealthy upper classes) were salaried employees. In 1870 the middle class represented 18.4 per cent of the total United States population. In 1935 that percentage had gone up to 25.5. It would seem that, contrary to Marxist predictions, the middle class was slowly growing. However, reproducing Lewis Corey's estimates in *The Crisis of the Middle Class,* Professor Leighton brings out that the 18.4 per cent who were "middle class" in 1870 were divided into only 4.8 per cent who were considered as salaried, and 13.6 per cent who were considered as "enterprisers." In 1935, out of the 25.5 per cent forming the middle class, 20.2 per cent had become salaried employees and only 5.3 per cent

[11] Leighton, *op. cit.,* p. 169.

of the same had remained as enterprisers. *"The composition of the entire middle class was radically altered. 'Independent enterprisers' fell from 74 per cent of the class in 1870 to only 21 per cent in 1935, while salaried employees rose from 26 per cent to 79 per cent."* "At the present time," concludes Leighton, "the middle class is a house divided against itself—a split personality." [12] The small businessman, ruthlessly driven out by the steam roller of chain-store expansion, knows that only too well.

There were, in 1935, some twelve million unemployed workers in the U.S.A.; twenty million people on relief. Six hundred thousand boys (in C.C.C. camps) worked for a net wage of *five dollars a month*—they were given thirty but had to send twenty-five dollars a month to their families. Said Amlie: "Eleven to sixteen million young men and young women, between the ages of nineteen and twenty-nine, members of the Lost Generation, found themselves unable to secure any place within the economic system."

To avoid generalizations which could seem hasty and unwarranted, I shall refer to one specific case: the miners who work in the Tri-State mining area (Missouri, Oklahoma, Kansas). Their plight has finally won nation-wide attention because they have been dying by the thousands—perhaps *seventy-five thousand in the last twenty-five years,* and of course "that's a lot o' men to die." [13] The cause of death, as we know, is the dreadful combination of silicosis and tuberculosis.

In 1937, 38 per cent of all the zinc mined in the United States came from the Tri-State. And there have been years when the area's contribution averaged 49 per cent. "According to the 1930 census figures, the Tri-State mining fields, extending over Ottawa County, Oklahoma; Cherokee

---

[12] *Ibid.,* pp. 173, 174.

[13] *A Preliminary Report on Living, Working and Health Conditions in the Tri-State Mining Area* (New York: Tri-State Survey Committee, Inc., 1939), Appendix B, p. 23.

County, Kansas; and Jasper County, Missouri, all have a native-born, white population of more than 90 per cent." [14]

The miners work in a region which has been rightfully called a "deathtrap." "The landmarks of these communities are mountainous piles of the useless, half-pulverized rock which is left as a residue when the ores mined in the district have been processed for shipment. Called chat, this rock is 90 per cent free silica." [15]

The town of Zincville, for instance, is built on the side of a chat pile. Visualize, if you can, this infernal life: "Every wind that blows across these piles raises a miniature dust storm and the dust is almost pure silica. When the wind subsides, the dust settles but not back onto the chat piles. Like a fine, powdery blanket it covers the community—the homes, the schools, the stores and the people walking on the streets. Nor are the houses free from it. Every time a door or a window is opened, a gust of wind may blow in the chat; and even when the doors and the windows are closed, the ever-present chat seeps in through the cracks around them. . . .

"Whether he [the miner] walks or rides, a trail of dust arises behind him in dry weather, and in wet weather he must either wade or ford puddles which, due to poor drainage, reach the size of miniature lakes." [16]

As a result of the constant absorption of silica, the deadly disease not only decimates the workers in the mines but their families living in the region.

According to Dr. A. J. Lanza and R. J. Vane, about 500,000 persons in the United States work in an "environment of employment likely to produce the disease." [17]

"The houses observed numbered 4,867, and of this total 3,541 were classed as unfit for habitation. . . . Houses were

[14] *Ibid.*, p. 13.
[15] *Ibid.*, p. 16.
[16] *Ibid.*, p. 18.
[17] *Ibid.*, p. 52.

made of tar-paper, scraps and cast-off packing boxes, and as the years passed, they were patched up with more tar-paper, more scraps and more packing boxes." [18]

Generally, entire families are contaminated, and "it is not unusual for a silicotic father, infected with tuberculosis, to share the same room or even the same bed with his children, even though he is continually showering the air with germs when he coughs." [19] And these miners are human beings, like you or me. They too have feelings and ideas. They too have dreams of an American way of life in which they could decently enjoy the comforts of modern civilization. Their school enrollment compares favorably with that of other towns of similar size. In Picher, there is a football stadium, equipped with floodlights. "This was built several years ago, and is a subject of considerable local pride." Parent groups formed a number of clubs devoted to the school children. The miners of Picher even boast of their children's long record of successful participation in state and county musical competitions. "But," continues the report, "behind these 'common-places' of American small-town activities, the rhythm of life in the Tri-State is the rhythm of the mines, and its symbol is the chat piles and the chat-filled air." [20]

One would think that these workers whose lives are sacrificed by wealthy corporations are at least well-paid and receive special attention—if not during their work, at least after they have contracted the disease. The report indicates that their yearly wages for a three-year period were around $550 a year *per family*,[21] less than $50 a month per family. And these haggard, emaciated, helpless victims have extracted from the earth a product whose aggregate value, in the forty-year period from 1899 to 1938, has been estimated at nearly eight hundred and twenty-seven million dollars.

[18] *Ibid.*, pp. 20, 21.
[19] *Ibid.*, p. 27.
[20] *Ibid.*, p. 31.
[21] *Ibid.*, p. 37.

As to health conditions and precautions, the report indicates that there was laxity in the enforcement of dust control measures; lack of adequate programs for educating the workers to understand their own role in successful dust control; defects in the installation or upkeep of mechanical ventilating equipment; and, finally, lack of proper sanitation in the mines.[22]

To correct the situation the report recommends the organization of shop committees. The shovelers are asked to wet down muck piles before starting to work, but "the working hours of these men are limited by regulations, and they receive their pay on a piece-work basis. The shoveler's weekly pay check is large or small on the basis of how many ore cans he has been able to load on each of his shifts. Naturally, such men have an incentive which amounts to absolute pressure to work at top speed shoveling the ore. Spending time on the shift in any other pursuit decreases their earning capacity.

"Under these conditions, delegating the responsibility for wetting down the muck to the shovelers is tantamount to asking them to finance the mine dust control program." [23]

Moreover, health services are utterly inadequate. The report shows that, from July, 1938, to April, 1939, one county with a population of nearly 39,000 spent only $2,145 for medical care. There were no county- or state-supported general hospitals in the Tri-State area. The rate paid for county patients at the nearest hospitals was $17.50 per week, in comparison with $22.50 per week charged to private patients. This means that "the majority of tuberculous persons in the Kansas and Oklahoma portions of the Tri-State probably receive no sanatorium care." [24]

Finally, I wish to close this one-sided criticism of the

22 *Ibid.*, p. 62.
23 *Ibid.*, pp. 64-65.
24 *Ibid.*, p. 80.

American way of life with a reference to another large group of distressed workers in the U.S.A.: the Mexican pecan shellers of San Antonio. Their problem caught the public attention in 1938 when their strike, for higher wages, organization, and collective bargaining was crushed largely through the hostile intervention of the authorities. In August, 1940, the Work Projects Administration published a detailed analysis of conditions related to this case.[25]

San Antonio has been the center of the pecan shelling industry for more than fifty years. Because of the low price of Mexican labor, averaging as little as one or two dollars per week during the depth of the depression, hand labor gradually displaced machines which, until a decade ago, were beginning to transform the industry. In round figures, the report shows that there were some twelve thousand workers employed in hand shelling. The average income for 1938 was only $251, for families averaging 4.6 persons. The $251 included all income, "payment in kind as well as in cash, wages from work relief and the value of surplus commodities and other relief contributions." This was the sum available for food, clothing, shelter, and incidentals for an entire family. It meant that only *15 cents* could be spent for each person in the family each day. "Incomes on this extremely low level can result only in suffering, malnutrition, disease, and high death rates." Only 12 per cent of the houses had running water. Only 9 per cent had inside sanitary toilets; and only 25 per cent had electric lights. In 1938, over 72 per cent of tuberculosis deaths in San Antonio were among Mexicans, although this group made up only 38 per cent of the population. In the same year, the Department of Health indicated that some 1,448 cases of tuberculosis were reported among children under thirteen years of age. Of these cases,

[25] Selden C. Menefee and Orin C. Cassmore, *The Pecan Shellers of San Antonio*. Washington (Federal Works Agency, Work Projects Administration, Division of Research): Government Printing Office, 1940.

77 per cent were Mexican children. Thus, nearly eight out of ten consumptive people, in that region, were Mexicans.

The only democratic way by which these uprooted, helpless people could better their conditions was to organize and bargain collectively. They tried but failed. The strike of 1938 was ruthlessly suppressed by the authorities. "From the beginning the union faced the opposition of the city authorities. On February 7, the police routed 300 pickets from the shelling plants. Over 1,000 pickets were arrested during the strike on charges of 'blocking the sidewalks,' 'disturbing the peace,' and 'congregating in unlawful assemblies.' Tear gas was used on six or eight occasions during the first two weeks of the strike, according to the testimony of Chief of Police Owen Kilday at the hearings of the Texas Industrial Commission on February 14."

Chief Kilday made the following highly significant statement: "You call it a strike; I call it a disturbance out of Washington, D.C." And this other: "I did not interfere with the strike. I interfered with a revolution." But impartial observers—including several newspapermen—reported, "The strikers were quite peaceable."

This brings us to the much discussed issue of Mexican labor in the U.S.A. Unrestrained exploitation of this foreign mass directly affects the standard of native American workers. Mexicans are utilized to undersell domestic United States labor. They are treated as mere commodities to be dumped on the market whenever native workers become scarce or too expensive. The situation of my countrymen is, moreover, aggravated by the systematic racial discrimination shown against people whose skin is not white. Mexican workers are segregated in sections of the town which are not unlike European ghettos. They share, with the Negroes, the burden of racial stigma. I have before me a heap of affidavits. They show that not only are Mexican workers, like the Negroes, segregated from the population called white, but, also like the Negroes, they are not given white men's salaries. Here is a typical case:

On the 4th day of May, 1942, I was hired by —— ———— ————, under foreman —— ————, as a furnace helper and slag brakeman. I gave my race as "French-Italian." My wages were 76 cents per hour or *$6.08 per day.* On May 14, 1942, when it was discovered that I was of Mexican ancestry, and not of French-Italian ancestry, I was demoted to plain laborer and my wages reduced to $4.20 per day. A few days prior to my demotion, I overheard a John Doe say that "the only ones that received $4.20 and never could or would receive more than $4.20 were Mexicans."

Even naturalized United States citizens of Mexican extraction, serving in the Army of the country of their adoption, suffer from racial discrimination. Here is a typical case:

We —— and —— from Camp ————, California, and —— from Camp ————, Texas, being sworn in accordance to law, depose and say, that we are privates in the regular Army of the United States of America, that we are on furlough and visiting relatives in the ——, —— District.

That on Saturday night May 9, 1942, we stopped at a place called The —— Cafe situated in the Camp of —— and asked for soft drinks. The clerk who serves on said place, refused to give us service under the excuse that he could not serve Mexicans; we asked him his name and he refused to comply with our request.

We also state that we were wearing our regular uniforms and he could not complain as to our identification. We are making this affidavit for the benefit of others who may come through this district and be humiliated as we were. This procedure on the part of the management can be interpreted as anti-American and result in bad feeling among our people at home, while we are trying with our own lives to bring victory to the principles of our Government.

CHAPTER V

Living and Dying: Latin American Way

A CRITICISM of the American way of living should in fairness cover all the nations of the continent. That alone would require an entire volume. It cannot be done here, not only because of lack of space but because there is unfortunately very little material from official or unofficial domestic sources. Only a few sister republics have undertaken scientific surveys of the situation. Besides, as indicated, the collection of works published in English, on *the other* America, is so abundant that many people in the United States are already acquainted with our economic plight. I shall merely try to throw light upon a few dark corners of our democracy, usually little known or else ignored.

First of all, as a Latin American, let me acknowledge that in spite of serious failures, some of which we have just recalled, the standard of life in the U.S.A. is, generally speaking, far *above* that of Latin America. A higher stage of industrialization, together with exceptional natural resources, relative benignity of climate, and last but not least, the precious foreign immigration, are factors which in themselves would suffice to explain the superiority of the United States, not only over Latin American standards but over European as well. However, it does not mean that democracy in the United States, in the field of social legislation or even distribution of wealth, is more advanced. It is evident that at least one country in the Hemisphere, post-revolutionary Mexico, can boast of government programs more advanced than those of the United States even during the progressive

administration of a Franklin D. Roosevelt. But we are dealing in this chapter with material conditions, not with national policies; with standards of living, not with constitutions or official decrees.

For a general survey of the Latin American way of living
and dying, I would recommend such works as Moisés Poblete
Troncoso's *El standard de vida de las poblaciones de América*,
just published in Chile; and also his *Problemas sociales y
económicos de América Latina (1936)*; the several studies
made by Dr. Ernesto Galarza, Chief of the Division of Labor
and Social Information at the Pan American Union; and
the figures intelligently compiled by the C.T.A.L. (Confed-
eración de Trabajadores de América Latina), especially the
volume on *Los Salarios de América* and the one on *Situación
de los Países Americanos en 1941.*

Contrary to popular belief, Latin American countries are
essentially poor. Exorbitant profits reaped by foreign investors have contributed to create the myth of Latin American riches. But the majority of the central and southern
republics are located within tropical or subtropical zones.
They have inaccessible mountains, impenetrable jungles,
endless deserts; and entire regions are without water, without
rivers or rain. Centuries of feudal exploitation have so weakened the native populations that sometimes they are regarded
as subhuman folk rather than as the nucleus of a promising
nation.

Again generalizing, I may say that the republics of Latin
America, especially those where Indians and Mestizos are
the majority, still remain in a feudal stage of development.
Vast rural domains, absentee landownership, agrarian economies, lack of industries, disease, illiteracy, fanaticism, and a
cleavage between wealthy minorities who do not work and
millions of underdogs who do all the working: such are some
of the evils characteristic of Latin America's backward economic pattern.

National budgets are amazingly low. Having no native industries to tax—in most of these republics no income tax at all—the government must rely on tariff duties.[1] National currencies are, with the exception of some five republics, worth only a fraction of a United States dollar. And yet, the population must import practically all the manufactured products.

The general death rate ranges from 10 per 1,000 population in Uruguay to 25 in Chile; the tuberculosis death rate, from 46.6 in Colombia to nearly 280 per 100,000 in Chile; and the infant death rate, from 95.6 per 1,000 live births in Uruguay to nearly 270 in Bolivia. These figures are for the years 1938–39. For the United States, the death rate in 1938 was 10.6; the infant death rate, 50.9—*less than a fifth* of that of Chile; the tuberculosis death rate 53.6, also contrasting with Chile's 280.[2]

There is sickness and there are no doctors. The statistics revealed by Miguel Othón de Mendizábal in *The Geographic Distribution of Doctors in Mexico* are eloquent. Basing his conclusions upon statistics from 1932 through 1936, he found that in towns of 10,000 inhabitants or fewer, 86.32 per cent of the people had died without any medical diagnosis, and only 13.68 per cent had been diagnosed in some way or other. In the entire Republic during that period, 60.80 per cent of the deaths were *without doctor's diagnosis,* and only 39.20 had medical certificates! [3] The United States has a physician for every 900 population; Europe, one for every 600. The League of Nations recommended, for Mexico, at least a doctor for every 2,000 inhabitants. Mexico City and some of the larger centers of population did have one physician for every 977 inhabitants. But in the rural districts, we find,

[1] See Chapter X, p. 180.

[2] All these figures are taken from statistics of the Pan American Sanitary Bureau in Washington, D.C.

[3] Verna Carleton Millán, *Mexico Reborn* (Boston: Houghton Mifflin Company, 1939), p. 295.

as pointed out by Mrs. Verna Carleton Millán, a radically different picture. There is one doctor for every 4,599 people in Yucatán; Michoacán, one for every 7,503; San Luis Potosí, one for every 9,207; and so on down the list to the State of Querétaro, where there is only *one doctor for every 52,669 inhabitants.*

According to other statistics, quoted in a paper by Dr. Charles A. Bailey, representative of the Rockefeller Foundation, to the First Rural Hygiene Congress, there were in that same period (1930–36) 84,452 cities, towns, villages, and other centers of population in Mexico. "Of these, 445, including the Federal District, possessed medical service, which left *84,007 places without any* [medical] *facilities whatsoever.* And as the census of 1930 estimated a total population of 16,552,772 inhabitants, 11,406,949 did *not* receive scientific medical attention." [4]

In a remote region of Yucatán, a careful and scientific investigation by the Carnegie Institution [5] revealed last year that *68.76 per cent of the population died before they were five years old,* and 7.93 per cent died between the ages of five and fifteen. So, *nearly 77 per cent of the population never lived beyond fifteen!* And after fifteen, the average age at death is 38.53. To understand the meaning of these figures, just think that the average United States citizen has a life span of 63 years. In other words, an American from that region of Yucatán goes to his grave when an average American from the United States practically begins to live.

Latin Americans have to fight all sorts of regional diseases: malaria, intestinal parasites, water-borne diseases causing typhoid and dysentery; also yaws, *carate* or *pinto,* snake bites, *Verruga peruana,* onchocerciasis, hydatidosis, jungle fever, and what not. Most of these deadly diseases can be wiped

[4] *Ibid.,* p. 296.
[5] Morris Steggerda, *Maya Indians of Yucatan* (Washington: Carnegie Institution of Washington, 1941), p. 231.

out through a systematic improvement of sanitary conditions, water and milk supplies, education, and whenever possible, vaccination. In some countries a great deal of work has been done, including the installation of sanitary latrines; examination and treatment of school children; draining, oiling, filling in, and otherwise destroying mosquito breeding places. According to these records, both Mexico and Brazil have concentrated on these problems in recent years and are rapidly installing modern systems in their most important cities. Colombia, Chile, Peru, Ecuador, and some of the Central American countries have modern installations or are working to improve their water supplies. Conditions, however, are still appalling.

The majority of Latin American countries are agricultural. Over 75 per cent of the economically active population of Mexico are engaged in some kind of agricultural work. And a similar situation prevails in most of the other republics. So, concentration of land in a handful of owners—upheld by reactionary domestic policies—is one of the main reasons for the pitiful state of Latin America's economic democracy. Let us take the case of Argentina, supposedly the most prosperous of them: it has been estimated that there are 26,700 owners of land and 57,300 share croppers and tenant farmers. In 1932 there was an important debate in the Congress of Argentina, in which it was brought out that fifty families owned nearly 11,750,000 acres. Fifteen of those families owned more than 250,000 each, the largest estate being 1,029,-845. Ten families owned between 175,000 and 247,500 acres each; seven families owned between 125,000 and 172,500 acres each; and eighteen families owned between 80,000 and 107,500 acres each.[6]

In Brazil, in 1920, large landowners held 77 per cent of the total agricultural area of the country. "Brazil is possibly

[6] Moisés Poblete Troncoso, *Problemas sociales y económicos de América Latina* (Ediciones de la Universidad de Chile, 1936), p. 85.

the country with the larger number of latifundia in America, which may be explained by its immense extension, the difficulties of communication, and the lack of a well-defined agrarian policy." [7]

In 1926 in Chile, large estates, latifundia (of more than 2,500 acres) composed more than 79 per cent of the total agricultural area of the country; in 1930, 78 per cent. "These data show that the problem of large agricultural property and latifundia constitutes an essential feature of the system of distribution of agricultural land in Chile and that their number does not diminish." Of the agricultural land of the country, 78 per cent was held by 2,690 owners. In Santiago, the most fertile of the provinces, sixty families owned two-thirds of the agricultural land. "The pattern of large agricultural holdings in Chile has created a privileged class, an agrarian oligarchy which has ruled the country for more than a hundred years." [8] That is the conclusion of Troncoso, himself a Chilean. In a more recent book, a North American comments: "They [the total of 202,000 agricultural properties] are the properties that are the true producers of the nation's agricultural wealth. They cover a total area of some 59,000,000 acres, of which 53 per cent is concentrated in estates of over 12,000 acres, owned by no more than 558 proprietors. On the other hand, some 63,000 farmers own about 1.7 per cent of the land in parcels ranging up to 50 acres in size. Fifty-five per cent of the owners studied by the census hold less than 2 per cent of the land, and one-half of 1 per cent of them hold 53 per cent of the land. And that, regardless of all considerations of social justice, regardless of all special pleas made by adherents of any special creeds, constitutes a great social problem for any nation." [9]

More or less the same situation exists in Paraguay and

[7] *Ibid.*, p. 89.
[8] *Ibid.*, p. 94.
[9] Earl Parker Hanson, *Chile, Land of Progress* (New York: Reynal & Hitchcock, 1941), p. 99.

Peru, Colombia, Uruguay, Ecuador and Venezuela. Also in Central America, especially in Guatemala. El Salvador is one of the most densely populated countries, but its agricultural land is in the hands of a few families.

I am dealing with Mexico separately because its case is exceptional. Before the 1910 Revolution there were in Mexico large agricultural estates (haciendas), some of them covering 1,729,700 acres. At that time 2 per cent of the population owned 75 per cent of the land. The first agrarian census, taken in 1930, showed that 2.5 per cent of agricultural properties formed 85 per cent of the total area of such properties. Before the Revolution Mexico was essentially a country of latifundia, and 1,831 haciendas, of more than 24,000 acres each, contained nearly 170,000,000 acres. If we assume (as is generally the case) that each hacienda was owned by one family, and if we place at five the number of the family members, we can say that approximately *one-twentieth* of 1 per cent of the population of Mexico owned one-third of the national territory! What the agrarian policy of the revolutionary governments of Mexico has done to correct this monstrous situation can be seen from the fact that, up to November, 1940, end of President Cárdenas' democratic administration, the government, after splitting large haciendas, had distributed some 76,000,000 acres of that land to nearly 2,000,000 peasants who for the first time could till a soil that was theirs, with a plow of their own.

However, the work of the Mexican Revolution in the field of agriculture, remarkable as it is, is far from reaching the goal. In 1940, there were nearly 4,000,000 individuals entitled to land. Of these, during twenty-five years of revolution, only 2,000,000 had received their land, most of them during Cárdenas' six-year term. Thus the agrarian reform has benefited so far only half of the peasant families of Mexico. It is only halfway on the road of complete agrarian democracy.

Statistics on concentration of land become more eloquent

when dealing with Latin America because its republics are *essentially agricultural.* For instance, almost 80 per cent of the people of Mexico make a living from the soil. That is almost four times the proportion found in the United States. Concentration of landownership means for us economic and political monopoly. And the result of this autocratic set-up has been national bankruptcy and misery.

According to domestic statistics, intelligently gathered by the C.T.A.L.—a pioneer in this worthy task—the average *hourly* wage of a United States worker in at least ten of the most common occupations (construction work, carpentering, mining, unskilled labor, printing, driving, painting, etc.) is $1.33. In contrast, the average hourly wage in other republics of the Hemisphere for more or less the same group of workers is: Canada, $0.56 per hour; Argentina, $0.30; Uruguay, $0.25; Cuba, $0.20; Colombia, $0.14; Mexico, $0.13; Costa Rica, $0.11; Bolivia, $0.09; Chile, $0.06; Ecuador and the Dominican Republic, $0.05 each. From $1.33 to five U.S. cents— a nickel, a package of chewing gum; so goes the scale of hourly wages, unevenly distributed among similar workers of our Hemisphere.

Some people try to becloud the issue by contending that such statistics mean nothing because the cost of living in Latin America is so low that you can almost buy there with cents, goods and services for which you must pay in the U.S.A. with dollars. That is wholly inaccurate! The same C.T.A.L. has compiled specific data which allow us to refute this silly argument. The data show, not what the workers of the Hemisphere comparatively *earn,* but what they *buy* with what they earn.

Let us consider only some of the essential items of food, such as bread, beef, milk, eggs, and sugar. In the United States the average worker earns, per hour, enough to buy 7.8 kilos of bread, while an hour's work by a Canadian worker in substantially the same occupation earns enough to buy only

4.3 kilos of bread; by an Argentine, 3.2; a Uruguayan, 2.9; a Cuban, 1.7; a Chilean, 1.4; a Mexican, 1.1; a Colombian, 1.0; a Costa Rican, 0.9; a Dominican, 0.5; an Ecuadorian, 0.4; and a Bolivian, 0.3. Thus, to take the two extremes only, a United States worker is paid, in bread, some twenty times as much as his fellow worker from Bolivia. In terms of beef, the situation is as follows: the United States, 2.0 kilos; Canada, 1.1; Argentina, 1.6; Uruguay, 2.0; Mexico, 0.6; Colombia, 0.3; Chile, Ecuador, Bolivia, 0.2 each; Dominican Republic, 0.1. That is to say, United States workers are paid, in terms of beef, ten times more than some of their fellow workers in Latin America. In milk, United States workers' pay is good for more than twelve times the amount that can be purchased by their Latin American brothers. In sugar, the situation is still favorable to the United States workers. They can buy with their wages thirty times as much sugar as, for instance, the workers of the Dominican Republic. It is sad to say that even in Cuba, which exports sugar in large amounts, workers can purchase only one-fifth of the amount which United States workers can buy with their wages. Finally, in terms of eggs, the hourly wage of the United States worker allows him to buy 53.4; Canada, 21.5; Argentina, 24.4; Uruguay, 16.6; Colombia, 8.0; Mexico, 7.5; Costa Rica, 6.4; Chile, 4.5; Ecuador, 3.3; Bolivia, 2.9; and the Dominican Republic, 2.4.

I could add to the statistics compiled by the C.T.A.L. others gathered by General Electric's President Gerard Swope. He has patiently figured out that a laborer in the United States needs to work 4.5 minutes in order to pay for a kilowatt of the electricity which he uses; whereas, for the same amount, a laborer in Argentina must work 31 minutes; in Brazil, 30; in Chile, 37; in Uruguay, 36. A United States worker can buy an electric light bulb with 0.25 hours of his work, whereas to buy this a worker in Argentina engaged in a similar occupation has to work 1.7 hours; Brazil, 3.8; and

Chile, 3.9. Lastly, a United States worker can buy a newspaper with three minutes of his labor time, whereas it would take an Argentine, similarly employed, twelve minutes, a Brazilian twenty-four minutes, a Chilean sixteen, and so on.[10]

Are those conditions compatible with our idea of a Pan American democracy? As long as they prevail, can we even think of our Hemisphere as a territory in which there is equality? Lastly, can democracy have the same meaning for the Bolivian, the Chilean, Haitian, Dominican, or almost any other underpaid Latin American worker, as it has for the workers in the United States? Still more simply: can democracy have *any meaning whatsoever* for the ill-housed, ill-clothed, ill-fed Latin American millions who have never known a concrete, tangible benefit of democracy? The issue raised here is the most important one in any factual discussion of Pan Americanism. It is the very meat of Pan Americanism. Any other consideration might be important, but relatively it is secondary.

If Latin Americans are to become more and more involved in the fate of democracy, they must become more and more acquainted with its tangible benefits. And if many last-minute Pan Americanists spoke less of spiritual and abstract conditions and studied more our material conditions for economic democracy, the importance and value of this wave of Pan American enthusiasm could never be overestimated. In dealing with Latin America, as in dealing with the United States or with any other part of the world, we must face the issue squarely. The naked truth is that of the one hundred twenty-six million Latin Americans, certainly *no fewer than eighty-five million are actually starving*. They have no houses, no beds, no shoes.

The most recent official statistics show that in Mexico there are slightly more than five million beds for a population of

10 Gerard Swope, "The Cost of Living in South America," *Atlantic Monthly,* Vol. CLXV, pp. 777-779 (June, 1940).

nearly twenty million, and that therefore fifteen million of my countrymen have no beds on which to sleep. Roughly, the per capita number of beds in Mexico is equivalent to that of automobiles in the United States, about one to every four people. Of the 3,884,600 houses in all Mexico, fewer than 265,000, sheltering some 2,500,000 people, have drinking and running water. Even in Mexico's stately capital, with 1,700,000 inhabitants, 500,000 lack those conveniences.[11] And Mexico is one of the most advanced of the Hemisphere republics, certainly the leader in labor legislation.

In Chile, children fourteen years old earn less than three cents American money a day.[12] It is not unusual to see nine people living in one single room. Tenant farmers receive less than two cents American money a day. For food, they receive hardtack and native peas three times a day. These data are derived from an investigation of ten thousand cases all over the country. Child shepherds make less than one cent American money a day—not even four dollars a year. And then this astonishing statement: "Of all the [ten thousand] cases investigated, only 2 per cent of the peasants ate meat, and only 6 per cent had *ever tasted milk*.[13]

In Peru the situation is similar. As a matter of fact, except for a number of workers in Mexico, Argentina, Uruguay, Brazil, and Costa Rica, the only change in the statistics is the difference in currencies. There are people in Bolivia who work twenty hours a day for a miserable wage. Most of the house workers receive *no* salary and are simply housed and fed.[14] The daily nutrition of these millions is one of starvation, and the days are not infrequent in which they eat absolutely nothing.

In fact, a great many of our Indian populations are sys-

[11] See the magazine *HOY*, published in Mexico City, May 2, 1942, pp. 4-5.
[12] Troncoso, *op. cit.*, p. 75.
[13] *Ibid.*, p. 78.
[14] *Ibid.*, p. 97.

tematically trained by the employers in the use of native drugs. I refer to the widespread habit among the Indians of southern Colombia, Bolivia and Peru, of chewing the leaves of coca, from which cocaine is derived. In an official, scientific publication, Dr. Piedrahita writes:

"It is easily explainable why the habit of chewing coca with alkaline bases is so widespread among the Indians of southern Colombia. At the present time this vice is encouraged by the landowners—the coca ration is used as wage money. Much of the day's work is paid in coca leaves which are cultivated on the haciendas.

"The chewers of coca skillfully hold the portion in one side of the mouth, every once in a while rechewing it or passing it to the other side. The saliva, filled with alkaloid, acts locally producing a superficial anesthesia of the buccal cavity. Once swallowed, it causes the same effect to the gastric mucus. All day long, the chewer changes the exhausted leaves for new ones, and thus maintains a permanent cocainization of the upper digestive tract. The resulting anesthesia appeases thirst, dulls the appetite and lessens hunger. Thus these men fool themselves and live on, burning their meager energies." [15]

This seems incredible; but it is a plain fact, which no one can deny. In order to extract the maximum of cocaine from the coca leaves, they are mixed with lime and ashes. The mixture is called *caccha*. In his study of living conditions of the Peruvian natives, published by the International Labor Office, Troncoso writes: "The inhabitants of the Sierra and the workers of the mines use great quantities of coca because they think it gives them more strength and helps them resist hunger, cold, and altitude. Unquestionably coca produces an anesthesia which suppresses the feeling of hunger. . . . All

[15] César Uribe Piedrahita, "Esquema para un estudio de la patología indígena en Colombia," *América Indígena*, Vol. II, p. 67 (Mexico, Jan., 1942).

the hygienists who have studied the use of coca among the Indians agree that its effects are profoundly devastating." [16] The vice is so embedded in the native population that when Indians from Peru went to work in the mines of Chile in 1925, employers requested their government to authorize importation of the drug. Dr. Long, a high official of the United States government then in Chile as technical adviser to the Secretary of Hygiene, exposed the harmful effects of coca and asked that only a restricted amount be allowed to enter the country. The Indian consumes *daily* from two to three ounces of these leaves. The employers and landowners claim that without coca the natives could not work. However, doctors agree that this benumbing herb creates dyspepsia, insomnia, and even insanity. Writes Troncoso: "Generally the Indian chews daily one hundred grams of coca, which according to investigators from Peru represents *3.88 weekly grams of pure cocaine.*" [17]

Finally, let us not forget the alarming percentages of illiteracy. In Honduras, Bolivia, Paraguay, Guatemala, Haiti, Ecuador, 73 to 83 per cent of the population is illiterate; in Peru, Nicaragua, Brazil, and Venezuela, around 70 per cent; in the Dominican Republic, Panama, and Cuba, 60 per cent; El Salvador, 55 per cent; Colombia, 50 per cent; Mexico, 45 per cent; Costa Rica, 32 per cent; Chile, 24 per cent; Uruguay, 20 per cent; Argentina, 12 per cent; the United States and Canada, 4.3 per cent.

In Latin America there are still people who say that there is nothing abnormal in the situation of the native populations, because the Indians are miserable, but helpless, hopeless and happy; that they would not know what to do if they were given shoes to wear, or beds on which to sleep, not to mention bathtubs, radios, and medicines. Whoever says that

[16] Moisés Poblete Troncoso, *Condiciones de vida y de trabajo de la población indígena del Perú* (Geneva: International Labor Office, 1938), pp. 170-71.
[17] *Ibid.*

is neither a true American nor a true human being. It would
be impossible to find on our good earth a nobler man than
the Indian or the mestizo. It would require an entire volume
to summarize their intellectual, artistic, and moral qualities.
In a moving appeal before the First Inter-American Congress
on Indian Life held in Mexico in 1940, Lázaro Cárdenas,
that great figure in the battle for Latin American democracy,
exclaimed:

"It is not correct to say that the Indian has rebelled against
his own betterment or that he has been indifferent to progress. If often he does not show his joy or his pain, but hides
his feelings like a sphinx, it is because he is accustomed to the
oblivion to which he has been relegated; he is used to plow-
ing fields which bring him no return for his labors, to weaving
cloth which he cannot use to clothe himself, to constructing
buildings which do not shelter him or improve his condition
of life, to overthrowing dictatorships only so that new dictatorships may be set up."

We share in common the problem of raising economic
standards for millions of people. This submerged population
must come to the surface. It must breathe, grow, expand.
We produce enough goods. The trouble lies not there but in
the distribution of what we produce. This aspect of the
problem was clearly stated in a remarkable address by Milo
Perkins, the Executive Director of the Board of Economic
Warfare: "This is a long, long fight to make a mass-production economy work. . . . The battle will be won when we
have built up mass consumption to a point where markets can
absorb the output of our mass-production industries running
at top speed. . . . Complete victory will not be won until
there is a full and increasing use of the world's resources to
lift living standards from one end of this planet to the other.
. . . We put up with a civilization which was commodity-rich
but consumption-poor too long to avert the present catas-
trophe. . . . *The job of the future will be to build up a mass*

consumption great enough to use this mass production." [18]

Capitalism, through private initiative and profit incentive, solved successfully the problem of production. We owe to it the efficient technique of mass production. However, capitalism has shown scant concern for the equally important problem of consumption.

On the other hand socialism seems more concerned with the distribution of goods. Its interest is consumption. It aims at creating mass consumption by lifting the standards of living and the purchasing power of the workers. In this way socialism tends to complete the job brilliantly initiated by capitalism. A democratic socialism would destroy none of the advantages of capitalism. It simply would begin where capitalism leaves off.

In the same address Milo Perkins reminds us that "if the peoples of Asia alone earned an extra *penny a day* it would open up a new market of *four billion dollars a year* for somebody."

The triumph of democracy will prepare the day when the native populations of all America will be able to plow their own fields, weave their own clothes, and live in the houses they have built. These people have survived four hundred years of injustice. After victory, the forces of democracy, in each country, must release the full potentialities of their submerged populations.

That day, America will be a better place in which to live. That day we shall speak with pride of our *American* standard of life.

[18] From the Commencement address of Milo Perkins, at Swarthmore College, Swarthmore, Pa., May 25, 1942.

Part Two: INTER-*America*

CHAPTER VI

Bolívar's Horizon

PAN AMERICANISM is unparalleled in the world's history. It is the first successful experiment in the friendly organization of an entire Hemisphere. There have been many "Pan" movements in history: for instance, Pan Islamism, an attempt at brotherhood through a common faith; Pan Slavism, an attempt at union through community of race; or Pan Germanism, an ideal of union through community of language. Pan Americanism does not exclude any religion or race or language. Its only boundaries are those of the Western Hemisphere. If it reaches full maturity, Pan Americanism will become an impressive demonstration that, given a climate of international decency, large and small nations, powerful and weak ones, can live side by side in peace. That would mean that not only individuals or nations but whole continents as well have outlived the law of the jungle, and that a reasonable solution of international difficulties may be found whenever there is the will to do so. Pan Americanism is a continental enterprise which embraces twenty-one countries living in all climates, in all types of geographical environment, with people of all races, worshiping different gods, and speaking many languages. The twenty-one countries present few common features, but among these are the facts that they *all* were at one time or another colonies exploited by European powers; that they *all* initiated their life as independent nations with a fight against Europe; that they *all* adopted, sooner or later, a republican form of government;

that today they *all* have officially recognized the existence of a common democracy throughout the Americas; and finally, that today they *all* have become aware of an increasing common threat—namely, Nazi military expansion.

Simón Bolívar, born in Caracas, Venezuela, on July 24, 1783, may well be hailed as the most abundantly rich personality of the New World. More than a century ago he abolished slavery, fought some two hundred battles in tropical jungles and snow-clad Andean peaks, freed half a dozen nations, personally drafted their political constitutions, and even traced the broad lines of their international policy—a policy that today we call Pan Americanism. His fight to keep the new nations together was as glorious as and perhaps even more dramatic than his fight to emancipate them from the Spanish yoke. He succeeded in freeing them but struggled in vain to keep them united. We can say that Bolívar was for South America a George Washington, a Jefferson, and a defeated Lincoln. Nearly a century and a half ago he advocated one great confederation—he liked to refer to it as the *Nation*—in which all the new countries of America would find themselves united. He also planned periodic meetings of a Pan American Congress. Moreover—and this prophetic side of Bolívar is less known—he explicitly and repeatedly proclaimed that, in order to survive, the Spanish American commonwealth had to rely on the strength and cooperation of both England and the United States. A Pan American Confederation allied with Great Britain was, in Bolívar's eyes, not only an invincible combination but one destined to make world history. In the field of international politics, Bolívar is the recognized father of international arbitration and of the idea of a League of Nations. To few men does mankind owe so much. Venezuela, Colombia, and the territory of what is today Panama, Ecuador, Peru, and Bolivia— the two latter with San Martín's cooperation—all owe their independence to the fortitude and genius of Bolívar, *El*

Libertador (The Liberator), as he was officially proclaimed. Bolivia was first named *República Bolívar,* in his honor and during his lifetime.

However, although Bolívar was the first to give definite shape to the idea of Pan Americanism in the Congress of 1826, other people before him had advocated permanent cooperation among the new independent countries of the Western Hemisphere. They were almost exclusively Latin Americans. We may therefore claim that Pan Americanism is essentially a Latin American creation. In 1797 General Francisco Miranda, the Precursor of Independence—*"El Precursor"*—founded in London a political society known as "The Great American Union." Such famous leaders as O'Higgins of Chile, Alvear, and the great San Martín of Argentina—besides Bolívar himself—were initiated by Miranda into their respective struggles for national liberation. But Miranda—in some respects the Thomas Paine of South America—who had fought as a soldier under George Washington and as a general under Napoleon, was to be only an apostle. Since their earliest movements for independence, the men of Central and South America had continental union in their hearts and in their minds. The Chilean Egaña in 1810 wrote, in a project of Declaration of Rights of the people of Chile, that "the states of America must unite for their external security against the aims of Europe." The tentative constitution of Chile asked for a *continental citizenship,* the formation of a General Congress of the Nation (America), and the adoption of a system of union and mutual security. Also in 1810 Bolívar, then a deputy from Venezuela, proposed a Spanish American League of Nations. To the London *Morning Chronicle* of September 5, 1810, he stated that "the Venezuelans will take care to invite all the peoples of America to unite in a single confederation." In 1811 the authorities of Buenos Aires granted naturalization to foreign officers fighting for the independence of Argentina. In 1817 Argentina and Chile formed an alliance—the first among nations of the Western Hemisphere. One year later Bolívar, fighting for the independence of Venezuela, promised his help to the inhabitants of Argentina and conveyed to them his project for the union of all the countries of South America. In 1821 Bolívar, the Venezuelan, wrote from Colombia (Nueva Granada) to O'Higgins, the Chilean, assuring him that the armies of Colombia were about to march into Ecuador with instructions to help the armies from Argentina and Chile to liberate Peru.[1] Those were glorious days for Pan Americanism!

Bernardo Monteagudo, another pioneer of Spanish American independence, in a study published after his death (1825), had gathered his ideas "on the necessity of a general federation of the Spanish American states," in which he suggested collaboration with Great Britain and the United States. José Cecilio del Valle, from Central America, expressed himself in these terms: "I would like to see a *General Congress* . . . which would endeavor to solve this problem: devise the most useful plan so that *none of the nations of America may be the object of foreign invasions.*"[2] The Uruguayan liberator, Artigas, stated in his *Ordenanzas de Corso Marítimo* that "it will be considered as enemy properly anything which constitutes a threat of subjugation or a new conquest of the Provinces of the Plata or *of any other one of the American continent.*"[3] Bernardo O'Higgins on May 5, 1818, said in his "Manifesto to the People Who Form the State of Chile" that "the simultaneous operation of our Forces . . . will determine whether it is possible to form, on

[1] Enrique Gil, *Evolución del Panamericanismo* (Buenos Aires: Librería y Casa Editorial de Jesús Menéndez, 1933), p. 21.

[2] Gaston Nerval, *Autopsy of the Monroe Doctrine* (New York: The Macmillan Company, 1934), p. 131.

[3] *Ibid.*, p. 131.

the American Continent, *a Grand Confederation.*" [4] The
Foreign Minister of Colombia, Pedro Gual, submitted to
the Congress of Bogotá: "First: that the American states
*ally and confederate themselves perpetually, in peace and
in war,* to consolidate their freedom and independence,
guaranteeing each other, mutually, the integrity of their
respective territories." [5] The Colombian Chargé d'Affaires
at Washington, Manuel Torres, proposed a continental
union in 1821; about the Holy Alliance project to establish
a monarchy in Mexico, he wrote to John Quincy Adams,
U.S. Secretary of State, "This is a new reason which ought
to determine the President of the United States no longer
to delay a measure which will naturally establish an American alliance, capable of counteracting the projects of the
European powers, and of protecting our republican institutions." [6] The Mexican Minister in London, José Mariano
de Michelena, made a similar suggestion to the Brazilian
representative in that capital. In the United States, the
lonely voice of Henry Clay was heard in 1820 in favor of "a
human freedom league" from Hudson Bay to Cape Horn.
I say "lonely" because the idea of union or even a casual
alliance with the American republics was immediately ridi-
culed and attacked by statesmen of the United States. To
them, what we call today Pan Americanism was absurd and
even dangerous to the sovereignty of the United States, as
John Quincy Adams expressed it after he became President
in 1825.

Pan Americanism, at its inception, was indeed a Latin
American affair. Expressions like "Congress of America,"
"Congress of the Nation," "General Federation," "General
Congress," a "Grand Confederation," "Perpetual Alliance
and Confederation," "American Alliance," "The Greatest

[4] *Ibid.*, p. 132.
[5] *Ibid.*, p. 132.
[6] *Ibid.*, p. 133.

Nation in the World" (meaning All America), "The American Pact," "A Cordial Confederation," "A Truly American League," "A Society of Sister Nations," and Bolívar's "Perpetual Union, League, and Confederation" were popular in the political vocabulary of early nineteenth century Latin America. Independence and confederation of nations—the two terms seemed at first inseparable; inseparable not only in theory but in practice. The first Latin Americans were inter-Americans. They acted as such. The shores of the continent were to them the only natural frontier. Within the Hemisphere they fought for the independence of their sister nations with as much fervor as they did for the independence of their own country. In the diplomatic archives of Peru I found the following description, which I quote in full because it illustrates this very important point:

"Colombians and Argentines completed the war of independence for Peru. An Argentine army freed Chile and another mixed army of Peruvians and Colombians gave the finishing blow, after Ayacucho, for the independence of Upper Peru. In all the proclamations of insurgent cabildos or assemblies of America, national elements mix with exiles from other countries who, instinctively naturalized in the new country, fight for liberty. The unanimity of the liberating feeling sweeps away still undefined narrow patriotisms. Not only in the armies are the various citizens of America merged but even in the exercise of political and diplomatic functions. Bolívar exercises the supreme command in *five* republics, and no one thinks of branding him as a foreigner. Sucre, a Venezuelan, governs Bolivia. And San Martín, an Argentine, governs Peru. Particularly in the diplomatic field is this continental solidarity demonstrated. The spiritual identity among all these born in America is so absolute that for functions, such as diplomatic ones, so jealously guarded in other parts of the world, they choose in Hispanic America citizens of other nations of the continent with the same con-

fidence as their countrymen. A Mexican, Miguel Santa
María, is the first plenipotentiary of Colombia in Mexico.
An Ecuadorian, Vicente Rocafuerte, is for many years a
diplomatic envoy of Mexico in London. The first diplomatic
representation of Peru in a foreign country is entrusted to
an Argentine, García del Río. A Peruvian, the seaman,
Eugenio Cortéz, is appointed plenipotentiary of Iturbide
before the emissaries who in 1823 carried Spanish proposals
to Mexico. Monteagudo, an Argentine, and Heres, a Colombian, are both secretaries of state for Peru. Ortiz de Zavallos,
a Colombian, is accredited as diplomatic agent of Peru in
Bolivia to sign treaties of confederation and territorial concession. Funes, an Argentine, acts in Buenos Aires as diplomatic agent of Bolívar. The first Peruvian minister in Central America, Don Manuel de Llano, learning upon his
arrival in that country that Central America has incorporated itself with Mexico, requests his own incorporation in
the Mexican army. The Argentine Republic takes steps to
obtain, during the days of Brazilian aggression against
Chiquitos, the appointment of common diplomatic agents
in the Brazilian Empire.

"Solidarity is so close that, when the hardships of war and
lack of communications sometimes leave diplomatic representatives penniless, they are aided with loans by the countries in which they are accredited. Such was the case of the
Bolivian Minister, Mendizábal, in Lima, and the Peruvian
Minister, Morales, in Mexico, at the time of the emancipation.

"Among the chancelleries the same brotherhood reigns
as among individuals. A true federated diplomacy is established among the diplomatic representatives of the New
World. The news of the sailing of a Spanish fleet, or of the
machinations of the Holy Alliance, or of the words of
Canning, is transmitted spontaneously from chancellery to
chancellery.

"To spiritual solidarity is united the fullest economic solidarity. Chile lends to Peru part of the money it has obtained, so that the latter may continue its war of independence. Peru defrays the expenses of the emancipating expedition in Bolivia without even previously fixing the amount of that tremendous enterprise. In 1826 Mexico lends Colombia 63,000 pounds so that the latter may pay the interest on a loan contracted in London, thus saving the credit of one American nation—which is the credit of all other American nations. Loans and requests for money are frequent among belligerent countries in spite of the economic distress caused everywhere by war." [7]

That, once more, is true all-inclusive Pan Americanism. However, the entire policy of that idea was shaped in the first international conference of American republics assembled in the Western Hemisphere. I do not mean the one held in Washington in 1889 but the Congress of Panama of 1826.

While an exile in the island of Jamaica in 1815 Bolívar wrote his now famous "prophetic letter," in which he declared: "I desire more than anybody else to see *the formation in America of the greatest nation in the world,* not so much as to its extension and wealth as to its glory and freedom. . . . How beautiful it would be if *the Isthmus of Panama should come to be to us what the Isthmus of Corinth was to the Greeks!* May God grant that some day we may have the happiness of installing there an august congress . . . to discuss and study the high interests of peace and war with the nations of the other three parts of the world!" [8]

In 1818 he wrote to Juan Martín de Pueyrredón, supreme director of the United Provinces of the Río de la Plata: "We shall hasten with the keenest interest to consummate on our

[7] Extract from *El Archivo Diplomático del Perú,* Vol. I, "El Congreso de Panamá" (1826), Recopilación y Prólogo por Raúl Porras Barrenechea, 1930.
[8] Nerval, *op. cit.,* p. 136.

part *the American pact,* which, *forming a political body of all our Republics,* holds America up to the world with an aspect of majesty and greatness without parallel among the older nations. America, thus united, Heaven permitting, can call herself Queen of the Nations and Mother of Republics." [9] Again in 1818 he invited Argentina to unite in order to form a single community; and to the President of Peru he wrote: "Southern America will most likely form *a cordial confederation* in the first few years of her life. I see this more and more feasible every day." [10] A similar idea was transmitted to General Alvear in Argentina. These were more than thoughts. Bolívar sent special envoys. Joaquín Mosquera went to Chile, Peru, and Buenos Aires, with the following instructions: "Nothing is more interesting at this time than the constitution of *a league, truly American.* . . . It is necessary that ours be *a society of sister nations* . . . *strongly and powerfully united, in order to defend themselves from the aggressions of foreign powers.*" [11]

Separate treaties of alliance were concluded by Colombia with Peru (July 6, 1822), with Chile (October 21, 1822), with Buenos Aires (March 8, 1823), and with Mexico (October 3, 1823). Their very name is significant: they are treaties of "Perpetual Union, League, and Confederation." So far no mention of the United States of America. It was simply not yet in the game. But because Bolívar seldom mentioned the United States, and because, at first, that nation was not invited by him to participate in the Assembly of Panama, it is completely inaccurate to infer that Bolívar's Pan Americanism did not include the powerful republic to the north. Bolívar's mind was much too broad to be accused of petty considerations. Bolívar not only finally welcomed the inclusion of the United States in his Pan American scheme

9 *Ibid.,* p. 136.
10 *Ibid.,* p. 137.
11 *Ibid.,* p. 137.

but also—and that is less known—that of Great Britain.
Following the tradition manifested in all Latin American
emancipators from Miranda on, Bolívar laid great stress
upon Great Britain's participation. His admiration for Great
Britain was such that he advocated the adoption by the new
Latin American republics of some kind of political system
similar to that of England—in his eyes, in spite of its mon-
arch, the most democratic of all the nations of the world.
In the second place, Bolívar understood perfectly well that
without the British fleet, the Western Hemisphere was vulnerable. And thirdly, Bolívar welcomed the inclusion of
Great Britain in the Pan American picture because her
influence would, to a great extent, serve to counterbalance
that of the United States.

In a document in the Archives of the Liberator at Caracas,
Venezuela, reproduced for the first time in Spanish in En-
rique Gil's book, *Evolución del Panamericanismo* (Buenos
Aires, 1933) and, to my knowledge, never published in
English, Bolívar summarized as follows his views on the
coming Assembly of 1826:

IDEAS ON THE CONGRESS OF PANAMA

The Congress of Panama will unite all the representatives of
America and the diplomatic agent of His British Majesty's Government. This Congress seems destined to form the largest, most
extraordinary, and strongest League of Nations that has yet appeared on the face of the earth. In comparison, the power of the
Holy Alliance will be inferior to that of this Confederation, provided that Great Britain wishes to take part in it as a constitutive
member. Mankind will give a thousand blessings to this League
of Salvation, and America, as well as Great Britain, will reap
benefits from it.

Political societies will be given a Code of Public Law to be
used as a rule of universal conduct in their relations.

1. The New World will be composed of independent nations,
all bound together by a common law that will determine their

external relations and offer them steady power in a General and Permanent Congress.

2. The very life of these new States would receive new guarantees.

3. Spain would make peace out of respect for England; and the Holy Alliance would give its recognition to these rising nations.

4. Internal order would be preserved intact among the different States and within each one of them.

5. None would be inferior to the others and none stronger.

6. A perfect equilibrium would be established in this truly *new order* of things.

7. The power of all would come to the rescue of any that might suffer from external aggression or anarchical factions.

8. Differences of origin and race would lose influence and strength.

9. America would no longer fear that tremendous monster that devoured the Island of Santo Domingo; neither would it fear the numerical preponderance of primitive inhabitants.

10. Finally, social reform would be reached under the holy auspices of liberty and social peace—provided that England holds the pointer of the balance.

Without doubt, Great Britain, through this arrangement, would reap considerable advantages:

(1) Her influence in Europe would be augmented progressively and her decisions would come to be those of destiny.

(2) America would serve her as a wealthy field of trade.

(3) America would be the center of her relations with Asia and Europe.

(4) The English would consider themselves equal to the citizens of America.

(5) Mutual relations between the two countries would in time become one.

(6) Americans would take on the British character and customs as normal elements of their future existence.

(7) Perhaps in the march of centuries, one Nation alone—the Federal Nation—will embrace the universe.

These ideas are already in the minds of Americans of the highest rank. They long with impatience for this initiative to be taken in the Congress of Panama, which can be the occasion of consolidating the union of the new States with the British Empire.

(Signed) BOLÍVAR.[12]

LIMA, February, 1826.

Today, when the connection between the fate of England and the Western Hemisphere has been once more recognized, it does good to underline this aspect of Bolívar's vision. Few people, even in our continent, know that it was not Franklin D. Roosevelt alone but Simón Bolívar who (more than one hundred twenty-five years ago) clearly understood that Pan Americanism would stand only as long as Great Britain remained unbeaten. "The great American Federation," he said in July, 1825, "cannot be achieved if the English do not protect it with their body and soul. . . . I know more than anyone else the inconvenience of this situation but as some one used to say, *I have my policy.*" [13] In March of that same year, in a letter to General Santander, Vice President of Colombia, Bolívar had defined his views in a declaration which could be subscribed to today by all conscious leaders of our American republics: "I believe America can be saved by these four elements: (1) *a large army* to command respect and insure protection; (2) a *European policy* to parry the first blows; (3) *England;* and (4) *the United States.*" And he added: "Besides, I insist upon a *Congress of all the American States,* as a fifth element of salvation." [14] What else could any American statesman add to this extraordinary advice? We find in it even the necessity of having a well-defined "European policy" to "parry the first blows" on the other side of the Atlantic before the threat comes to our shores. In Bolívar's time

[12] Gil, *op. cit.,* pp. 24-25.

[13] Enrique Finot, *Bolívar Pacifista* (New York: L. and S. Printing Co., 1936), pp. 111-112. Quoted from Vicente Lecuna, *Cartas del Libertador,* Vol. V, p. 25 (Caracas, 1929).

[14] Lecuna, *op. cit.,* Vol. IV, p. 288.

there were Napoleon and the Holy Alliance; in President Roosevelt's time there are Hitler and the Axis. In both cases the threat is similar; the remedy, identical.

The circular invitation addressed by Simón Bolívar to the governments of Colombia, Mexico, Central America, the United Provinces of Buenos Aires, Chile, and Brazil, is dated from Lima, Peru, December 7, 1824. In it the Liberator reminded his "great and good friends" that "it is time the interests and relations uniting the American republics should have a fundamental basis," and that "to initiate that system and concentrate the power of this great political body implies the exercise of a sublime authority. . . . Such a respectable authority can exist only in an assembly of plenipotentiaries." [15] He reminded the Latin American governments that in 1822 invitations had been sent Mexico, Peru, Chile, and Buenos Aires "to form a confederation and hold on the Isthmus of Panama or some other point agreeable to the majority, a congress of plenipotentiaries from each state that should act as a council in great conflicts, to be appealed to in case of common danger, and be a faithful interpreter of public treaties, when difficulties should arise, and conciliate, in short, all our differences." Bolívar referred to the future congress as the "august act of America" and ended the invitation with the following words: "The day our plenipotentiaries make the exchanges of their powers will stamp in the diplomatic history of the world an immortal epoch. When, after a hundred centuries, posterity shall search for the origin of our public law, and shall remember the compacts that solidified its destiny, they will finger with respect the protocols of the Isthmus. In them they will find the plan of the first alliances that shall sketch the mark of our relations with the universe. What, then,

[15] *International Conferences of American States, 1889–1928* (New York: Oxford University Press—for the Carnegie Endowment for International Peace—1931), p. xix.

shall be the Isthmus of Corinth compared with that of Panama?"[16]

After the invitation, Bolívar issued on May 15, 1825, instructions that were to govern the conduct of his ministers plenipotentiary. He sent the 1822 invitation in his capacity as President of Colombia and the later instructions of 1825 as head of the government of Peru. The delegates were instructed among many other things: (a) to secure the great compact of Perpetual Union, League, and Confederation against Spain, and against foreign rule of any character (Article 6); (b) to decide about the fate of Cuba and Puerto Rico (Article 9); (c) to issue a proclamation containing an endorsement of the Monroe Doctrine (Article 13); (d) to negotiate a treaty by which all the new American states attending the Congress would be united by a close alliance, both offensive and defensive; (e) to secure the territorial *status quo* of all the American nations at the time of their independence *(uti possidetis juris)* (Article 18); (f) to enact measures for the suppression of the slave trade in America; and (g) to promulgate the treaties agreed upon at Panama as the public law of America and make them obligatory on all the states which were parties thereto.[17]

Bolívar's Pan Americanism—in reality the only Pan Americanism possible and certainly the only Pan Americanism acceptable to Latin Americans—was a continental policy of equal rights and mutual obligations. It was meant to be a dialogue, not a monologue, like President Monroe's. It was to be a Pan Americanism of partners, not one in which a self-appointed tutor assumes the responsibility of protecting his weaker neighbors if and when convenient to his own national interests. The Monroe Doctrine was at its best a mere expression of the right of self-defense—and as such claims no originality. Bolívar's pattern of a truly continental

[16] *Ibid.*, p. xx.
[17] *Ibid.*, pp. xxii-xxiv.

order was then and is still today Pan Americanism.

The United States was invited to the Congress of Panama, although not at first. The Liberator had an instinctive fear of the United States and its growing power. Besides he was afraid that too intimate a connection with the United States would be resented by England. And it was England and not the United States that helped Bolívar and the Spanish American nations in their fight for freedom. I have referred to the British connections of Miranda. The participation of British legionnaires, under Bolívar's command, in two of the outstanding battles of Spanish America's war of independence—Boyacá and Carabobo—is symbolical of the close friendship and collaboration between the English people and the first free Spanish Americans. Wrote Bolívar: "Federation with the United States is going to compromise us with England because the Americans are the only rivals of the English in regard to America." [18] And again: "I will repeat again that federation with the United States seems to me very dangerous because our interests are going to merge with those of Great Britain." [19] And finally: "I do not think that the North Americans should enter the Congress of the Isthmus. This step will cost us trouble with the British, even though the whole United States administration be favorable to us, as I do not doubt it, considering its fine make-up." [20]

But when the United States was invited, at the suggestion of Mexico, Colombia, and later on Central America, Bolívar welcomed the step. He wrote: *"I am glad that the United States sends delegates to the Isthmus, be it as it may."* [21] Either Bolívar had by then overcome his distrust of the United States and his fear that the presence of United States

[18] Lecuna, *op. cit.*, Vol. IV, p. 306. Letter to Vice President of Colombia, April, 1825.

[19] *Ibid.*

[20] Lecuna, *op. cit.*, Vol. V, p. 140.

[21] *Ibid.*, p. 273.

delegates at Panama would displease Great Britain, or maintaining both, he finally came to the conclusion that for the sake of true Pan Americanism the United States had to play an active role in this first act of that all-important policy.

This quotation from Bolívar, together with many other of the Liberator's ideas, shows how absurd and untrue are the contentions of some anti-American so-called Hispanistas of today, who use the name of the hero of Latin American independence as a banner in their fight to sabotage Pan Americanism. Bolívar was not at all anti-American. Quite the contrary. His only outspoken aversion was against Spain, never against the United States. Few people have written more caustic attacks on Spain than Simón Bolívar. In fact, his anti-Spanish feelings, which outlasted the fight for independence, were so vehement that at times they seem unfair. Bolívar understood quite clearly that the two natural allies of the Latin American countries were Great Britain and the United States. Referring to the dangers of the Holy Alliance, he wrote: "The palliative to all this is the great congress of plenipotentiaries in the Isthmus . . . *and an alliance most intimate and narrow with England and North America.*" [22]

The Vice President of Colombia, General Francisco de Paula Santander, in his reply to Bolívar's circular, wrote on February 6, 1825, in regard to the United States: "I have thought it advisable to invite them to join us in the August Assembly at Panama, as I am firmly persuaded that none among the allies will fail to see with satisfaction those sincere and enlightened friends take part in our deliberations upon subjects referring to our common interests." [23] President Victoria of Mexico, in his reply to Bolívar dated February 23 of the same year, also stated: "As I am persuaded that the cause of independence and liberty does not belong ex-

[22] *Ibid.*, Vol. IV, p. 291.
[23] *International Conferences, etc.*, p. xxi.

clusively to the Republics which were Spanish colonies, but that *it is also the cause of the United States of the North,* I have directed the Mexican Minister to make a suggestion to that effect to the President of that country, so as to enable him *to send his envoys, if he so wishes, to that assembly."* [24] Both the Mexican Minister in Washington, on November 1, 1825, and the Colombian Minister, on the following day, officially transmitted the invitation. The Mexican Minister delivered it to President Adams, the Colombian representative sent it to Secretary of State Clay.

The invitation to Panama met strong opposition in the United States, not unlike that manifested later on by isolationists against Secretary of State Blaine's proposal to convoke a Pan American conference in Washington in 1881; and later still, the opposition of similar elements against President Woodrow Wilson's League of Nations and Franklin D. Roosevelt's world policy. After a long debate during which several outstanding isolationist congressmen denounced Bolívar's invitation as a dangerous policy of foreign entanglement and alliances, the Government at Washington was finally authorized by the Senate of the United States to nominate Richard C. Anderson of Kentucky and John Sergeant of Pennsylvania to be envoys extraordinary and ministers plenipotentiary to the Assembly of American Nations at Panama. William B. Rochester of New York was to be secretary to the mission. Sergeant's trip was delayed by the discussions at the Senate. He arrived in Panama after the Congress had adjourned. Anderson, United States Minister in Bogotá, never reached Panama. He died at Cartagena during the trip. So, although fervently solicited to participate in the Assembly, no United States delegates were present. It was not President Adams' fault nor Henry Clay's. Both did everything within their power to overcome congressional opposition. In order to achieve that end, they

[24] Nerval, *op. cit.,* p. 143.

even distorted the true purpose of the meeting. The President, trying to reassure the members of the House of Representatives, stated that the acceptance of the United States did not imply foreign entanglements. In a message to the Senate on December 26, 1825—while requesting the nomination of the above-mentioned delegates—President Adams (the same man who as Secretary of State under President Monroe is credited by historians with having drafted the original text of the Monroe Doctrine) stated: "An agreement between all the parties represented at the meeting, that *each will guard by its own means* against the establishment of any future European colony within its border, may be found advisable. *This was more than two years since announced by my predecessor.*" [25] That predecessor was Monroe himself. Thus, as clearly shown here in the words of Monroe's ex-Secretary of State, the Doctrine never meant to imply any obligation of any kind for the United States to do something in case of European intervention in the affairs of the Western Hemisphere. The United States was simply committed by that historical message to denounce such interventions, as acts implying "unfriendly disposition" toward the Government at Washington. The obligation of the United States was strictly that and no more. From there on it was *"each by its own means."* How far this policy seems to us from Bolívar's contractual Pan Americanism of obligatory and mutual aid! Bolívar's idea was not each one for himself but one for all and all for one. That is again the core of Pan Americanism today.

President Adams sent another message to Congress on March 15, 1826: "The purpose of this Government is *to concur in none [measure] which would import hostility to Europe or justly excite resentment in any of her State*s. Should it be deemed advisable to contract any conventional engagement on this topic, our views would extend *no further*

[25] *Ibid.*, pp. 146-47.

*than to a mutual pledge . . . to maintain the principle in
application to its own territory,* and to permit no colonial
lodgments or establishment of European jurisdiction *upon
its own soil."* [26] *"Its own territory," "its own soil"*—always,
from the first United States Pan Americanists, was this fear
of foreign commitments, even to defend the integrity of the
other sister republics! How far from this limited declaration
to the legend of the Monroe Doctrine as the expression of
a policy intended to protect the whole continent!

On April 21, 1826, the government of the United States
was finally authorized to send delegates to the Congress of
Panama, but on condition that "the people of the United
States should be left free to act in any crisis in such a
manner as their feelings or friendships toward these republics and as their own honor and policy may at the time
dictate." To send delegates, under those circumstances, was
really an insult to Bolívar's invitation. Even Secretary of
State Henry Clay who is usually acclaimed as a pioneer
of Pan Americanism, in his instructions to the appointed
delegates underlined that "each State will, consequently, be
governed and left free, *according to its own sense of its
particular interests. All notion is rejected of an amphic-
tyonic council* [which was on the contrary what Bolívar
wanted] . . . There can be no necessity at this time for an
offensive and defensive alliance between the American
powers. . . . Such an alliance, under present circumstances,
*would be worse than useless, since it might tend to excite
feelings in the Emperor of Russia and his allies* [the Holy
Alliance.]" [27] Today, it seems incredible that, at the beginning, the foreign policy of the United States could have been
so timid and so mindful of European sensibilities. Anything,
even European intervention in America, rather than for the
United States to engage in foreign entanglements. The truth

[26] *Ibid.,* p. 148.
[27] *Ibid.,* p. 150.

is that the United States had to expand. It needed freedom
of action. It felt secure, at least as long as Great Britain was
on its side. Therefore, what did it care about the fate of
Latin American nations? In his important instructions to
the much discussed United States delegates to the Congress
of Panama, Secretary Clay admitted at the most the possibility of "a joint declaration of the several American States,
each, however, acting for and binding only itself, that,
within the limits of their respective territories no new European colony will hereafter be allowed to be established." [28]
And he took pains to reassure that such a joint declaration
*"is not intended to commit the parties . . . nor is it proposed
to commit them to a joint resistance against any future
attempt to plant a new European colony."* Those were the
words of a Secretary of State of the same nation which,
today, courageously upholding the principles of Bolívar, has
become the aroused champion of Pan American rights and
Pan American freedom.

Brazil, which was at that time an empire, Argentina, which
was uneasy at the hegemony of Bolívar's Colombia, and
Chile sent no delegates to Panama, although they endorsed
the purpose of the meeting. Colombia (including then what
is today Venezuela, Panama, and Ecuador), Central America
(including what is today Guatemala, Costa Rica, Nicaragua,
Honduras, and El Salvador), Mexico, and Peru sent delegates.

The Congress approved four treaties, the most important
one being that of Perpetual Union, League, and Confederation (July 15, 1826). The three others were: an agreement
providing that the Congress should meet periodically at
Tacubaya, Mexico; a convention fixing the contingent of
troops of each republic for a permanent army of 60,000
men, and their support; and an agreement additional to the
convention on contingents, regarding the organization of
the army. The Congresses of Peru, Mexico, and Guatemala

[28] *Ibid.,* p. 150.

failed to ratify these documents. Only Colombia approved them partially.

The Treaty of Confederation had thirty-one articles, its outstanding features being: (a) A pact of *confederation* to maintain in common, defensively and offensively, the sovereignty and independence of each and all of the confederated powers of America against foreign subjection and to secure to themselves from that time forward the enjoyment of unalterable peace (Articles 1 and 2). (b) The organization of an *inter-American army* for mutual defense against the enemies of all or any of the nations concerned, and measures to insure that warships and fleets of whatever number and grade belonging to one or more of the contracting parties should have free ingress and egress to and from the ports of each and all of them, and that they should be properly protected against attacks of common enemies (Articles 3, 4, and 5). The term "naval bases" was unnecessary among those early good neighbors. (c) Article 10 stood for what we call *"no separate peace."* "No one of the parties shall make peace with the common enemies of their independence without including therein specifically all the other allies." (d) *Meetings* were to take place every two years in time of peace and every year during the present and future common wars, in a general assembly, composed of two ministers plenipotentiary on the part of each party (Article 11). (e) The principles of *conciliation* (Article 13) and *arbitration* (Article 16) were adopted and have ever since been a main topic in any Pan American conference. (f) None of the contracting parties were to conclude *treaties* with any foreign power without previously consulting the others (Article 14). (g) The treaty established that there should be not only no separate peace but *no separate war*. "In case any of the confederated powers deem it advisable to declare war or commence hostilities against any power foreign to this confederation, it shall first solicit the good offices, interposition, and mediation of its allies" (Article 18). (h) The parties "solemnly obligate and bind themselves to uphold and defend the integrity of their respective territories, earnestly opposing any act of *colonial settlement* in them" (Article 21). (i) The citizens of all the contracting parties were to enjoy the rights and *privileges of citizens* of the republic in which they resided if they made an oath of allegiance to the constitution of the nation they adopted (Article 23). (j) The contracting parties obligated and bound themselves to cooperate for the complete abolition and extirpation of the African *slave trade* (Article 27).[29]

Where do we find a pact containing principles more important to the Western Hemisphere? The essence of what we call Pan Americanism was in Bolívar's thought. Very few improvements could we add. And practically none of Bolívar's great ideas could we afford to suppress. Had he accomplished nothing more than to inspire the meeting of Panama, he would still deserve to be considered the undisputed Father of Pan Americanism. However, the immensity of his mission becomes visible as we follow the successes and setbacks of Pan Americanism. Young countries selfishly insisted upon strengthening their narrow nationalism. Others, more powerful and ambitious, ignored Bolívar's romantic appeal because they wanted to keep unrestricted freedom of action in order to expand, even to the detriment of their neighbors. But the international idea of Bolívar was formulated with such clarity and so forcefully set to work that it was able to overcome all obstacles. Whatever the difficulties encountered, Pan Americanism—Bolívar's dream—is steadily shaping world history.

[29] See *International Conferences, etc.*, pp. xxiv-xxix.

CHAPTER VII

U.S. *Against* Us

AT THE time of its enunciation, the Monroe Doctrine was intended to be, essentially, a policy toward Europe; not a policy for the Hemisphere. It was a toothless warning indeed, but one definitely aimed at Europe. As such, there is nothing that we can hold against it. To reject its original intention would be tantamount to accepting the right of Europe to meddle with the nations of our Hemisphere: and that, no Latin American wants.

It is only by virtue of later interpretations—or rather "misinterpretations"—that the momentous Message was gradually fashioned into a Machiavellian policy for *intra*-Hemisphere consumption. From a candid but commendable United States gesture against European interference, the Doctrine was turned into a ruthless axiom, utilized by Washington administrations to suit the interests of what is known as *"Yankee Imperialism."* Because the Doctrine—certainly through no fault of its victims—was perverted to the point of being invoked as a justification for attacks against the sovereignty of the nations which it claimed to protect, it bulks large today as a stumbling block in the way of inter-American relations. "Paramount Interests," "Manifest Destiny," "Big-Stick Policy," "Watchful Waiting," "Dollar Diplomacy," "Paternalism," "Protectionism"—in short, "Yankee Imperialism"—those slogans have become irrevocably connected, in the minds of Latin Americans, with the two words, *"Monroe Doctrine."*

Yes, it may be said that historically there are *two* Monroe Doctrines: the one, promulgated by the President; and the other, the distorted Doctrine of the Corollaries. But the authentic one has been pushed into the background. Today people have not in mind the mild offering of the fifth President of the United States, but the subsequent concoction into which entered all the imperialistic ingredients added by more voracious occupants of the White House, among whom Theodore Roosevelt—twenty-sixth President of the United States of America—stands out conspicuously.

"The Monroe Doctrine, first enunciated by President Monroe in 1823," writes Professor Schuman, "was a warning to the European powers to keep out of the American Hemisphere and, by implications and successive reinterpretations, an assertion of the hegemony of the United States over the American continents." [1] That is precisely the point! The Doctrine has come to mean "an assertion of the hegemony of the United States over the American continents": a policy of bloody military occupation and outright diplomatic intervention.

Practically any Spanish American could put forward an impressive list of perfectly legitimate reasons why he rejects vehemently the Monroe Doctrine. A striking sample of genuine Latin American attitude in this respect, can be found in Gaston Nerval's book, significantly entitled *Autopsy of the Monroe Doctrine*.

"Autopsy" is perhaps wishful thinking. The *original* Doctrine is not dead. The Axis has given it a shot in the arm. To handle the *original* Doctrine as if it were dead would be not "autopsy" but vivisection. It is not dead, yet the weight of its additions places it beyond redemption. The Corollaries have become an intrinsic part of it. We cannot and must not forget them. No historical or diplomatic

[1] Frederick L. Schuman, *International Politics* (New York: McGraw-Hill Book Company, Inc., 1937), pp. 469-70.

surgeon could sever the Doctrine from the acts of aggression committed in its name; not even Professor Perkins, family doctor of Monroe's troublesome child, nor official interpreter Reuben Clark and his authoritative Memorandum. After all, a political Doctrine should not be judged by its intent only, but also by its results. Scores of charges can be leveled at the Monroe Doctrine by a Latin American. For the sake of clearness, I will limit the counts of my indictment to five:

1) It is *unilateral*.
2) It proved *inefficient*.
3) It was *perverted*.
4) It is *unpopular*.
5) It has become *outmoded*.

1) There can be no argument concerning the first count. Practically all historians, Anglo-Saxon as well as Latin, agree on that. Even Dr. Perkins writes: "The Monroe Doctrine was not, and was not intended to be, anything else than a unilateral declaration of policy. From that day to this American statesmen have insisted upon its purely American character, upon the right of the United States to interpret it in its own fashion, and on the basis of its own interests."[2] That point is so incontrovertible that we find, for once, Gaston Nerval and Dr. Perkins completely in accord. Nerval writes: "If there is anything at all upon which the statesmen of the United States, from Monroe to our day, agree in their views of the Monroe Doctrine, it is on the unilateral, nationalistic nature of the Doctrine."[3] Even so unbiased a critic as Stephen Duggan acknowledges that "the Monroe Doctrine is a unilateral statement made by, maintained by, and interpreted by, the United States alone, without consultation with any other country."[4] Also Reuben Clark,

2 Dexter Perkins, *Hands Off* (Boston: Little, Brown & Company, 1941), p. 70.
3 Nerval, *op. cit.*, p. 13.
4 *The Two Americas* (New York: Charles Scribner's Sons, 1934), pp. 146-47.

most unbiased *official* United States interpreter, writes: "The United States determines *when* and *if* the principles of the Doctrine are violated, and when and if violation is threatened. We *alone* determine what measures, if any, shall be taken to vindicate the principles of the Doctrine, and *we* of necessity determine when the principles have been vindicated. No *other* power in the world has *any* relationship to, or voice in, the implementing of the principles which the Doctrine contains. It is *our* Doctrine, to be by *us* invoked and sustained, held in abeyance, or abandoned as *our* high international policy or vital national interest shall seem to *us,* and to *us alone,* to demand." [5] Here again, I have italicized some words to bring out the point. There is nothing the matter with a *unilateral* policy. But its interpreters have no right to make it multilateral. The Monroe Doctrine was never meant to be anything but a one-sided policy. To pretend otherwise, is to commit historical heresy. It is not saving the Monroe Doctrine but rather confessing, by implication, that it has ceased to exist.

The Doctrine was a *monologue,* not a dialogue. It assumed, after the Theodore Roosevelt Corollary, an order of things entirely created and maintained by a self-appointed *guardian;* not one agreed to by equal partners. Why speak of "Americanization" or "continentalization"? Whatever rabbits Monroeist magicians pull out of their hats, that thing called Pan Americanism will never come out of it!

The Doctrine was unilateral not only in its proclamation, definition, and application, but also in its original motive, which was not the safety of the Hemisphere, but the security of the United States. So well known an authority as Professor Charles Edward Chapman, states: "The benevolent feature never was, and is not, the primary purpose of the doctrine. Its fundamental idea has always been *the se-*

[5] State Department, *Memorandum on the Monroe Doctrine,* prepared by J. Reuben Clark (Washington, 1930), p. xxiv.

curity of the United States. In this all-important respect, the Monroe Doctrine has not 'changed,' as so often alleged." [6] The security of the United States: again, there is nothing the matter with that. Pan Americanism also includes it—but does not stop there. It cares not only for the security of the United States but for that of all and each of the American Republics. *Good-Neighbor Pan Americanism is a joint enterprise freely undertaken by partners with equal rights and mutual obligations.* And that is precisely what the Monroe Doctrine is not!

2) *The Doctrine proved inefficient.* To be accurate, one should say that it was created impotent. It was the expression of a wish: to remove from the Western Hemisphere the threat of European military or political interference. But there was never mention of specific measures to be taken, should that wish go unheeded. Every North American statesman made it clear that the Doctrine never implied the slightest pledge by the United States actually to fight for the sovereignty of any American Republic. The man who as Secretary of State is credited with the drafting of the Message read by President Monroe to Congress—John Quincy Adams—said in a Message to the Senate December 26, 1825, after he had become President of his country: "An agreement between all the parties represented at the meeting [7] that each will guard *by its own means* against the establishment of any future European colony within its border may be found advisable. This was more than two years since announced by my predecessor." [8] It could not be clearer: *"each by its own means."* From the outset and from the lips of the statesmen who played the principal parts in the elaboration of the Doctrine, the world was advised that it was up to every country by its own means to uphold Monroe's

6 Charles Edward Chapman, *Republican Hispanic America* (New York: The Macmillan Company, 1937), p. 143.

7 Of Panama. See Chap. VI, p. 106.

8 *Messages and Papers of the Presidents* (Washington, 1896), Vol. II, p. 319.

recommendation, with the inference that, should any European nation violate such recommendation, the United States would not consider itself obligated to act; nor, of course, the other American republics. The Monroe Doctrine was too platonic to be effective. Later on, President Adams' Secretary of State, Henry Clay, in his instructions to the United States delegates—who did not reach Panama in time for Bolívar's Congress [9]—made a similar statement: "The President wishes you to propose a joint declaration of the several American states, each, however, acting for and binding only itself, that within the limits of their respective territories no new European colony will hereafter be allowed to be established." [10] *Each* by its *own* territory, binding only *itself:* that is the only type of Pan Americanism which legitimately could be built on the foundation of the real Monroe Doctrine. That, again, is as different from our modern concept of Pan Americanism as anything we can think of. A policy along those lines is precisely what our Pan Americanism does not want to be! In the same document, Secretary Clay goes further: "It is not intended to commit the parties . . . to the support of the particular boundaries . . . nor is it proposed to commit them to a *joint* resistance against any future attempt to plant a new European colony." [11] Here again we find the genuine expression of what Monroe's Message originally meant: a commendable but timid admonition. When there is no sanction, any transgressor is willing to take the risk. To consider European infringements as "the manifestation of an unfriendly disposition toward the United States," was not enough. Monroe did not say "act of hostility" but simply "unfriendly disposition." Little wonder that European interventions, of all kinds, took place from 1823 on.

[9] See Chap. VI, p. 105.
[10] *International American Conference: Reports of Committees and Discussions Thereon*, Vol. IV, pp. 113-49.
[11] See Chap. IX.

The Doctrine was appealed to in vain by some Latin American countries because of optimistic misinterpretations (improving the essence of the Message, not perverting it). The Doctrine did not bind the United States to any joint resistance against Europe. It never placed upon the United States the heavy burden of protecting the Hemisphere. The Corollaries of the Doctrine tended in that direction, but Monroe and the original Monroeists took pains to make it clear that it made no promise as to the international action of the United States.

It was appealed to in vain by Colombia in 1824; by Venezuela, Peru, and Ecuador, in 1846; by Nicaragua in 1848; again by Nicaragua, plus Honduras and El Salvador in 1849; by Mexico in 1862; by Venezuela, on five occasions (1876, 1880, 1881, 1884, 1887); by the Dominican Republic in 1905; and by Argentina in 1902–1903. Although impressive, this record is far from complete. I quote from Professor Perkins: "We must not imagine, however, that, speaking broadly, the United States, in the period with which we are dealing, pursued a consistent policy looking to the discouragement of a show of force against American republics by the states of the Old World. The recurrent chastisement of the Haitians, for example, never seems to have been regarded with much emotion in Washington. France in 1869, Spain in 1871, Germany in 1872, Great Britain in 1877, France, Spain, and Great Britain in concert in 1883, Russia in 1885, Great Britain again in 1887, resorted to force or the threat of force against the black politicians of Port-au-Prince without a word of protest from the State Department. The British in 1874, the Germans in 1878, the French in 1882, made minatory gestures against the Nicaraguans without arousing any concern in the United States. The Italians had a short-lived brawl with Colombia in 1886 which awakened no mention of the Monroe Doctrine. The French used coercive measures against the Dominican Republic in 1893 without the lifting of a hand at Washington." [12] There were other violations, treated in detail by Nerval in a chapter significantly entitled "Violations Wholesale": [13]

"In 1833, the United States did not prevent, nor even oppose, the seizure of the Argentine Islas Malvinas, or Falkland Islands, by Great Britain." Two years later, "the United States failed to support the government of Central America against the colonization which England was carrying on in Honduras Bay." "In 1838 France, and in 1845 France and England jointly, intervened by armed force in the Río de la Plata." "New British encroachments on territory of Central America occurred in 1838, when the Bay Islands, of which the most important was Ruatán, were seized by the authorities of British Honduras." "In 1837, a British squadron, in reprisal for alleged indignities heaped upon a British consul, proclaimed the closing of the ports of New Granada (Colombia) and actually blockaded the main port of Cartagena." In 1838 again French naval forces blockaded the Mexican port of Veracruz, "in order to insure the collection of private claims of French citizens from the Mexican government." In 1850 the United States and Great Britain signed the Clayton-Bulwer treaty which "provided for construction of a ship canal from the Atlantic to the Pacific Ocean by way of the San Juan River and the lakes of Managua and Nicaragua." "Thus," writes Nerval, "intervention by a European power in Latin America was not only accepted, but, in this case, invited and solemnly sanctioned by the country which had given the Monroe Doctrine to the world." In the same year "the government of the United States, after confidential conversations in Washington between the Secretary of State and the British and French Ministers, agreed to join France and England in a mediation to bring about the conclusion of the war between the Dominican Republic and

[12] Perkins, *op. cit.*, pp. 170-71.
[13] Nerval, *op. cit.*, p. 155.

Haiti." "In 1861, Spain, following several years of open intermeddling with the domestic affairs of the Dominican Republic, finally proclaimed its annexation to the Spanish Crown." "In 1864, the greatest violation of the Monroe Doctrine, and by far the most famous one, was consummated. This was the overthrow of the republican form of government in Mexico by French troops, and the enthronement of the Archduke Maximilian of Austria as the Emperor of Mexico."

These are the ten major violations of the original Monroe Doctrine. Nerval mentions "secondary" violations: "the invitation by the United States to England and France, in 1862, to aid in insuring the free transit through the Panama Isthmus and in restoring internal order in Colombia; the seizure of the Chincha Islands by Spain as a reprisal against the Peruvian government, in 1864; the bombardment of Valparaíso, major Chilean port, by Spanish naval forces, in 1866, as a coercive measure; the collective intervention of the United States and certain European powers, suggested by the former though never materialized, during the Cuban insurrection of 1868–78; the retrocession of the Island of St. Bartholomew by Sweden to France, in 1877; the refusal of the United States to prevent German military action against Haiti, in the controversy of 1897; etc., etc." [14]

Three major instances are commonly mentioned by those who claim the efficiency of the Monroe Doctrine. One is the French intervention in Mexico, 1861–67. The second is the Venezuelan boundary dispute with Great Britain in 1895. The third is the incident in which Venezuela was involved with Germany, England, and Italy, in 1902.

That the Monroe Doctrine had little or nothing to do with the French abandonment of Emperor Maximilian in Mexico is admitted even by Professor Perkins when he writes: "All these considerations taken together make it

[14] *Ibid.*, pp. 156-81, *passim.*

clear, as must frankly be admitted, that the Empire of Maximilian might have come to an inglorious end, and the French
troops been withdrawn from across the seas without the
intervention of the United States." [15] As a matter of fact,
in Perkins' more recent book, I was happy to find a statement to the effect that "there is much reason to believe
that such an assumption [that had it not been for the position of the United States, new, ambitious enterprises might
have been attempted on this side of the Atlantic] is a false
one; and that the developments of the period from 1865
to 1895 would not have been materially different if Monroe
and his successors had not interposed a veto upon the
colonization of the New World, or the subversion of its
republican governments." [16] I would be, of course, *the last*
to disagree with such a statement. But, safely backed by
Professor Latané, I may say that the three instances so
popular among the stubborn defenders of the Monroe Doctrine (plus its Corollaries) worked out for the good of the
Hemisphere, not because of the Doctrine, but because, Monroe or no Monroe, the European powers involved in Western
Hemisphere interventions had to abandon their adventures
on account of European conditions involving the problem of
European balance of power. Professor Latané maintains that
the French (aside from the heroic resistance put up by the
thousands of Mexican citizens who died for the freedom of
their country, under the leadership of the immortal Juárez)
would have been obliged to withdraw all support of the Aus-
trian-born Mexican Emperor because, coincidently with what
amounted to an ultimatum from Abraham Lincoln, word
had reached Napoleon III of Bismarck's determination to
force a war with Austria over the Schleswig-Holstein controversy. "Napoleon realized that the territorial aggrandize-

[15] Dexter Perkins, *The Monroe Doctrine: 1826–1867* (Baltimore: Johns Hopkins Press, 1933), p. 521.
[16] Perkins, *Hands Off*, p. 150.

ment of Prussia . . . would be a serious blow to his prestige and in fact endanger his throne . . . in order to have a free hand to meet the European situation he decided to yield to the American demands. As the European situation developed he hastened the final withdrawal of his troops and left Maximilian to his fate. . . . Thus," Professor Latané concludes ironically, "the Monroe Doctrine was vindicated." [17]

As is well known, the dispute of 1895 originated from the conflicting contentions of Venezuela and Great Britain on 30,000 square miles of territory on the border of the South American republic and British Guiana. In a message to Congress, President Cleveland declared that the acquisition of territory, in America, by a European power, was a clear violation of the Monroe Doctrine; and he asked Congress to take steps for the appointment of a commission to determine the true boundary. "Here was a bold and unqualified defiance of England. No one before had ever trod so roughly on the British lion's tail with impunity. The English-speaking public on both sides of the Atlantic was stunned and amazed. . . . But here again," writes Latané, "the true explanation is to be found in events that were happening in another quarter of the globe." Cleveland's Venezuelan Message was sent to Congress on December 17th. At the end of the year came Dr. Jameson's raid into the Transvaal, and on the 3rd of January the German Kaiser sent his famous telegram of congratulation to Paul Kruger. The wrath of England was suddenly diverted from America to Germany, and Lord Salisbury avoided a rupture with the United States over a matter which after all was not of such serious moment to England in order to be free to deal with a question involving much greater interests in South Africa. The Monroe Doctrine was none the less effectively vindicated." [18]

[17] John Holladay Latané, *From Isolation to Leadership* (New York: Copyright by The Odyssey Press), p. 48.
[18] *Ibid.*, pp. 49, 50.

In 1902, a second Venezuelan incident occurred. This involved, besides Venezuela, three European countries: Germany, England, and Italy. The three made a naval demonstration against the South American republic for the purpose of forcing her to pay certain claims of their subjects. "How England was led into the trap," continues Latané, "is still a mystery." Once again the United States protested, and Admiral Dewey stated publicly "that the entire American fleet was assembled at the time under his command in Puerto Rican waters ready to move at a moment's notice." Why did Germany, with a powerful navy, back down? "The reason why the Kaiser concluded not to measure strength with the United States was that England had accepted arbitration and withdrawn her support and he did not dare attack the United States with the British Navy in his rear. Again the nicely adjusted European balance prevented the Monroe Doctrine from being put to the test of actual war." [19]

But ineffectiveness implies exclusively a negative criticism. A more serious charge could be made against the Monroe Doctrine when it was fashioned into a positive, aggressive policy.

3) *The Doctrine was perverted.* Originally it meant, "America not for Europe," but the Corollaries made it say, "America for the U.S.A." Cuba, Puerto Rico, Panama, the Dominican Republic, Haiti, Nicaragua—six United States "protectorates" in less than fifteen years. Outright interventions, with Marines landing, occupying territories, setting up governments and running the country: in Cuba from 1898 to 1903, then from 1906 to 1909, again in 1912, and finally from 1917 to 1922; in the Dominican Republic, from 1916 to 1924; in Nicaragua, from 1912 to 1933, practically without interruption; in Haiti, from 1915 to 1934. We can mention these facts because they represent a policy which belongs to the past. We *must* mention them because, since they cannot

[19] *Ibid.*, pp. 51, 52.

be forgotten, we expect the United States at least to admit them and never to minimize their historical significance. Wrongs belong to the past only when you are able to talk about them and still be friends. That is precisely our attitude today: do not keep wrongs bottled up inside. Friendship is a positive, driving force. Frustrated rancor cannot be taken for love. Not to fear is necessary but not sufficient. Friendship is not restraint but forward impulse.

The Monroe Doctrine is guilty—not only because it did not prevent but because it even was invoked to justify manifestations of imperialism. Rather, not the original Message, but its inglorious additions. There are a good many Corollaries. I will mention the most significant ones:

In 1825, Secretary of State Clay declared that the United States could not consent to the occupation of Cuba and Puerto Rico, by "any other power than Spain." [20] The idea was good, as is often the case in the history of Monroe's Problem Doctrine. It is better known today as the "No transfer" principle, reiterated by Van Buren in 1829, Forsyth in 1840, Webster in 1843, and consecrated at the Habana 1940 Conference. Yet the timely warning did not apply to the United States, which, for too many years, made of Cuba a virtual Protectorate. Until 1936, when Franklin D. Roosevelt's Administration renounced the right of intervention granted to its country by the well known Platt Amendment, Cuba was freed from Spain but remained subjugated to the U.S.A.

In 1845, President Polk—of whom Abraham Lincoln said, "He feels the blood of this [Mexican] war, like the blood of Abel crying to heaven against him" [21]—added his Corollary, intended to justify the annexation of Texas. Said he: "We can never consent that European powers shall interfere to

[20] Clay to Brown, Minister of France, Oct. 25, 1825. MS. Instructions to U.S. Ministers, in the State Department, Vol. X, p. 404.

[21] Carl Sandburg, *Abraham Lincoln: The Prairie Years* (New York: Harcourt, Brace & Co., 1926), Vol. I, p. 368.

prevent such a union [of Texas and the United States] because it might disturb the 'balance of power,' which they [European countries] may desire to maintain upon this continent." [22] So, having promulgated the Doctrine to redress and maintain the balance of power *in Europe,*[23] a North American President claimed that Europe, in turn, had no right to be concerned over changes in the balance of power of the Western Hemisphere.

The second of the so-called "Grant Corollaries," in 1871 conceded the Dominican Republic the right to annex itself to the United States. President Grant stated: "I believed . . . that *our institutions were broad enough to extend over the entire continent* as rapidly as other peoples might desire to bring themselves under our protection. . . . In view of the facts which had been laid before me, and *with an earnest desire to maintain the 'Monroe Doctrine,'* I believed that I would be derelict in my duty if I did not take measures" in regard to the annexation of the Republic of Santo Domingo.[24]

Under President Cleveland, Secretary of State Bayard said that the United States had "proclaimed herself *the protector of this Western World,* in which she is by far the strongest power." [25] Then, in 1895, came the arrogant Olney Corollary, added by that Secretary of State who shouted to the world: "Today the United States *is practically sovereign on this continent and its fiat is law* upon the subjects to which it confines its interposition . . . its infinite resources combined with its isolated position render it *master of the situation* and practically invulnerable as against any or all other powers. . . ." [26] It is recorded in history as "Olney's Fiat." The

[22] Annual Message to Congress, Dec. 2, 1845, in *Messages and Papers of the Presidents,* Vol. IV, pp. 398-399.
[23] See Chapter XI.
[24] Message to Congress, Apr. 5, 1871.
[25] Nerval, *op. cit.,* p. 205.
[26] *Ibid.,* p. 207.

word of the United States was to be a command, not only to
European meddlers but to the "subjects" of Latin America's
protectorates—and this bombastic attitude was based on the
fact that "its infinite resources combined with its isolated
position render it *master of the situation* and practically invulnerable as against any or all other powers"! How foolish
it all sounds today! Nothing could be more opposed to contemporary Pan Americanism, nothing less acceptable to Latin
America. Olney's Fiat was a new expression of United States
hegemony. So was the well known Theodore Roosevelt addition: the famous Roosevelt Corollary which dealt the Doctrine its death blow.

On December 6, 1904, "Big Stick" T. R. solemnly declared: "Any country whose people conduct themselves well,
can count upon our hearty friendship. If a nation shows that
it knows how to act with reasonable efficiency and decency
in social and political matters, if it keeps order and pays its
obligations, it need fear no interference from the United
States. Chronic wrongdoing or an impotence which results
in a general loosening of the ties of civilized society, may in
America, as elsewhere, ultimately require intervention by
some civilized nation, and in the Western Hemisphere the
adherence of the United States to the Monroe Doctrine may
force the United States, however reluctantly, in flagrant
cases of such wrongdoing or impotence, to the exercise of an
international power." [27]

No document has proved more harmful to the prestige of
the United States in the Western Hemisphere. No White
House policy could be more distasteful to Latin Americans—
not even, perhaps, outspoken imperialism. Latin Americans
are usually inclined to admire strength, force, a nation *muy
hombre*. This was imperialism without military glamour:
this was imperialism *à la* Tartufe, not even *à la* Napoléon.
Moreover, it was a total distortion of the original Message.

[27] *Messages and Papers of the Presidents*, Vol. XVI, pp. 7053-54.

Monroe's Doctrine was defensive and negative: defensive, in that it was essentially an opposition to eventual aggression from Europe; negative, in that it simply told Europe what it *should not* do—not what the United States *should* do. The Monroe Doctrine of later Corollaries became aggressive and positive: aggressive, because even without actual European attack, it urged United States "protection" of Latin America —and that was outright intervention; positive, because instead of telling Europe what *not* to do, it told the United States what it *should* do in the Western Hemisphere. From a case of America *vs.* Europe, the Corollaries made of the Doctrine a case of United States *vs.* America. President Monroe had merely shaken his head, brandished his finger, and said to Europe, "Now, now, gentlemen, if you meddle with us, we will not love you any more," while Teddy Roosevelt, brandishing a big stick, had shouted, "Listen, you guys, don't muscle in—this territory is ours."

In still another Corollary, enunciated to justify United States intervention, the same Roosevelt said: "It is far better that this country should put through such an arrangement [enforcing fulfillment of financial obligations contracted by Latin American states] rather than to allow any foreign country to undertake it." [28] To intervene in order to protect: to intervene, in order to prevent others from so doing. It is the "Invasion for Protection" corollary, so much in the limelight recently, in other parts of the world.

Some people say that the Monroe Doctrine has nothing to do with its later interpretations. We have rejected the argument. Let me add Professor Chapman's significant conclusion: "It is not too much to say that the Monroe Doctrine has become the Roosevelt Corollary, despite several minor twists and turns hereinafter considered." [29] After Theodore

[28] Annual Message to Congress, Dec. 5, 1905, *Messages and Papers of the Presidents,* Vol. XIV, pp. 6994-97.
[29] Chapman, *op. cit.,* p. 147.

Roosevelt, the already unpopular Doctrine took an irrevocable turn for the worse. "Sending marine forces is not regarded as war," wrote ex-President Calvin Coolidge as late as January 5, 1931. And in true T. R. hypocritical style, he added: "Our government does not like to do this and avoids it when possible. But if we failed to do it . . . European governments would send their forces there to protect their corresponding interests." [30] It is the echo of T. R.'s words.

In fact, the Roosevelt Corollary has left so decisive an impression upon the Doctrine that not only thoughtless politicians but scholarly professors have been contaminated. Professor Chapman thinks: "The barest common sense shows that he [Coolidge] was right. . . . Interventions are *not* a good electoral maneuver. Yet, they take place." And, what is worse: "One can understand why a Hispanic American . . . might find something aggressively sinister in them, but it is impossible that any honest, intelligent, well-informed citizen of the United States should think so, if he gives the matter the slightest consideration." [31] The consideration obviously being that, for such citizens, financial investments count more than international law; that property rights must prevail over national rights; that what is good for the United States is good—*period*.

4) Thus, in the light of historical facts—laying aside considerations of theoretical value—one can easily understand why the Monroe Doctrine became so *unpopular* not only among Latin Americans but also among an increasing number of people of the United States. Those who do not yet see the point would do well to put themselves, by a stretch of the imagination, in the victims' shoes. Latin Americans— Professor Chapman to the contrary [32]—are just as patriotic and liberty-loving as Anglo-Americans. Unless you begin

[30] Calvin Coolidge, "Comment on Timely Topics," Oakland, Calif., *Tribune*, Jan. 5, 1931.
[31] Chapman, *op. cit.*, p. 148 n
[32] *Ibid.*, p. 160.

your analysis on that assumption, you are not qualified to judge the problem of inter-Americanism. Latin Americans, even those who admire the technical superiority of their powerful industrial neighbor, do not recognize the political or moral tutelage of the United States. We have seen that some Latin American countries are ahead of the United States in social legislation. Mexico's agrarian policy, for instance, is certainly more advanced than that of the United States. I could name many other important fields in which Latin America maintains a moral leadership. But one should avoid unnecessary comparisons. It is enough to proclaim that Latin Americans love "life, liberty, and the pursuit of happiness" as ardently as their northern neighbors. So, any reminder directly or indirectly connected with brutal attacks from without, whoever the aggressor, automatically revives legitimate Latin American resentment.

Many authorized spokesmen of public opinion in the United States have been as frank as Latin American critics. On December 28, 1933, President Roosevelt, commemorating the birthday of Woodrow Wilson, admitted: "I do not hesitate to say that if I had been engaged in a political campaign as a citizen of some other American republic I might have been strongly tempted to play upon the fears of my compatriots of that republic by charging the United States of North America with some form of imperialistic desire for selfish aggrandizement." [33]

Also referring to those dark years of inter-American relations, a distinguished United States authority on Latin America, Professor Rippy of Duke University wrote: "It is in vain that we plead our innocence of imperialism. Our whole history gives a lie to such a plea . . . A policy which has brought under our virtual domination some nine to twelve republics in a generation, may differ from European imperialism in form; but it is very near that imperialism,

[33] *New York Times*, Dec. 29, 1933; quoted in Nerval, *op. cit.*, p. 289.

in substance." [34] And a recent well known interpreter of Hemisphere conditions wrote in even stronger words: "In the past whenever we wanted territory we took it. We took Texas, New Mexico, and California from Mexico. We took Cuba from Spain. We took Panama from Colombia. And we were more forthright than the German, Italian, or Japanese aggressors. 'I took the Canal Zone,' said Theodore Roosevelt bluntly. We were equally forthright about landing the United States Marines to defend the property of banking and fruit companies in what we contemptuously referred to as 'banana republics.' And at one moment North American officials directed the financial policies of eleven of the twenty Latin American countries, while in six these banking agents were backed by American bayonets on the spot. In our conquests and in our interventions we frequently cited the Monroe Doctrine." [35]

The Monroe Doctrine, with its imperialistic connotations, is loaded with the kind of explosive that endangers the Pan American structure. That explains why United States Presidents sincerely concerned with their neighbors' feelings, from Abraham Lincoln to Franklin D. Roosevelt, have found no need to mention the Monroe Doctrine. Not even during the meeting of foreign ministers of the Americas, held at Rio de Janeiro in January, 1942, did the skillful United States delegate, Sumner Welles, mention the name of that unhappy Doctrine which for the last fifty years has been the greatest stumbling block in the way of genuine inter-Americanism. And there is no doubt that the situation discussed at the Rio Conference was one which, had the Message of 1823 not been perverted, would have fallen within the jurisdiction of the original Doctrine. But, right or wrong, the delegates knew that the emotional connotations of the words "Monroe

[34] J. Fred Rippy, *Latin America in World Politics* (New York: Alfred A. Knopf, 1928), p. 265.

[35] John T. Whitaker, *Americas to the South* (New York: The Macmillan Company, 1940), p. 3.

Doctrine" were such that they could not be pronounced without stirring up legitimate ill feelings. *The moment Monroe's distorted shadow enters a Pan American Conference, the Good Neighbors disband.* The silence made around the Monroe Doctrine at the historical meeting at Rio is more eloquent than any indictment ever uttered against it.

5) Finally, in the light of authentic, genuine Pan Americanism *à la* Bolívar [36] or *à la* F. D. Roosevelt,[37] it is obvious that the Doctrine seems completely *outmoded.* The days in which a single country—however powerful—could claim the exclusive right to behave, on the world stage, as a "rugged individualist," are gone forever. Ask Napoleon, ask the Kaiser, or ask Hitler! Civilized order is a joint enterprise, freely accepted by all partners. Mankind does not allow gangsters, be they individuals or nations. Order was established, first among the members of the family, then among the residents of the community, later among the citizens of a nation. Finally the day is near when a cooperative international order will be established among the nations of the earth. That order, whether local or national, continental or international, can be conceived only as a joint enterprise. America was the first continent in history to struggle for the establishment of such order. There can be no room in this continent for a doctrine which, even at its best and in its original intention, rests essentially on the arbitrary decision of one self-appointed "leader." The hour of selfish nationalism is past. There is no room for anarchy in organized society. Because the welfare of the many must prevail over that of the few, Monroeist Pan Americanism has been gradually but irrevocably displaced by democratic Pan Americanism.

The Monroe Doctrine may not be dead, but there is little use for it today. And there certainly will be less room for it in the world of tomorrow.

[36] See Chap. VI.
[37] See Chap. IX.

CHAPTER VIII

Blah-Blah Pan Americanism

BOLÍVAR'S Pan Americanism may have been considered, by some, as too idealistic—and perhaps it was; but Monroe's was certainly too realistic. Only in its third stage does Pan Americanism begin slowly to combine idealism with realism. Only then, also, do we see for the first time *continental* Pan Americanism; a movement in which *all* the republics of the Western Hemisphere have become interested parties. Latin American nations, exclusively, joined in Bolívar's act. And, as previously shown, the United States alone was legitimately concerned with the Monroe Doctrine. The First International Conference of American Republics, held in Washington in 1889, was a continental enterprise. From there on, the all-American movement began to take shape.

Bolívar was the romantic hero of our first act; Monroe, the star of Act II; United States Secretary of State James G. Blaine, the principal character of Act III; and one of America's greatest, Franklin D. Roosevelt, is the hero of Act IV— a hero who, not unlike Bolívar, moves in an atmosphere of war and glory. Blaine's act, the least known, is also the least exciting of the four. Yet without it—without the Pan American Union and the first six International Conferences of the American Republics—there would be no Pan Americanism at all. The year 1889 must be remembered because it was then that contemporary Pan Americanism was born. By remarkable coincidence it was also the year in which Adolf Hitler was born. Perhaps history will record that these two diametrically opposed forces, Pan Americanism and Hitler, were born in the same year. It was kind of Destiny to provide the world, from the very first, with the antidote to so deadly a poison. Pan Americanism and Hitler were born in 1889. But there is no room for both of them. There never was. The former will crush the latter. It has already begun to do so.

According to Lockey,[1] the *New York Evening Post* was first to use the adjective "Pan American"—on June 27, 1882, in connection with Secretary Blaine's proposal for a conference of American states. If so, the word was coined some sixty years ago, seven before the actual meeting of the proposed first conference, and about a hundred after the first ideas on Pan Americanism had been advocated by well known statesmen.

Secretary Blaine met with an opposition similar to that which, fifty-six years before, Secretary Clay had encountered when he asked the Congress of the United States to authorize the appointment of United States delegates to the 1826 Panama Congress—the same opposition, based on the same ground, *isolationism*. The United States was not to indulge in any policy of foreign entanglements. The word "entanglement," like "alliance," or "commitment," was taboo, and almost anything having to do with continental or world policy could, of course, be so labeled. Secretary Blaine's fight started in July, 1881, when President Garfield and he agreed to convoke a congress of American states in the city of Washington. The first setback suffered by Blaine came after the assassination of President Garfield. The Vice President, Arthur, became Chief Executive. He decided to keep Blaine at the head of the Department of State. He even authorized him to send invitations for the Inter-American Conference, through a circular letter addressed on October 29, 1881, to

[1] Joseph Byrne Lockey, *Pan Americanism: Its Beginnings* (New York: The Macmillan Company, 1920.)

the Latin American envoys accredited in the capital of the United States. In that circular letter, the aim of the meeting was carefully described by Blaine as "finding a way of permanently averting the horrors of a cruel and bloody combat between countries oftenmost of one blood and speech, or the even worse calamity of internal commotion and civil strife." [2] The conference was thus to confine its attention strictly to *peace:* peace within national boundaries and also within the boundaries of the Hemisphere. This time, Pan Americanism officially began as a pacifist international movement. It was not an alliance for war but an understanding for peace. In spite of its inoffensive beginnings, even this design of timid Pan Americanism was considered too dangerous by traditional isolationism. As it did in 1826, for the Congress of Panama, the government of the United States took pains to notify the American republics that it would not embark on any continental adventure liable to involve the powerful North American republic in international obligations of any kind. But, in 1881 as in 1826, isolationists endeavored to block the rising Pan Americanist movement. The administration at Washington, in order to defeat such unreasonable opposition, used the usual tactics. It tried to reassure Congress on the ground that the contemplated meeting was to be strictly limited; that it was not to commit the United States in any way. Isolationists should have no fear.

Unfortunately, when this second battle for Pan Americanism was only half fought, Secretary Blaine was replaced in the State Department by Frederick Theodore Frelinghuysen. Frelinghuysen followed the isolationist line. On January 9, 1882, he sent to William H. Trescot, United States Minister in Chile and Peru, a communication from

[2] *International Conferences of American States, 1889–1928* (New York: Oxford University Press—for the Carnegie Endowment for International Peace—1931), p. 448.

which I take the following paragraph: "The United States is at peace with all the nations of the earth, and the President wishes hereafter to determine whether it will conduce to that general peace, which he would cherish and promote, for this government to enter into negotiations and consultation, for the promotion of peace, with selected friendly nationalities, without extending a like confidence to other peoples with whom the United States is on equally friendly terms. If such partial confidence would create jealousy and ill will, peace, the object sought by such consultation, would not be promoted." [3] Thus, in an official document, a Secretary of State practically canceled Blaine's momentous invitation, because Pan Americanism might irritate the feelings of European powers!

However, Blaine kept on fighting. On February 3, 1882, he wrote indignantly to President Arthur, in an open letter: "The suggestion that a Congress of all American nations should assemble in the city of Washington . . . was warmly approved by your predecessor. . . . You received the suggestion with appreciable consideration and, after carefully examining the form of invitation, directed it to be sent. . . . I was greatly surprised to find a proposition looking to the annulment of these invitations, and I was still more surprised when I read the reasons assigned. . . . If I correctly apprehend the meaning of these words, it is that we might offend some European powers if we should hold in the United States a Congress of 'selected nationalities' of America. . . . European Powers assemble in Congress whenever an object seems to them of sufficient gravity to justify it. I have never heard of their consulting the Government of the United States in regard to the propriety of their so assembling, nor have I ever known of their inviting an American representative to be present; nor would there, in my opinion, be any good reason

[3] *Papers Relating to the Foreign Relations of the United States . . . 1882* (Washington: Government Printing Office, 1883), p. 58.

for their so doing. . . . If that movement is now to be arrested for fear it may give offence in Europe, the voluntary humiliation of the United States could not be more complete, unless we should petition European Governments for the privilege of holding the Congress.

"It is difficult to see how this country could be placed in a less enviable position than would be secured by sending in November a cordial invitation to all the Independent Nations in America to meet in Washington for the sole purpose of devising measures of peace, and in January recalling the invitation for fear it might create 'jealousy and ill will' on the part of monarchical governments in Europe. It would be difficult to devise a more effective way for the United States to lose the friendship of its American neighbors." [4]

All this seems just plain common sense in 1942. In 1882 it seemed reckless and wild to cautious isolationists. The President, after receiving Blaine's letter—and probably because he did not want to take the responsibility of annulling the invitation, submitted to Congress the question of whether or not the conference should be held. Between June 5 and August 7, 1882, twenty-three petitions were introduced in the two houses of Congress requesting the Peace Conference to be called. Since Congress took no action, however, Secretary of State Frelinghuysen gladly declared in a note of August 9 that the conference was indefinitely postponed. It seemed, for a while, that Blaine's project would never recover from this blow; that the Pan American movement had been crushed at its very inception. In 1826, after Bolívar's failure, clouds equally dark hovered over the Pan American horizon. But again there would be light.

Six years had elapsed when on May 24, 1888, a bill providing for a conference of American nations became a law in the Congress of the United States. Blaine had been vin-

---

[4] Gail Hamilton (i.e., Mary Abigail Dodge), *Biography of James G. Blaine* (Norwich, Conn.: Henry Bill Publishing Co., 1895), pp. 521-22.

dicated. Pan Americanism would be born. Secretary of State
Thomas Francis Bayard signed invitations which were sent
on July 13, 1888. The *First Pan American Conference* was
called to meet in Washington in October, 1889. This time
the delegates of the United States could not miss the Conference: it was held right in their own capital. It so happened, too, that by that time James G. Blaine had again
been appointed Secretary of State and was thus able to enjoy
the triumph of the cause which he had been the first to
sponsor, and into which he had put so much effort.

As two contemporary historians have not failed to see,
the United States' motives behind this first meeting were
the increase of commerce and profitable investment of capital,
and maintenance of peace, "without which investments would
be neither safe nor remunerative." On the other hand, as
far as Latin America was concerned, the stress was laid not
on commerce but on security, and against aggression from
any source. Says David R. Moore, "Latin Americans on their
side were more interested in their own security and political
independence than in any purely economic gains." [5] Kirkpatrick makes a similar comment: "In these Conferences the
United States and Latin America were aiming at different
things. Latin America, especially the smaller peoples, wanted
security, whereas the aims of the United States were economic." [6] I mention this because the situation today is, if
anything, completely reversed.

Since the outbreak of World War II, the United States
sees more and more in Pan Americanism a measure of security, while to Latin America Pan Americanism is becoming
more and more an economic problem. There is an explanation. When Pan Americanism began, the United States felt
secure, free from attack. Its interest was in commerce. Since

[5] *A History of Latin America* (New York: Prentice-Hall, Inc., 1938), p. 738.
[6] F. A. Kirkpatrick, *Latin America* (New York: The Macmillan Company,
1939), p. 433.

the military threat of mechanized Hitlerism, the United States, for the first time, has had a taste of insecurity. And that feeling is so strong that it overshadows economic considerations. Today the United States has consented to pay the price for Hemisphere security: that price is the Good Neighbor Policy.

On the other hand, Latin America, feeling secure, because it has faith in the Good Neighbor Policy, becomes more and more concerned with the economic implications of Pan Americanism. The United States went from trade to security. Latin America is beginning to move from security to trade. This change in the respective motives of the Americas must be seriously considered if one is to understand the problems of 1942 Pan Americanism. In the long run, both security and trade will be assured to our entire Hemisphere through sound, integral Pan Americanism.

Secretary Bayard in 1889, as Blaine in 1881, and Clay in 1826, took great care to quiet the ever present isolationist opposition. "I have to call your particular attention," he warned, in his circular instructions to the American diplomatic representatives accredited to the governments of Mexico, Central and South America, Haiti and the Dominican Republic, "to the scope and object of the Conference suggested, which as will be observed, is consultative and *recommendatory* only. The proposed Conference will be *wholly without power to bind any* of the parties thereto and it is not designed to affect or impair in any degree the treaty relations now existing between any of the States which may be represented." [7] In spite of the timidity of the first steps on the road of Pan Americanism, the United States, by promoting the First International Conference of American Republics, had definitely launched the movement.

The *First Conference of the American Republics* met in Washington from October 2, 1889, to April 19, 1890.

[7] *International Conferences, etc.*, p. 6.

Eighteen countries were represented; that is to say, all the nations of the Hemisphere, save the Dominican Republic. Cuba had not won her independence. Panama did not exist as a separate country. In agreement with the wishes of the United States principally, no conventions or treaties were approved—merely *recommendations:* one, on the construction of an intercontinental railway; three, on sea communications with the Caribbean, the Atlantic, and the Pacific. It was agreed that great advantages would accrue in the commerce between the nations with the use of coin that would be current, at the same value, in all the countries represented in the Conference; and therefore, it was recommended that an international American monetary unit be established. Also a Customs Union of the Americas was recommended, so that the nations of our Hemisphere would collect import duties under substantially the same tariff laws and reciprocally receive as domestic goods, free of duty, their respective natural or manufactured products. "It might be necessary," reads the recommendation, ". . . to create two bodies, one representing the population, and the other the states, in the manner in which a like problem was solved in the Constitution of the United States of America. But this step would require a partial sacrifice of the national sovereignty of the American nations." [8] The resolution acknowledged that, at the time, the project was impractical on a continental scale but recommended that the end should be approached by gradual steps. "The first and efficient step in direction being the negotiation of partial reciprocity treaties among the American nations whereby each may agree to remove or reduce the import duties levied by it on some of the products of any of the other nations, in exchange for similar and equivalent advantages." If, after this had been tried, the results proved satisfactory, the number of articles on the free list might be enlarged. The project advocated thus a pro-

[8] *Ibid.,* pp. 33-34.

gressive implantation of a Customs Union in our continent.
Then the First Conference created "a Commercial Bureau
of the American Republics," better known today as the Pan
American Union. Suffice it to say for the moment that the
report creating this bureau of information mentions for the
first time "the international union of American Republics."
But that union existed then exclusively "for the prompt
collection and distribution of commercial information." The
organ of that international union was called significantly
the "Commercial Bureau of the American Republics." Slowly
but steadily this modest bureau transformed itself into the
powerful and imposing Pan American Union.

A plan of arbitration was adopted at the First Conference. It reminds us of Article XVI of Bolívar's 1826 Treaty.
In both documents the American republics reiterated their
faith in arbitration as a principle of international law.

The right of conquest was again denounced in a recommendation adopted April 18, 1890. Article I reads: "The
principle of conquest shall not be recognized as admissible
under American public law." Also a recommendation on
claims and diplomatic intervention adopted the following
principle of American international law: "A nation has not,
nor recognizes in favor of foreigners, any other obligations
or responsibilities than those which in favor of the natives
are established in like cases by the constitution and the laws."
This recommendation was opposed by the delegates of the
United States, who voted in the negative.

The *Second Pan American Conference* was held in Mexico
City from October 22, 1901, to January 21, 1902. This time
every country of the Hemisphere was represented. Arbitration, peace, and international law were the main topics of
discussion. It was agreed to join the Hague Conference for
settling international disputes by peaceful means. The creation of a Pan American Bank was recommended. A convention for the formation of codes on public and private inter-

national law was voted; also a "Treaty for the Extradition of Criminals, and the Protection against Anarchism." It was agreed (Article II), that extradition should not be granted for political offenses. Then a convention regulating the "rights of aliens" was signed by fifteen of the delegates. Its implications are so important that the convention, by itself, would justify, in my opinion, the entire Second Conference. Article II reads: "The States do not owe to, or recognize in favor of, foreigners, any obligations or responsibilities other than those established by their constitutions and laws in favor of their own citizens." This had been said before. But another paragraph explains: "Therefore, the States are not responsible for damages sustained by aliens through acts of rebels or individuals and in general for damage originating from fortuitous causes of any kind, considering as such the acts of war, whether civil or national . . ." The United States did not sign this document either. As a matter of fact, for a long time it has sustained an entirely opposite view. It has upheld the theory that United States citizens should receive cash for precisely such damages as those explicitly rejected by the convention.

This is very important. The majority of Latin American republics have had and probably will have political upheavals, civil strifes, revolutions. Because of the deficiencies in their political life, very often those apparent disorders are the only weapons left to people determined to save democracy. But, whatever we think of revolutions, it seems to me that any person who chooses to make a living in a foreign country should be willing to share its good as well as its bad moments. Unless this principle is accepted, foreigners established in Latin America will find themselves placed in a privileged position. Foreign citizens established in Mexico, for example, should not expect to enjoy all the advantages of Mexican life without taking any of its risks. If they had *all* of the advantages and *none* of the risks, they would find themselves, I repeat, in a unique situation. Financially speaking, they could never lose. Their expatriation would automatically grant them an *insurance against losses originating from political conditions.* Being away from their native land, they would be naturally immune to financial losses caused by political trouble at home. And, being protected by their governments against similar losses in foreign lands, they would be equally immune to such losses abroad! Again, they would certainly be better off than both their compatriots and the citizens of the foreign country in which they have established themselves. Having no property at home, they could not lose there. And having property *but* diplomatic protection abroad, they could not lose there either.

The *Third Conference* met in Rio de Janeiro in 1906. The atmosphere was tense. President Theodore Roosevelt's intervention in Panama, Colombia, and the Dominican Republic, in fact, the whole policy of "Manifest Destiny" and the "Big Stick" was more and more drawing all Latin America together against the United States. Nevertheless, a convention was signed for the renewal of the treaty concluded in Mexico for the arbitration of pecuniary claims. Also worth mentioning was the convention providing for the creation of an international commission of jurists, to formulate codes of international law for the American nations. Secretary of State Elihu Root visited the conference and gave a memorable address from which I quote the following: "We wish for no victories but those of peace; for no territory except our own; for no sovereignty except the sovereignty over ourselves. We deem the independence and equal rights of the smallest and weakest member of the family of nations entitled to as much respect as those of the greatest empire, and we deem the observance of that respect the chief guarantee of the weak against the oppression of the strong. We neither claim nor desire any rights, or privileges, or powers that we do not freely concede to every American republic."

There we have, in theory, a pioneer of the Good Neighbor policy. As a matter of fact, I happen to know that, when he was in his eighties, Elihu Root was so convinced of the importance of Latin America that he undertook to learn Spanish. But who could, in Latin America, believe in the good faith of any United States delegate at that time?

Very little that is worthy of mention happened during the *Fourth International Conference of American States*—as these Pan American Conferences are called today—held at Buenos Aires in 1910. In those years Pan Americanism was at a low ebb. American marines landed in the Mexican port of Veracruz on April 1, 1914; and in 1916 the United States government sent a "punitive military expedition," led by General Pershing, against Pancho Villa. Between these dates, an illustrious President of the United States, Woodrow Wilson, came out with one of the most outspoken pleas for Pan Americanism, in his message to the Congress on December 7, 1915. He said: "The moral is, that the states of America are not hostile rivals but cooperating friends, and that their growing sense of community of interest, alike in matters political and in matters economic, is likely to give them a new significance as factors in international affairs and in the political history of the world. It presents them as in a very deep and true sense a unit in world affairs, spiritual partners, standing together because thinking together, quick with common sympathies and common ideals. Separated, they are subject to all the cross-currents of the confused politics of a world of hostile rivalries; united in spirit and purpose, they cannot be disappointed of their peaceful destiny. This is Pan Americanism. It has none of the spirit of empire in it. It is the embodiment, the effectual embodiment, of the spirit of law and independence and liberty and mutual service." But as long as United States marines occupied Latin American territories, all this was blah-blah Pan Americanism.

Between the Fourth and the Fifth Conference, held in

Santiago, Chile, in 1923, thirteen years elapsed, the main reason being the World War of 1914–1918. At the *Fifth Conference* the matter of a Pan American Court of International Justice was referred to a commission of jurists; and, something which seems to us more important today, Uruguay spoke of the creation of a real Pan American league of equals "with mutual pledges to maintain national independence and territorial integrity." That country tried in vain to end the unilateral nature of the Monroe Doctrine. The United States refused to change the doctrine or even to define it.

Anti-American sentiment was climaxed when the *Sixth Pan American Conference* was held in Habana in 1928. How could such a conference stand on any solid ground when the government in Washington was still pursuing a policy of systematic official interference and military intervention in the weaker countries south of the Rio Grande? In 1928 the United States still continued to occupy Nicaragua and Haiti. It was in vain, I think, that President Calvin Coolidge attended the opening session. And very little was accomplished by the good-will tour of Charles A. Lindbergh to Mexico and the Caribbean countries. Lindbergh reached Habana while the conference was in session. The conference was a dramatic affair that culminated in the sensational exit of Charles Evans Hughes, chairman of the United States delegation, when the delegates were to discuss United States interventions in Latin America. Technically much was accomplished: sixty resolutions and over twenty conventions and motions were adopted, most of them economic or cultural. Aggressions were condemned; they were even labeled international crimes, but since no definition was given, the term "aggression" remained too vague to mean anything. Latin Americans failed to have the principle of nonintervention adopted as a part of international law. We had to wait until 1936 to see the United States accept this principle, without which there would be no Pan Americanism.

Summing up, one can say that during these conferences, which stand like the six scenes of the third act, Pan Americanism was pitifully thwarted. Pan Americanism and Big Stick policy *à la* Theodore Roosevelt, or Dollar Diplomacy *à la* Taft, or even Big Brother policy *à la* Wilson, cannot mix. They did not, and they never will. Precious time was wasted, if not entirely lost; precious speeches were made, but found no echo. Precious projects were elaborated, but found no ground on which to stand. The climax of the third act—Blaine's act—was Secretary of State Hughes' pathetic and spectacular exit during the Habana Conference in 1928. Something was definitely wrong. Rather something was lacking. That something Franklin D. Roosevelt described in two words: "Good Neighborliness." Pan Americanism is a game which only good neighbors can play. Perhaps the only thing worth while, salvaged from this cycle of abortive attempts, was the *Pan American Union*.

Erected in 1910, through the generosity of Andrew Carnegie and contributions of the American republics, on land given by the Government of the United States, the building is the shrine of a continental ideal. The Union, created by the First Pan American Conference (Washington, 1889–1890), was at its inception a mere *"Commercial Bureau"* of the American republics, set up under the supervision of the United States Secretary of State; that is to say, practically a branch of the American government. In 1896, a Permanent Executive Committee was created, composed of five representatives of the member nations, four to be selected in rotation, the order of rotation by lot and the Secretary of State of the United States as chairman. The Union began to lose its almost exclusively North American character. At the Second Inter-American Conference (Mexico, 1901–1902), the Commercial Bureau became the *"International Bureau"* of the American republics. As shown by the change of title, the Union was becoming more ambitious and more determined to widen its field of action. First it was run exclusively by the State Department in Washington; next by *five* representatives of the American nations. Next the management of the organization was entrusted to a governing board composed of *all* the diplomatic representatives of the American republics in Washington and the Secretary of State of the United States. That is to say, it was growing more inter-American. The Third Conference (Rio de Janeiro, 1906) formally recognized it as a continuing secretariat of conferences. For the third time the name was changed, at the Fourth Conference (Buenos Aires, 1910), to *"Pan American Union."* It still keeps that name, and probably will keep it for a long time.

After the Fifth Conference (Santiago, Chile, 1923), members of the governing board did *not* have to be the diplomatic representatives of the governments accredited at Washington. Special delegates might be appointed; and every Latin American state was entitled to membership in the Union, regardless of whether it was on friendly terms with the United States government. This was a very important step. Before this change occurred, any government *not* recognized by Washington was deprived of any possibility of participating in the activities of the Union, even if its country continued to be a paying member. It was further agreed that the chairmanship of the governing board was to be an elective office, no longer to be filled automatically by the Secretary of State of the United States. The advantages of this great step have never been tested, since the chairman of the board has always been the Secretary of State in Washington. Not only the chairman of the board, but *all* the directors general of the Union have been citizens of the United States. It is almost a law that it shall be so. But, if the Union continues to become more democratic and more Pan American, the day will come when not only the chairman of the governing board but the director general as well will be a citizen of *any* of the Latin American countries. After all, even some of the Popes in Rome were non-Italians!

The Union has been highly praised and severely criticized; but Pan Americanism would be inconceivable without a *permanent* organization. Far from losing ground, the Union is becoming more important lately through the many international, technical, administrative, and political functions that it performs. Since 1920 Dr. L. S. Rowe has been Director General, the eighth in a line of distinguished United States citizens who have worked earnestly to widen the scope and to strengthen the prestige of this unique international body. Like the Union, Dr. Rowe has been both highly praised and severely criticized. In all fairness, it should be stated that he has performed an extremely delicate task with undeniable success. If the Union has been called "America's clearing house of good will," Dr. Rowe well deserves to be known as the first career *Pan American.*

As to the Union, if there is anything wrong with it the trouble lies not with the institution or with its director, but with the members of the governing board, who are vested with full powers to introduce any pertinent modifications whenever they wish to do so. The means to accomplish the task are in the hands of the twenty-one members of the governing board, representing all our republics. If they fail to use the tools, they alone are to blame, not the Union!

The Pan American Union needs *America*-minded people, of the Bolívar type. Unfortunately, our *Homo Americanus* is too rare a specimen. It will take years of something more than official, smiling, blah-blah Pan Americanism to create him. However, the fact that he exists at all and that the climate of the Good Neighbor Policy is favorable to his propagation, gives cause for optimism.

I do not see why the director of an *all*-American organization should always be a citizen of the United States. But if it must be so, one may safely predict that the future directors of the Pan American Union will be youthful, unbiased, continentally minded citizens, of the Laurence Duggan type. I might have said of the Henry A. Wallace, the Justice Douglas, or the Ambassador Winant type, but these men will be needed to carry on after victory the gigantic task courageously initiated by Franklin D. Roosevelt.

CHAPTER IX

Good Neighbors

WE SHALL see how deeply the foreign policy of Franklin D. Roosevelt is rooted in early American history; how directly it grows from the sagacious thought of George Washington and that of Thomas Jefferson.[1] However, there is another branch which springs from the lofty conception of a later prominent statesman, Woodrow Wilson. Were the Good Neighbor Policy merely a theory without practical meaning, one would acclaim as its herald Woodrow Wilson, not Franklin D. Roosevelt. The essence of the doctrine for inter-American relations advocated today by Roosevelt had been outlined, in even more precise terms, by the other Democratic wartime President of the United States.

The gallant Knight of the League of Nations was, like the second Roosevelt, no die-hard isolationist. Inspired by Washington and Jefferson, he abandoned the smug isolationist stand when he deemed it imperative for the good of his country. Woodrow Wilson was a great American because he outgrew native provincialism. He was, like Roosevelt today, a great American because, being fully conscious of the material and moral dimensions of his country, he wanted it to assume a corresponding responsibility in the making of a new world. He, like Roosevelt, never feared universality. As a true American, he was a citizen of the world. And, in spite of his last-minute political setback, one may affirm that Wilson was,

[1] See Chap. XI.

in reality, never defeated: he merely had come a generation ahead of his time. His apparent failure does not reflect upon him but upon his contemporaries. Isolationism was too imbedded in the majority of his people. His hands were tied by foreign intrigue and by local politics, when he needed them most to complete the task which he had valiantly undertaken. Congress rejected *his* League of Nations. Thus, the child was born an orphan. But today Woodrow Wilson's dream has been vindicated. Isolationism has lost. Once more, idealism has paradoxically become realism; and realism, the realism of an impossible isolationism, has been abandoned because everyone considers it now too idealistic. National independence and world *inter*dependence have become so closely interwoven that they cannot be separated even for the sake of academic discussion. This time, it seems that Franklin D. Roosevelt, backed by the will of an aroused nation—and, I might add, by that of a unified continent—will materialize the international ideal of his predecessor. It is fortunate for the United States that in the two decisive tests of modern history, World War I and World War II, when giants were needed, the White House was not occupied by dwarfs.

The Geneva institution was not successful, precisely because it was literally a "League *of* Nations," of *some* nations, not of *all* nations. Also, it failed because it was made powerless, from its inception. It was a court without police force; a court from which the offender could simply walk out if and when he did not like the decision rendered. It was an ethical, not a judicial, tribunal, relying almost exclusively on moral force. We know better now.

As early as 1913, President Wilson declared [2] that the future of our Hemisphere was going to be "very different"

[2] Address before the Southern Commercial Congress at Mobile, Ala., Oct. 27, 1913. Quoted in John Bassett Moore, *The Principles of American Diplomacy* (New York: Harper & Brothers, 1918), pp. 398-400.

from the past; that the states lying to the South would be "drawn closer . . . by innumerable ties." The states of Latin America, Wilson said, were "also going to see an emancipation from subordination to foreign enterprise, such as had resulted from the granting of concessions to foreign capitalists." Here we find, in Wilson's lips, another prediction come true: the states of Latin America—led in this instance by Mexico—have become more and more aware of the necessity, for them, to achieve at least some degree of economic independence, without which territorial, political, or any other kind of independence is only an illusion. Those who wish to becloud the issue by spreading "patriotic" rumors to the effect that so healthy a move endangers the foreign trade of the United States either do not see far enough or are deliberately misleading public opinion at home in order to maintain dishonest advantages abroad. No country can prosper long at the expense of its neighbors, however weak they are. Besides, the great liability of inter-American trade is precisely the low standard of living in most of the Latin American countries. The higher that standard can be raised, the better for all concerned; and that includes United States exporters and investors. The only way to raise that standard is to enforce not exclusively political but also *economic* equality. Only when integral democracy may function freely in every one of our American republics, shall we all enjoy the full benefit of our geographical neighborhood. The theory according to which the Western Hemisphere should remain divided in two—on the one hand, a powerful, industrial nation in which workers receive high wages and wealthy industrialists export manufactured products, and on the other hand, a sad group of weak, primitive nations in which the people must endure *sub*human conditions of living in order to provide the towering industrial giant with raw material and cheap labor—that theory belongs definitely to the past. Intelligent businessmen are beginning to understand it. And when selfish, individual interests stand in the path of democratic progress they must be removed. The United States, said Woodrow Wilson on that same occasion, *"should be the first to take part in assisting that emancipation."* May I add that it will never regret this. The markets of highly civilized countries always bring higher profits to the exporter. And democracy alone will raise the purchasing power of Latin American masses. Mexico is a better market for United States exporters, since its governments have vigorously pursued a policy of social betterment for its working people.

Also, President Wilson reiterated that the United States "would never again seek one additional foot of territory by conquest," and that it should regard it as "one of the duties of friendship to see that from no quarter are material interests made superior to human liberty and national opportunity." America—North, Central, and South—was to be united into "a family of mankind devoted to the development of true constitutional liberty." [3] Simón Bolívar and Franklin D. Roosevelt spoke that same language.

Secretary Lansing, in addressing the Second Pan American Scientific Congress, observed that the "essential qualities" of Pan Americanism were "those of the family—sympathy, helpfulness, and a sincere desire to see another grow in prosperity, absence of covetousness of another's possessions, absence of jealousy of another's prominence, and above all, absence of that spirit of intrigue which menaces the domestic peace of a *neighbor.*" [4] We find here even the word "neighbor." Lansing also said that, while the Monroe Doctrine is the "national policy of the United States," Pan Americanism is the "international policy of the Americas"; that Pan Americanism "extends beyond the sphere of politics and finds its application in the varied fields of human enterprise"; that

[3] *Ibid.*
[4] *Ibid.*

it is "an expression of the idea of internationalism" and the "most advanced" and "most practical form of the idea," and has been "made possible" by our "geographical isolation," "similar political institutions," and "common conception of human rights." All that is, essentially, Pan Americanism *à la* Good Neighbor policy—but Wilson went further: in the winter of 1914–15 he sounded the representatives of some Latin American countries at Washington as to the conclusion with the United States of a treaty for "the mutual guarantee of territorial integrity and political independence, under republican forms of government." Later on, the proposal was transmitted to *all* the nations of the Hemisphere. The draft of that proposed Pan American Treaty should be known by all. It reads as follows:

ARTICLE I. That the high contracting parties to this solemn covenant and agreement hereby join one another in a common and mutual guarantee of territorial integrity and of political independence under republican forms of government.

ARTICLE II. To give definite application to the guarantee set forth in Article I the high contracting parties severally covenant to endeavor forthwith to reach a settlement of all disputes as to boundary of territory now pending between them by amicable agreement or by means of international arbitration.

ARTICLE III. That the high contracting parties further agree: First, that all questions, of whatever character, arising between two or more of them which cannot be settled by the ordinary means of diplomatic correspondence shall, before any declaration of war or beginning of hostilities, be first submitted to a permanent international commission for investigation, one year being allowed for such investigation; and second, that, if the dispute is not settled by investigation, to submit the same to arbitration, provided the question in dispute does not affect the honor, independence or vital interests of the nations concerned or the interests of third parties.

ARTICLE IV. To the end that domestic tranquillity may prevail within their territories the high contracting parties further severally covenant and agree that they will not permit the departure from their respective jurisdictions of any military or naval expedition hostile to the established government of any of the high contracting parties, and that they will prevent the exportation from their respective jurisdictions of arms, ammunition or other munitions of war destined to or for the use of any person or persons notified to be in insurrection or revolt against the established government of any of the high contracting parties.[5]

Except for the all-embracing Treaty of Confederation drafted by Bolívar and signed at the historic Assembly of Panama in 1826,[6] this was the most important plea for union made by any of the American leaders. Its importance lies in the fact that it contains an implicit abandonment of the narrow, unilateral spirit of the Monroe Doctrine. All genuine Pan Americanism must necessarily follow this trend. This was a Pan Americanism of *"partners,"* with no self-appointed "guardian" as sole beneficiary. That Wilson had this pact very much at heart, is evident. A scholarly biographer of the great President wrote: "His heart was indeed set upon the achievement of the new pact, for its implications were far flung. If he was to ask the war-torn world to accept the basic elements of such an agreement in forming a League of Nations, he must omit no effort to apply it practically in the Western Hemisphere. It would make us 'partners' with South and Central America, 'rather than guardians.' He thought it a 'great step in advance.' " [7] The whole Pan American movement is today, I repeat, based on this idea of an *American partnership*. Woodrow Wilson understood it clearly. Remember his wise criticism of the Monroe Doctrine. Unfortunately for Wilson's fame, there was little correlation between ideas and deeds. His intervention in Latin America—especially in Mexico—weakens his claim to leadership in the Pan American movement, whose essential principles, however, he understood so well and expressed with so ardent a conviction.

[5] Quoted in John Bassett Moore, *op. cit.*, p. 408.
[6] See Chap. VI.
[7] Ray Stannard Baker, *Woodrow Wilson: Life and Letters*, Vol. VI (New York: Doubleday, Doran & Co., 1937), p. 85.

As a shining example of Wilsonian Pan Americanist, I must mention here Josephus Daniels, ex-Ambassador in Mexico City. This distinguished statesman did more to promote Mexican-American friendship than any other United States Ambassador. He won not only the esteem of the government but—what is more difficult—the affection of the working classes of the country to which he was accredited.

In the slow development of the Good Neighbor policy, only Herbert Hoover fills up the gap between Woodrow Wilson and Franklin D. Roosevelt—a gap of some twenty years of exciting political life. Hoover, like Wilson, and all the American Presidents until Franklin D. Roosevelt, inherited Latin America's ill will, created by his predecessors. The public utterances of the eminent Republican President on inter-American problems are not numerous. However, some incidents of his political life must be recorded here if we want to complete, even superficially, a survey of the antecedents of the Good Neighbor policy. Hoover's outstanding contribution to that trend was his extended trip, as President-elect, to various countries of South America at the end of 1928 and the beginning of 1929.

Later, in his Inaugural Address, President Hoover declared: "We have no desire for territorial expansion, for economic or other domination of other peoples." [8] Also, there is no doubt that the first official interpretation of the Monroe Doctrine, given with the authorization of the State Department by Undersecretary Clark, was good news to the Latin American republics, since it took away from that unpopular doctrine some of its most objectionable corollaries.

Finally, also under President Hoover's administration, the treaty providing for the withdrawal of American marines was signed with Haiti; and in January, 1933, two months before Roosevelt's inauguration, the last marines left Nica-

[8] Quoted in Thomas A. Bailey, *Diplomatic History of the American People* (New York: F. S. Croft & Co., 1940), p. 730.

ragua. At that moment, Pan Americanism took a sharp turn for the better.

To appreciate fully the change undergone by inter-American policy, I shall say that in 1928 one of the most distinguished North American historians of Latin America, Professor J. Fred Rippy, in his remarkable analysis *Latin America in World Politics*, had arrived at the conclusion that Latin American suspicion was well founded, and that *"never have the Latin peoples of America been more bitter* toward the United States than they are now." [9] Yet some eight years later, on January 3, 1936, a President of the United States could emphatically say in his annual message to Congress: "At *no time* in the four and a half centuries of modern civilization in the Americas has there existed—in any year, any decade, or any generation in all that time—a greater spirit of *mutual understanding,* of common helpfulness . . . than exists today in the twenty-one American Republics and their neighbor, the Dominion of Canada." [10] A few weeks before, on December 6, 1935, the very able Sumner Welles, Assistant Secretary of State, had made a similar remark: "There exists today, in my considered judgment, a closer and more understanding friendship between the United States and its sister republics of the western world than has existed since the earliest years of the independence of the American Republics." [11]

Thus, in 1928, an authorized critic could say that never had the relations between the Americas been *worse;* and in 1935 and 1936 a United States high official and the President of the United States could with equal emphasis state that

[9] J. Fred Rippy, *Latin America in World Politics* (New York: Alfred A. Knopf, 1928), p. 253.

[10] Franklin D. Roosevelt, Annual Message to Congress, quoted in *Public Affairs Bulletins,* Bull. No. 7 (Library of Congress, Washington, D.C., June, 1941), p. 3.

[11] Address, "The Good Neighbor Policy on the American Continent," under auspices of Center of Inter-American Studies of The George Washington University, *Ibid.,* p. 18.

never had those relations been *better*. That change from "the worst" to "the best" describes, quite accurately, the ground that was gained in the field of inter-American friendship, by the proclamation and the subsequent maintenance of the Good Neighbor policy. Yes, some ten years ago it did seem that Pan Americanism could be nothing but a dream. In the previous fifty years, the United States had intervened some sixty times in the affairs and territories of its Latin American neighbors—especially in the Caribbean. United States Marines had occupied Cuba almost without interruption from 1898 to 1922, the Dominican Republic from 1916 to 1924, Haiti from 1915 to 1934, Nicaragua from 1912 to 1933. Mexico itself, which had lost (between 1845 and 1848) *more than half* of its territory to the United States, again had seen American marines land in Veracruz in 1914 and American troops cross the Rio Grande under Wilson's General Pershing, in 1916. How could one speak seriously of inter-American solidarity, Pan Americanism, or Good Neighborliness when the stumbling block in the path of good relations was nothing less than the most powerful republic of the Hemisphere? The situation could change only if and when the United States decided to abandon once and for all its imperialistic interventionism.

The phrase "Good Neighbor Policy" was coined by President Roosevelt in his First Inaugural Address on March 4, 1933. Then was publicly stated for the first time the essence of the fair rule in international conduct, happily adopted by the new Administration in Washington. It was a memorable occasion in the annals of Hemisphere relations. Said the President: *"In the field of world policy, I would dedicate this nation to the policy of the good neighbor:* the neighbor who resolutely respects himself and, because he does so, respects the rights of others—the neighbor who respects his obligations and respects the sanctity of his agreements in and with a world of neighbors." [12] Because the phrase "good neighbor" sounded familiar, its meaning was easy to grasp. It caught the public's ear immediately; and because it has won the right to be considered as something more than nice but empty words, "Good Neighbor Policy" has become in 1942 the foundation of contemporary Pan Americanism. When a high official of the State Department said, "I make the prediction that this Rooseveltian phrase will go down in history as the keynote of a philosophy and a policy which will become as well known and as important as Washington's dictum 'no entangling alliances,' " [13] he made a sound prophecy indeed. The Rooseveltian phrase *will* go down in history as a dictum of American policy more important to the Hemisphere than any related to Washington, Jefferson, or Monroe.

On April 12, 1933, President Franklin Roosevelt, in an address before the special session of the Governing Board of the Pan American Union at Washington, enlarged upon the statement quoted from his First Inaugural Address: "The essential qualities of a true Pan Americanism must be the same as those which constitute a good neighbor, namely, mutual understanding and, through such understanding, a sympathetic appreciation of the other's point of view." [14] From there on, the President has mentioned quite often the popular Good Neighbor Policy. "There was nothing particularly new about these sentiments. What was new was their immediate *translation* into practical effect," Laurence Duggan, then Chief of the Division of American Republics, said very pertinently in an address on the Good Neighbor policy on September 12, 1938.[15] Mr. Duggan, a few months before, had already said: "A careful examination will disclose no

[12] *Ibid.*

[13] Hugh G. Grant of the Division of Western European Affairs, Department of State, address to American Association of University Women, Birmingham, Ala., May 21, 1935.

[14] *Public Affairs Bulletins*, Bull. No. 7 (June, 1941), p. 1.

[15] *Ibid.*, p. 28.

period in our relations with the other American Republics when there has been a closer *correlation* between declared purpose and fulfillment, between theory and fact, as during the past five years." [16] Yes, many other North American statesmen had used and abused the official language of friendship, but whether these people were sincere or not, no Latin American could afford to accept them seriously, because of the irritating discrepancy between words and deeds. Even some of the fiercest enemies of Latin America had dared to speak officially as "good neighbors." But Franklin D. Roosevelt's was no siren song.

The last United States Marines left Haiti in 1934. And on May 29 of that year, second of the Roosevelt first Administration, the island of Cuba "was released from the intervention trammels of the Platt Amendment." [17] The same month (August, 1934) in which the last marines were withdrawn from Haiti, a pact was signed with Panama by which "some of the iniquities of the Hay-Bunau-Varilla Treaty were removed." [18] That treaty was not approved by the Senate of the United States until July 25, 1939. Thus, from the beginning of his Administration, President Roosevelt proved with concrete facts that he meant precisely what he said. Today, after nine years in the White House, President Roosevelt is the first Chief Executive of the United States who, to use his own words, can "look us in the eye and take our hand." No other leader of so powerful a nation could use his language and expect weaker nations to believe him. "We believe in democracy," said he. "We believe in freedom; we believe in peace. . . . We offer to every nation of the world the handclasp of the Good Neighbor. Let those who wish our friendship look us in the eye and take our hand." [19]

[16] Address before the Academy of Political and Social Sciences, Apr. 2, 1938, *Ibid.*, p. 26.

[17] Bailey, *op. cit.*, p. 738.

[18] *Ibid.*

[19] Address at Chautauqua, New York, Aug. 14, 1936.

With the *Seventh Pan American Conference,* held in Montevideo in 1933, contemporary Good Neighbor Pan Americanism officially came into existence. The conference was held during the first year of President Roosevelt's Administration, close on the heels of the economic depression. High tariff barriers had been raised. To give a picture of the international setting, I refer to Moore: "Haiti wanted the withdrawal of American financial and military occupation. Cuba wanted the abolition of the Platt Amendment. Mexico was anxious for a Pan American bimetallic currency. Argentina seemed to be as far estranged from the United States in policy and cooperation as it was in geographical distance. It did not accept the Monroe Doctrine. It disliked Pan Americanism because the United States held such a leading place in it. It had refused to sign the 1923 Gondra Treaty, which, arising out of the Fifth Pan American Conference, was designed to avoid or prevent international conflicts. It had refused also to have anything to do with the Inter-American Conciliation Convention of 1929 or the Inter-American Arbitration Treaty of the same year, or the Kellogg-Briand Pact of Paris. A few months before the Montevideo Conference was to meet, the Argentine Minister of Foreign Affairs, Señor Carlos Saavedra Lamas, had announced a new pact, to be known as the Argentine Anti-War Pact, a scheme similar to but not quite so thorough as the Kellogg Pact. It had obtained the signatures of Brazil, Chile, Paraguay, and Uruguay. Argentina apparently did not like the United States and was herein trying to displace American by Argentine leadership." [20]

Undoubtedly inspired by the general feeling of his President, Secretary of State Hull, presiding over the American delegation, proceeded with utmost tact and kindness. He succeeded first in dispelling suspicion and secondly in securing cooperation. He signed the Argentine Anti-War Pact. And

[20] Moore, *op. cit.,* pp. 751-52.

that undoubtedly won Argentina and saved the Conference. Later Argentina adhered to the Kellogg Pact, the Gondra Treaty, the Inter-American Conciliation Convention, and the Inter-American Arbitration Treaty. Secretary Hull succeeded also in having the conference adopt a resolution for lower tariffs, reciprocal trade agreements, and similar policies. It was agreed to call a financial and economic conference at Santiago, a technical, commercial one at Buenos Aires. Other outstanding results of that conference were the truce between Bolivia and Paraguay and the decision to cooperate with the League of Nations Commission in Montevideo.

As in Habana, the most critical discussion centered around the question of the United States Latin American policy. Giving shape to the Good Neighbor Policy outlined by President Roosevelt, Secretary Hull declared that his government was "doing its utmost, with due regard to commitments made in the past, to end with all possible speed engagements which have been set up by previous circumstances. . . . Every observing person must by this time thoroughly understand that under the Roosevelt Administration the United States Government is as much opposed as any other government to interference with the freedom, the sovereignty or other internal affairs or processes of the governments of other nations . . . No government need fear any intervention on the part of the United States under the Roosevelt Administration." So far Secretary Hull has been right: *"under the Roosevelt Administration."* But, in the light of regrettable historic facts, can we of Latin America feel assured that this friendly policy will continue under *any* United States administration? The answer implies a faith in the United States, a faith which only time can justify. At any rate, that Conference of Montevideo was, I repeat, a turning point in Pan Americanism.

From then on, Pan American meetings have ceased being mere social functions or formal diplomatic gatherings. They take root in political reality. The Buenos Aires *Inter-Ameri-can Conference for the Maintenance of Peace* (1936) met on the initiative of the President of the United States and at the invitation of Argentina. It convened under most happy auspices. It reaffirmed the commitments entered into by the twenty-one American republics to settle their international differences by recourse to the pacific means provided by existing treaties. Moreover, improving upon the machinery for the maintenance of peace, it introduced the increasingly important principle of *consultation,* the moment the peace of the continent is threatened. At the same time the conference adopted a number of conventions and resolutions to promote closer economic and cultural relations. Its three outstanding documents are a convention for the "Mainte-nance, Preservation, and Establishment of Peace"; an "Addi-tional Protocol Relative to Nonintervention"; and a "Dec-laration of Principles of Inter-American Solidarity and Cooperation."

The first stipulates that in the event the peace of the American republics is menaced, the governments of the Americas shall consult together "for the purpose of finding and adopting methods of peaceful cooperation." In the event of war between American states, the governments represented at the conference shall undertake without delay the necessary *mutual consultations;* and in the event of an international war outside America "which might menace the peace of the American republics," such consultation shall also take place.

The Protocol Relative to Nonintervention, presented by the Mexican delegation under the able leadership of its chairman, Ambassador Francisco Castillo Nájera, and adopted by the Conference, is so essential to the understanding of contemporary Pan Americanism, that one could say it alone justifies the Buenos Aires meeting. For the *first* time, an official delegation of the United States signed a pledge condemning intervention in the most emphatic terms. Article I reads: *"The high contracting parties declare inadmissible the intervention of any one of them, directly or indirectly, and for whatever reason, in the internal or external affairs of any other of the parties."* The violation of the provisions of this article "shall give rise to mutual consultation."

The Declaration of Principles of Inter-American Solidarity and Cooperation is also greatly significant because it acknowledges in the Americas "a common likeness in the democratic form of government"; defines Pan Americanism as "a moral union of all the American republics in defense of their common interests based upon the most perfect equality and reciprocal respect for their rights of autonomy, independence, and free development"; and, summing up, declares in its conclusions that "the American nations, true to their republican institutions, proclaim their absolute juridical liberty, their unrestricted respect for their several sovereignty, and the existence of a common democracy throughout America." It was also the first time mention was made of *"a common democracy throughout America."* That "common democracy" is the very motto of our modern, dynamic Pan Americanism.

The *Eighth* and latest of the periodic International Conferences of the American Republics met in Lima, Peru, December 9–27, 1938. It followed the general policies of the Seventh Conference and the Buenos Aires Peace Conference. But more emphasis was placed on the *political* aspect of the Pan American problems. Two new declarations, adopted at Lima, rightfully compete in popularity with the three just mentioned, approved at Buenos Aires two years before. They are another "Declaration of the Principles of the Solidarity of America" and, especially, a clear-cut "Declaration of American Principles." The first reaffirms that "the peoples of America have achieved spiritual unity through the similarity of their republican institutions" and mentions "their unshakable will for peace, their profound sentiment of humanity and tolerance, . . . their absolute adherence to the principles of international law, equal sovereignty of states, and individual liberty without religious or racial prejudices." Then, on the basis of such principles the governments of the American states, first, reaffirmed their "continental solidarity"; secondly, declared their "decision to maintain them [these principles] and to defend them against all foreign intervention or activity that may threaten them"; thirdly, reiterated the all-important procedure of consultation; and fourthly, "in order to facilitate the consultations . . . the Ministers for Foreign Affairs of the American Republics, when deemed desirable and at the initiative of any one of them, will meet in their several capitals by rotation." This declaration, officially known as the "Declaration of Lima," approved on Christmas Eve, 1938, is the basis of the three meetings of Ministers of Foreign Affairs later held on this continent, about which a few words will be said later.

The *Declaration of American Principles* should be read on Pan American Day in every school and university of this continent. Since it embodies the essential principles of Pan Americanism, one may well consider it as a sort of Constitution of the Americas. It is very brief. The first four articles read:

1. The intervention of any State in the internal or external affairs of another is inadmissible.
2. All differences of an international character should be settled by peaceful means.
3. The use of force as an instrument of national or international policy is proscribed.
4. Relations between States should be governed by the precepts of international law.

That was not all the work of the Lima Conference. The topic of a League of American Nations, so dear to Woodrow

Wilson, was introduced this time by the governments of Colombia and the Dominican Republic. However, the chairman of the Colombian delegation declared that neither Colombia nor the Dominican Republic, nor the group of states supporting the proposal for a League, wished to hasten developments; that they preferred to wait until sentiment had more definitely "crystallized." So the matter was simply referred to a committee of jurists! We know what that means. But it is evident that "sentiment" in favor of such project is rapidly "crystallizing."

The conference also recommended that the indigenous populations have preferential rights to the protection of the authorities, and that the governments should promote policies tending to the complete integration of indigenous populations into national life. And finally, on the basis of a project submitted by the Mexican delegation and of a suggestion of the Cuban delegation in favor of a convention on the Civil and Political Rights of Women, a document known as the "Lima Declaration in Favor of Women's Rights" set forth the rights of women to political treatment on the basis of equality with men, the enjoyment of equality in civil status, full protection in and opportunity for work, and the most ample protection for mothers. It further urged the American republics to enact legislation to carry these principles into effect. Still dealing with women, the conference approved a resolution recommending that measures be taken to improve the conditions of work of rural women; and again, on the basis of another Mexican project, a resolution was approved recommending that the Pan American Union study the possibility of convening an Inter-American Congress of Women, preparing its agenda and determining the place and date of meeting. It was the first time that so much attention had been given in a Pan American gathering to women's contribution to the life of our continent.

The *First Meeting of Ministers of Foreign Affairs* was at

Panama, September 23 to October 3, 1939. We were still optimists. The keynote was *neutrality.* A general Declaration of the Neutrality of the American Republics was approved, the preamble of which asserted that "the attitude assumed by the American Republics has served to demonstrate that it is their unanimous intention not to become involved in the European conflict." The resolution provided for the establishment of an Inter-American Neutrality Committee. A Joint Declaration of Continental Solidarity was also approved, based on projects presented by Colombia, Cuba, and Mexico. It reaffirmed the Lima "Declaration of Solidarity," reiterated the determination of the American republics to maintain and strengthen the peace of the continent, and expressed a fervent hope for the reestablishment of peace throughout the world, on the basis of law and justice.

A sensational document was the Declaration of Panama, which established a *"zone of security"* around the American continent, to be kept free of belligerent activities. This declaration entails no sanction for the violation of such a neutrality zone. It evidently relies entirely on "moral" weight. How efficient that can be was proven by the fact that some of the most spectacular naval fighting of the European war took place precisely within the waters of that "security zone"! I refer to the pursuit and eventual scuttling of the *Graf Spee,* at the very entrance of the Montevideo harbor.

Also on the basis of projects presented by Mexico, a resolution was approved on the "transfer of sovereignty of geographic regions of the Americas held by non-American States," providing for a consultative meeting among the American republics whenever a geographic region of America subject to the jurisdiction of a non-American state—in other words, a European colony in the Western Hemisphere —should be obliged to change its sovereignty and there should result therefrom a danger to the security of the American continent. Finally, another resolution suggested the desirability of a Second Meeting of the Ministers of Foreign Affairs on October 1, 1940.

The Committee on Economic Cooperation created an Inter-American Financial and Economic Advisory Committee, to be composed of twenty-one experts, one from each country, and to begin its activities not later than November 15, 1939, in Washington. The Advisory Committee, which still functions, is to continue during the emergency arising out of the European war. In general terms, it deals with problems affecting the economic situation of the American republics.

The *Second Meeting of Ministers of Foreign Affairs* was held at Habana, Cuba, July 21–30, 1940. The European threat was looming nearer and nearer. So, the object of this second consultation was *defense* rather than neutrality. A convention was approved on the provisional administration of European colonies and possessions in the Americas in case of a Hitler victory. This is one of the most important problems directly connected with the outcome of the European war. What would be the fate of English, French, or Dutch colonies in the Western Hemisphere should Hitler win the war? Would America sit still and allow any transfer of those territories? Would it allow Germany to obtain a foothold on this Hemisphere? Two agreements were reached: The convention mentioned above, and the Act of Habana.

The first makes it clear that any transfer of territory on the American continent from one non-American power to another would be regarded by the American republics as against American principles and the rights of American states to maintain their security and political independence. Accordingly, the convention sets forth a procedure for the temporary administration of such territories by one or more

American states. For that purpose an Inter-American Commission for Territorial Administration is formed. The provisional administration is to be exercised in the interest of the security of America and for the benefit of the region in question "until such time as the region is in a position to govern itself or is restored to its former status." The first administration shall cover a period of three years and, if necessary, shall be renewed for successive periods of not longer than ten years. Like the convention, the Act of Habana recognizes the danger of the transfer of European possessions. It creates an Emergency Committee composed of one representative of each of the American republics; this committee, in case of emergency, and even before the coming into effect of the convention, shall apply its provisions and assume the administration of the region threatened. America is taking no chances. The Act goes further: it stipulates that, should the emergency be so great that action of the Committee cannot be awaited, *any* of the American republics, individually or jointly with others, shall have the right to act in the manner which its own defense or that of the continent requires. In plain words, this would give the United States the right to land Marines in Martinique, for example, should Hitler win in Europe. A further provision of the Act makes it equally clear that, once the reason for such an extraordinary measure passes, the territory shall be organized as an autonomous state or be restored to its previous status.

Of special significance also is the Declaration of Reciprocal Assistance and Cooperation for the Defense of the Nations of the Americas, according to which *"any attempt on the part of a non-American State against the integrity or inviolability of the territory, the sovereignty or the political independence of an American State shall be considered as an act of aggression against the States which sign this declaration."*

Any European aggression against a country of this continent will be considered as an act of hostility toward the United States.

The United States, in proclaiming the much discussed Monroe Doctrine, became the *self*-appointed "guardian" of the continent. But, as we have indicated elsewhere,[21] the Monroe Doctrine was an exclusive policy of the United States. With this policy so clearly defined at Habana in the declaration just referred to, the warning to Europe is re-affirmed, but this time, *each and all* of the twenty-one countries of the Western Hemisphere consider themselves guardians of the continent and pledge their mutual help in fighting the common threat. In that sense—and thanks to Roosevelt's Good Neighbor Policy—one could say that the Monroe Doctrine has become *multilateral*. On the other hand, it could be argued—more logically—that that doctrine has ceased to exist, since the nature and scope of this new *multilateral* declaration now render Monroe's completely useless and outmoded even in its only aspect acceptable to Latin Americans: its well-intentioned—but platonic—opposition to European intervention.

Rio de Janeiro was designated as the seat of the next meeting of the Ministers of Foreign Affairs, the third; but it was ruled that thereafter the place of meeting should be determined by the Governing Board of the Pan American Union.

The *Third Meeting of Ministers of Foreign Affairs* met in Rio de Janeiro from January 15 to 28, 1942. This time the United States was at war. An American republic had been treacherously attacked. The declaration of reciprocal assistance and cooperation adopted in the previous meeting of Habana, was at a test. On December 9, 1941, the Minister of Foreign Affairs of Chile, and on the following day the Government of the United States, had addressed communications to the Pan American Union asking for the meeting in Rio. The

[21] See Chap. VII.

Chilean note based the request for consultation on the fact that "unjustified aggression against the United States by a non-American power" had taken place. It emphasized also that "pursuant to Resolutions XV and XVII" adopted by the Habana meeting, the request of Chile was well founded. It certainly was. The American note read in part: "The American Republics, at the Inter-American Conferences held in Buenos Aires, Lima, Panama, and Habana have jointly recognized that a threat to the peace, security, or territorial integrity of any American Republic is of common concern to all. . . . On December 7, 1941, without warning or notice, and during the course of negotiations entered into in good faith by the Government of the United States for the purpose of maintaining peace, territory of the United States was treacherously attacked by armed forces of the Japanese Empire. . . . The wave of aggression has now broken upon the shores of the New World. In this situation that menaces the peace, the security and the future independence of the Western Hemisphere, a consultation of the Ministers of Foreign Affairs appears to be of urgent desirability." [22]

The principal object of the meeting was to adopt *unanimously* a Hemisphere policy in face of Nippo-Nazi-Fascist aggression. Colombia, Mexico, and Venezuela presented jointly a project which was *obligatory* in character and would have required the signatory governments to sever diplomatic relations with Japan, Germany, and Italy—the first mentioned for having attacked, and the other two for having declared war on, an American state. Most of the delegates were willing to accept this, but the representatives of Argentina and Chile "advocated modifications that would require such action only with the approval of the respective constitutional organs." [23] With a view to preserving the

[22] *Report of the Third Meeting of the Ministers of Foreign Affairs of the American Republics, Rio de Janeiro, January 15-28, 1942* (Washington: Pan American Union, 1942), p. 2.
[23] *Ibid.*

principle of unanimity, characteristic of Pan Americanism, it therefore became necessary to find a formula that would meet with the approval of all the governments. Thus, thanks in great part to the serenity of Under Secretary of State Welles, United States representative at the meeting, the principle of unanimity was saved, in spite of the gravity of the hour, and in spite of the clearly contractual character of the Habana declaration of solidarity in the face of non-American aggression. Only time will tell whether, in order to save unanimity, it was wise to sacrifice the Habana declaration, signed even by the delegates of the two sister republics later unwilling to approve the breaking of diplomatic relations with non-American aggressors.

The resolution finally and *unanimously* approved merely stated that "the American Republics, in accordance with the procedure established by their own laws and in conformity with the position and circumstances obtaining in each country in the existing continental conflict, recommend the breaking of their diplomatic relations with Japan, Germany and Italy." [24]

It was generally acknowledged that Secretary of State Padilla from Mexico was the man of the Conference. In his address at the opening meeting, January 15, 1942, the tall, dignified and brilliant orator said, amidst thunderous applause: "It was not only an attack on the United States, on an American nation; it is an onset by a totalitarian power against the whole of America! The men who gloriously fell on Wake Island and in the Philippines . . . have not fallen in the defense of the honor and sovereignty of the United States alone. They have also met their death in the defense of human liberties and the free destinies of these Americas."

So ends, for a while, the first cycle of genuinely *Pan* American gatherings, *all* of them, significantly, held during President Roosevelt's administration. Any one of the six means

[24] *Ibid.,* p. 8.

more to the history of our Hemisphere than all the other six held from 1889 to 1933, during nearly half a century of thwarted blah-blah Pan Americanism. The Good Neighbor Policy had been put to test. Montevideo (1933), Buenos Aires (1936), Lima (1938), Panama (1939), Habana (1940), Rio de Janeiro (1942), all sound like so many victories, won by the American republics in their battle for Pan Americanism. Simón Bolívar had been vindicated. Could his portentous voice reach us today, it would declare, "Well done, fellow Americans!"

Today, for the first time in the history of the Western Hemisphere, we of Latin America may confidently clasp the open hand extended us by a President of the United States.

CHAPTER X

Trade for Democracy

THE Latin American republics won their territorial independence not long after the United States. Later on, like Mexico under Juárez, some gained political separation from the Church. But, unlike the United States, they have yet to win their vital struggle for economic emancipation. This does not mean that Latin America must fight United States capital. The intelligent cooperation of that capital is needed to build up the national economies of some twenty Hemisphere republics. Moreover, for their participation in this continental task, United States investors will be not only morally but financially rewarded. We do need capital—but an entirely different type of capital.

With its main sources of income virtually all under foreign ownership, and under the control of a very few people, Latin America is seriously handicapped in creating national wealth. For, contrary to the contention of the interested parties, foreign monopoly investments do not help the development of a country. Rather, they hinder it by the very nature of their purpose, which is the artificial control of prices in order to insure high and steady returns to distant speculators for whom countries are not nations inhabited by human beings, but mere commodities. The stockholders at home, not the native workers or the native population, thousands of miles away, are the principal concern of powerful foreign monopolies with large investments in Latin America.

"So far Latin Americans have not had the capital to develop their resources," writes Mrs. Raushenbush. "Billions of dollars from Europe and the United States have been poured into their countries. But the profits were taken out. In recent years several Latin American nations decided to keep more of the nation's wealth at home." [1] That is clear. Assistant Secretary of State A. A. Berle, Jr., is perhaps even clearer when he gives the following concrete example: "Where an entire enterprise is in the hands, say of Chileans, and it sells its product overseas, Chile, through her nationals, has the full price of that product to use for imports to meet Chilean needs. In other words, she gets the full advantage of the product in, let us say, dollars, when sales are made here; and these dollars are substantially all used by Chileans to buy, for Chileans, what Chileans need and want. But when a Chilean enterprise is owned entirely by Americans, the product is developed in Chile, and once exported, is converted into dollars which remain in the treasury of the American corporation, and are held in New York. Only that proportion of them which is needed for actual running expenses in Chile finds its way back to take care of Chilean needs. *Consequently, the foreign ownership of natural resources in Latin American countries operates as a net deduction from the proceeds of Latin American products which can be used to satisfy Latin American needs.*" [2] That is precisely the point: investments for exploitation operate as a net deduction. They do not add anything to the wealth of the exploited country. They subtract something from it. More so, they are a constant source of economic and therefore political instability. "If development of any country is due principally to a flow of capital, and if that capital is attracted by high return, but wishes the privilege of swift

[1] Joan Raushenbush, *Look at Latin America.* (New York: Foreign Policy Association, Headline Books, 1940), p. 24.

[2] A. A. Berle, Jr., "Peace Without Empire," *Survey Graphic,* Vol. XXX, p. 106 (March, 1941).

withdrawal whenever there is danger, doubt, or fear, then the development will be halting and insufficient, and the economic life of any country involved may be shaken at any time." [3]

Capital for exploitation, as it is found in Latin America, generally takes one of the following forms: (a) concession, (b) monopoly, (c) tariff protection, (d) foreign loans. These are not healthy investments, but abuses. And yet one of the charges frequently leveled at Latin American governments is that they seem slow or even unwilling to pay the loans made to them. It should be said, in all honesty, that quite often these loans could never be repaid. Years ago, speaking of Mexico, President Woodrow Wilson said: "What Mexico needs more than anything else is financial support which will not involve the sale of her liberties and the enslavement of her people. I am speaking of a system and not uttering an indictment. The system by which Mexico has been financially assisted has in the past generally bound her hand and foot and left her in effect without a free government. It has almost in every instance deprived her people of the part they were entitled to play in the determination of their own destiny and development." [3a] Quite along that line, although much more recently, Mordecai Ezekiel wrote: "Incidentally, one of the reasons why South America has had difficulties in paying back previous loans has been that the interest and financing charges were often so heavy that *it would have been impossible for any industry in any country to pay back the loan, regardless of how effectively the money was used.*" [4]

Experience has taught us to fear absentee capitalism. We do not want great sums of money invested from distant for-

[3] *Ibid.*

[3a] Article by President Wilson appearing in *Ladies Home Journal*, October 1916.

[4] Mordecai Ezekiel, "Economic Relations Between the Americas," *International Conciliation* (Carnegie Endowment for International Peace), No. 367, Feb. 1941, p. 3.

eign markets by one powerful monopoly, but numerous small investments placed by people directly and personally interested in the country that will provide them with the means of living. We need people who, for instance, would come to Mexico with five, ten, or fifteen thousand dollars each, determined to make of their investment a human and not a market experience, a wholesome adventure involving not only their pocketbooks, but also their brains and their hearts. We want people willing to settle, learn the language, adjust themselves to the customs, and mingle in brotherly fashion with the native population. In short, we need and welcome an immigration with the moral qualities, the dynamic initiative, and the loyalty of the North American pioneers. Of course we need capital—but an understanding, cooperative capital, not for the *exploitation* of Latin America, but for its economic *development*. The era of exploitation is gone forever in this Hemisphere of Neighbors.

I do not believe in "reformed" capitalists; but I know there are plenty of intelligent ones. It is to them I make this appeal. In our countries they will find untold opportunities to show their enterprising genius. Money will be safe—because in the long run it is safe only when it is used fairly. In fact all rights, not only property rights, are safe only when they do not infringe on the rights of others.

The businessman of tomorrow either will understand that the era of exploitation has given way to that of cooperation, or will have to disappear. Quite often, men lose *all* because they insist on retaining *too much*. The people of the United States have shown exceptional flexibility. Not being overburdened with prejudices born of outmoded traditions, they have been able to adjust themselves to changing circumstances. Pan Americanism, if it means anything, is another turning point in American history. The price for it is domestic and inter-American democracy; not only the formal, theoretical, political democracy of our several constitutions, but the material, tangible, economic democracy in our peoples' way of living.

Intellectuals may spend leisurely hours interpreting the tenets of democracy; but when democracy is in danger, it is the people who do the fighting. And those who are willing to die for democracy should be allowed to live under it. United States investors must become fellow workers in the cause of Latin American democracy. They must not, they cannot, as in the past, consciously or unconsciously block the liberal policies proclaimed by domestic administrations determined to release the full potentialities of the heretofore inarticulate Latin American masses.

In a very keen analysis of "Inter-American Trade and Financial Problems," Eduardo Villaseñor, Director General of the Bank of Mexico, writes: "I think the future of the United States is irrevocably linked to that of Latin America. It is up to them whether they want to be linked to a poor Latin America or a rich Latin America." A sound businessman will agree with Villaseñor that there is only one possible choice. A rich client is always a better client. This is precisely what Professor Watkins makes very plain when he states: "Permanent expansion of inter-American trade is not likely to be assured unless the United States, together with the governments of Central and South America, takes an active interest in the elevation of the standards of life for the great mass of Latin Americans." [5]

Some people will say that a Pan Americanism resting on economic Hemisphere democracy is a dream which will never be realized. These skeptics are blind to the youth, the intelligence, and the purity that are characteristic of the man of America; the Man, for whom Secretary Padilla of Mexico has been the brilliant herald.

[5] Gordon S. Watkins, "The Impact of the War on the Economic Relations of the United States and Latin America," in *The Meaning of the War to the Americas* (Berkeley, Calif.: University of California Press, 1941), p. 81.

To systematic un-American pessimists I would say: A dream, yes, perhaps. But an American dream! And American dreams have made history. Because of that, we feel safe in predicting that this other American dream—of an integral Hemisphere democracy, based on the enjoyment of rights, economic as well as spiritual—will some day become a reality; and that, as such, this new American reality will shape the world of tomorrow.

If Pan Americanism is to be more than wishful thinking, it must rest on a plausible inter-American economy. I do not mean, by this, that business and trade considerations alone suffice to create international good will, but merely that, in the field of international relations as well as in the domestic field, economic situations are a necessary foundation for any policy. It is therefore pertinent to analyze at least some of the essential aspects presented by our Pan American—or rather Pan American*ist*—economy.

First, a rapid survey of Latin America's foreign trade reveals that our twenty-one republics cannot be considered as *one* unit, but rather form two distinct groups. On the one hand, those which sell at least half of their exports to the United States of America; on the other, those which do not. Considering the figures for 1937 (a normal prewar year) we find that only nine countries belong to the first group, eleven to the second.

Panama sells to the United States 90 per cent of its exports; Honduras, 89 per cent; Cuba, 81 per cent; Colombia and Guatemala, 64 per cent; El Salvador, 61 per cent; Mexico, 56 per cent; Nicaragua, 55 per cent; Costa Rica, nearly 50 per cent.

In the other group, we find, also by decreasing order of percentage, the following: Brazil, selling 36 per cent of its exports in United States markets; Dominican Republic, 35 per cent; Ecuador, 33 per cent; Haiti, 28 per cent; Peru, 22 per cent; Chile, 22 per cent; Venezuela, 14 per cent; Uruguay, 14 per cent; Argentina, 13 per cent; Paraguay, 8 per cent; Bolivia, 7 per cent.

In the light of these figures, Pan Americanism cannot mean the same thing for a country like Panama, which exports 90 per cent to the U.S.A. as for a country like Bolivia, which exports only 7 per cent of its products to the U.S.A. Anyone would admit that, in strict business sense, a client who buys 90 per cent of the goods is more precious than a client who buys only 7 per cent. You must try to keep the first, whereas you can afford to lose the second.

Export figures become particularly significant when you deal with the Latin American Republics, because a substantial percentage of their total annual production is sold not in domestic, but in foreign, markets. The United States export trade takes less than 10 per cent of the total production; while Latin American countries export from one-third to one-half of their commodity output; and in some the ratio rises as high as 70 to 80 per cent.[6] Writes Professor Watkins: "In Chile, Colombia, and Venezuela about nine-tenths or more of all mineral production is exported, and in Peru about three-fourths. Most agricultural exporting countries, such as Brazil and Colombia, export about one-half of their farm output. The Argentine exports two-thirds of its crops and three-fourths of its livestock, and Cuba, with its intensive sugar production, exports more than three-fourths of her farm produce."[7] Eliminate, as the war has done, European trade and markets, and you will see that raw materials worth something like five hundred million dollars, nearly 30 per cent of Latin America's total yearly output, find *no* markets. I shall quote from another source a few figures which will show perhaps more vividly the plight of Latin American trade in the world at war.

Let us take some chief agricultural exports of the repub-

[6] *Ibid.*, pp. 50-86.
[7] *Ibid.*, p. 64.

lics to the south: 93 per cent of Latin America's meat (almost all from Argentina) went to Europe before the war. To Europe went also: 86 per cent of Latin America's corn (also mainly from Argentina), 85 per cent of the cereals (more than half from Argentina), 74 per cent of the cotton (mostly from Brazil), 73 per cent of the wool (half of it from Argentina), 64 per cent of the linseed (almost all from Argentina), and 66 per cent of the hides and skins (exactly half from Argentina). Among Latin America's chief agricultural exports those bought by the United States are: bananas (79 per cent of which are sold in United States markets), from Colombia and Central America; sugar (72 per cent of which is bought by the United States), mostly from Cuba; cacao (67 per cent), mostly from Brazil; and coffee (57 per cent), also mostly from Brazil.[8]

This is not the worst. Not only does the trade of Latin America depend upon *foreign* rather than national markets (in contrast to the United States and, even more so, to Soviet Russia), but, in too many cases, their exports consist of *one* or *two* products; they are *one*-commodity exports.

For instance, 91.9 per cent of Guatemala's exports are coffee and bananas; 90.5 per cent of Venezuela's, oil and its by-products; 86.9 per cent of El Salvador's, coffee; 78.9 per cent of Bolivia's, tin and silver; 78 per cent of Cuba's, sugar; 76.4 per cent of Costa Rica's, coffee and bananas; 74.3 per cent of Colombia's, coffee and oil; 73.6 per cent of Panama's, bananas. The other Latin American republics are in a better position since, with a more diversified production, their trade income does not depend exclusively upon the world price of *one* commodity. A country whose trade is predominantly *foreign,* and almost exclusively of *one* commodity, may be independent in name, but economically it is completely at the mercy of the market which buys that

[8] Joan Raushenbush, *Look at Latin America* (New York: Foreign Policy Association, Headline Books, 1940), p. 45.

specific commodity. And since, in most cases, that market is controlled by *one* monopoly the firm behind that monopoly holds in its hands the fate of that particular country.

These figures show that the economies of Latin America remain colonial to a large extent. Many other statistics confirm this. For instance, a comparative analysis of government revenues brings out the fact that import duties rather than income tax or any levies on commercial transactions, provide most of the national income of Latin American governments. A study made some years ago showed the following percentages of total ordinary revenue derived from customs and shipping duties: Argentina, 27 per cent; Brazil, 42 per cent; Bolivia, 41 per cent; Chile, 57 per cent; Colombia, 57 per cent; Ecuador, 46 per cent; Paraguay, 63 per cent; Peru, 28 per cent; Uruguay, 41 per cent; Venezuela, 51 per cent.[9]

Colombia, the Dominican Republic, and El Salvador obtain more than 40 per cent of the national revenue from import and export duties; Chile, Costa Rica, Guatemala, Haiti, and Paraguay, from 50 to 85 per cent; whereas, only 6 per cent of the United States government revenue comes from duties upon foreign trade and nearly 60 per cent of it from the income tax. So long as the Latin American republics remain in their primitive, agricultural stage of economic development, tariffs will constitute their main source of income—which was true of the United States for many years after its independence. And such trade barriers are a hindrance.

Latin American republics are still subject to primitive exploitation for the benefit of foreign monopolists. They are, to the latter, lands of raw material and cheap labor. It is, of course, to the selfish interest of these prosperous monopolists to maintain these primitive conditions of exploitation; but

[9] James S. Carson, "Tomorrow's Shape of Things in Latin America," *George Washington University Bulletin,* Jan., 1942, p. 54.

it is obviously not to the benefit of the millions of people to eke out a miserable existence in their own "rich" territories. The result of so untenable a situation is: quick and fantastic returns for foreign investors, but unbelievably low standards of living for the native populations.

The war has created, for the republics of the Hemisphere, the problem of disposing of *surplus products*. In normal times we buy from the United States substantially more than we sell. We pay for our United States imports partly with money obtained from European buyers. The war has closed European markets. What can we do about these agricultural surpluses? There are people who believe that the United States should buy *all* of Latin America's production. Thus, they think, our Hemisphere could become a closed system, an independent trade unit. It would be continental economic isolation. Could it be done? "In crude terms, it would cost the United States a maximum of $1,200,000,000 annually to underwrite Latin America's 1936–38 average exportable surplus sold outside the Western Hemisphere. If this had been done in 1938, the United States would have bought about 10,000,000 more bags of coffee, 700,000 tons of meat, at least 5,600,000 bags of sugar, 200,000 tons of wool, 1,500,000 bales of cotton, 200,000 tons of hides and skins, 1,950,000 tons of wheat, 2,737,000 tons of corn, and 900,000 tons of nitrates, as well as large quantities of other products, such as copper and petroleum, all in addition to normal imports and domestic supplies." [10] But even if it could be done—if the United States were in the position wisely or generously to dispose of *all* the Latin American production—would that be a convenient solution for Latin America? Frankly, I think not. It would be equivalent to putting all our eggs into one basket. We should then be entirely at the mercy of United States markets. First, we

[10] William T. Stone, *America's Choice Today* (New York: Foreign Policy Association, World Affairs Pamphlets, No. 9, July, 1940), p. 34.

fear that situation. Secondly, we do not want isolationism of any kind, whether national or continental. It would be unsound to organize our economies on the basis of war conditions. War is transitory; victory is near. There will be a Europe again; as a matter of fact there will always be a Europe. Inter-American cooperation must not exclude the participation of our Hemisphere in any world enterprise, whether cultural or economic.

Let us say more about the problem of exclusive inter-American trade. In a speech at Des Moines, Iowa, Earl N. Bressman, former Assistant Director of the Office of Foreign Agricultural Relations, United States Department of Agriculture, analyzed the possibilities of the United States buying more noncompetitive goods from Latin America. Dr. Bressman reminded his listeners that the United States at present imports each year from the American republics goods with an average value of approximately $200,000,000. Those goods are strictly noncompetitive as far as domestic agriculture is concerned. "This sum," he said, "might conceivably be *raised* to over $650,000,000 a year. If production in Latin America of certain tropical crops needed by the United States were expanded, this would give our Latin American neighbors almost $450,000,000 *more* purchasing power each year for industrial and manufactured goods and for temperate zone agricultural products of the Western Hemisphere. Here indeed lies the largest potential source of increased intra-Hemisphere consumption." Then Dr. Bressman mentioned some of these noncompetitive materials that might be produced in Latin America—rather than in any other continent—to satisfy United States needs. They are crude rubber; cinchona bark, from which quinine is made; abacá or Manila hemp, from which rope is made; rotenone-bearing plants, extremely valuable for insecticidal purposes; kapok, used for insulation; cocoa; tea; tapioca; certain types of vegetable and industrial oils; silks; and a number of tropical fruits and nuts. Most of these products are or could be produced in the Western Hemisphere. Some of them, he reminds us, are of American origin. Pouring $450,000,000 into the Latin American republics through the purchase of goods which the United States needs and buys from other continents, would certainly contribute toward building up an isolationist, Pan American economy. But, again, I question the soundness of adopting an emergency measure as a permanent solution.

To confirm the contention that trade reasons alone do not suffice to unite nations, it is pertinent to say a word on the trade of Latin American countries among themselves. That trade is practically *nonexistent;* and yet Latin America is always referred to as a solid, coherent block of nations. With the outstanding exception of Paraguay, all the Latin republics do many times more business with the U.S.A. than with any one of themselves. It does not hurt to make business among friends. Quite the contrary, it consolidates good relations. But a broad international political movement, especially one the size of the Hemisphere, with all the inherent historic complexities, certainly requires more than business grounds.

Only 5.7 per cent of Latin America's exports find a market in the Latin American republics, as contrasted to 34 per cent sold in the United States.[11] In the year 1938, last normal prewar year, Mexico, Guatemala, Panama, the Dominican Republic, Haiti, Colombia, and Venezuela sold less than 1 per cent of their exports to other Latin American countries; Cuba, only 1.6 per cent; Costa Rica, 2.6 per cent; Honduras, 3.9 per cent; Bolivia, 4.0 per cent; Chile, 4.6 per cent; Nicaragua, 5.4 per cent; Brazil, 6.3 per cent; El Salvador, 7.1 per cent; Argentina, 11.1 per cent; Uruguay, 14.1 per cent; Peru, 20.1 per cent; Ecuador, 22.9 per cent; and

[11] *Panamérica Comercial,* Vol. X, Nos. 4, 5, 6 (1941), published by Pan American Union, Washington, D.C.

landlocked Paraguay, 48.5 per cent. With the outstanding exception of Paraguay—which sold during 1928–30 an average of 92.5 per cent of its exports to Latin America alone—one may say that there is little or no international trade among the sister Latin republics.[12] Finally, better to illustrate this feature of Hemisphere trade, I will add that *less than one-half of 1 per cent* of the exports from any of the Latin American republics (except Panama with 0.55 per cent) goes to Mexico. Three Latin American republics sell *nothing at all* in Mexico. And Mexico's quota in Brazil's exports is only two hundred-thousandths of 1 per cent![13] Yet, who would doubt that, in the field of diplomacy and official relations, Mexico and Brazil are close sister Latin republics?

Another point which needs clarification is the relative unimportance of Latin America in total United States foreign trade. In the year ending August, 1941, total United States exports reached the sum of $4,190,000,000 which represents an increase of $177,000,000 over the previous year. Of this total almost 66 per cent went to the United Kingdom and Egypt, and only 18.7 per cent to Latin America.[14] During the same year, the second of the war, the United States increased its imports by 16 per cent. That meant some three billion dollars, the highest since 1936–37. Here again Great Britain provided the U.S.A. with 45 per cent of the total, whereas Latin America's contribution was only 28 per cent.

To understand the Hemisphere trade situation fully, it should also be said that, when World War II broke out in 1939, the United States stake in the trade of its neighbors was not only not decreasing but steadily increasing. Latin American trade with Germany was increasing in much larger

[12] *Panamérica Comercial*, Vol. X, No. 8 (Aug. 1941).

[13] C.T.A.L., *Situación de los países americanos en 1941* (México, D.F., México).

[14] "Comercio Exterior de los Estados Unidos en el Segundo Año de la Guerra," *Boletín de la Unión Panamericana*, May, 1942.

proportion; however, it was not at the expense of the United States but at that of Great Britain. To substantiate this interpretation, let us keep in mind that in 1913 the trade ratio of rival American and European great powers was as follows: of Latin American exports, the United States took 30.8 per cent. Germany 12.4 per cent, and the United Kingdom 21.2 per cent. World War I completely eliminated Germany; but a few years after Versailles, Germany began to take more and more products from Latin America, and Hitler's Reich was able to acquire 10.3 per cent of Latin America's goods in 1938, as compared to 31.5 per cent taken by the United States—more or less the same proportion as in 1913 —and 15.9 per cent by the United Kingdom—a substantial loss from the 1913 figures. In the field of imports, we find a similar situation: the U.S.A. and Germany not only holding their own but steadily improving their gains, and the United Kingdom steadily losing ground. In the year 1913 Latin American imports from the United States totaled 25 per cent, from Germany 16.6 per cent, and from the United Kingdom 24.4 per cent. The war cut Latin America off from German imports; but in 1929, when the United States ratio had gone up to 38.7 per cent, Germany had come back and provided 10.8 per cent, while the United Kingdom had gone down to 14.9 per cent (an absolute loss of more than 40 per cent). In 1938 the United States ratio had slightly diminished, to 35.8 per cent, but it was still over the 1913 figure by 10 points. The German quota had gone up to 17.1 per cent, even higher than in 1913. And the United Kingdom was still losing ground with a ratio of 12.2 per cent. In other words, on the eve of World War II the proportion of British exports to Latin America was exactly one-half that of 1913. It is evident that if World War II had not occurred and the trend shown here had continued, the United Kingdom would finally have been eliminated from the Latin American market; and in the resulting rivalry between Germany and the United States, the former would have had better chances to win, largely because of the barter-trade system adopted by the Nazi government. Over the free exchange followed by Great Britain and the United States, that system had the apparent but only immediate advantage of eliminating currency in all transactions. Latin American products were simply exchanged for products from Germany. Of course we had to take from Germany whatever we could get. Since no money was involved in the transaction, not only did it keep other countries out of the way in each specific instance, but it left the Latin American countries without money to buy anything else from other countries. Thus, in this commercial struggle among three powerful countries, the U.S.A., the United Kingdom, and Germany, we provided the battlefield. And we are still feeling the effects of that regrettable situation.

So, when it is not because of the more or less conscious policy of ruthless economic exploitation by big United States monopolistic investors, we have to suffer in our own territories the consequences of a traditional conflict of foreign rival business interests. It would be difficult to prevent the international rivalries between the United States and Europe; but United States investors must be reminded, as we have tried to do, that they could modify their policy for the mutual benefit of all concerned.

In his address before the Southern Commercial Congress at Mobile, Alabama, on October 27, 1913, President Woodrow Wilson, referring to Pan Americanism (to which, in spite of his Hemisphere policy, he was sincerely devoted), said that the future was "going to be very different for this Hemisphere than the past"; that the states lying to the south would be "drawn closer to us by innumerable ties" into a spiritual union, so that the opening of the Panama Canal would also open the world to "a commerce that she has not known before, a commerce of intelligence, of thought, and sympathy between North and South."

The states of Latin America, he said, were also going to see an emancipation from subordination to foreign enterprise, such as had resulted from the granting of "concessions" to foreign capitalists. The United States *ought to be the first to take part in assisting in that emancipation.* "Human rights, national integrity and opportunity as against material interests"—this, in the memorable words of the other great World War President, was the issue to be faced.[15]

All we ask is that United States businessmen and investors face it squarely. That they also, and not only their government, adopt an *economic* Good Neighbor Policy which will complement the other and be the foundation for a more cooperative democratic trade.

Many a sad experience has shown the disastrous consequences of not harmonizing trade and national policy. A country cannot safely tolerate the coexistence of autocracy in business and democracy in politics. The price of such paradox is chaos and conflict. This applies to foreign as well as domestic conditions. The case of United States trade with Japan is a good illustration.

In a sober, factual analysis of American trade relations with Japan, published a year before Pearl Harbor, by the American Academy of Political and Social Science, T. A. Bisson, specialist in Far Eastern affairs for the Foreign Policy Association, comes to the definite conclusion: "For nearly three years the United States has garnered the profits from war trade with an aggressor, even while it was condemning that aggressor for violation of mutually shared obligations. Throughout this period it has been the overwhelmingly greatest supplier of Japan, with the next largest proportion

[15] J. B. Moore, *The Principles of American Diplomacy* (New York: Harper & Brothers, 1918), pp. 398-400.

(roughly 30 per cent) being furnished by the British, French and Dutch empires combined. *The United States must therefore assume the major share of responsibility for arming Japan in the latter's assault on China."* [16] To prove this statement, Mr. Bisson analyzes in detail Japan's imports of war materials for the years 1937 and 1938. From the twenty items in his table—which includes even rubber—I single out the percentages of U. S. share corresponding to petroleum and products, metal-working machinery, scrap or old iron and steel, copper, aircraft and parts, automobiles, ferro-alloys, metals and alloys. Without these articles, Japan could not have waged war against China or prepared its treacherous attack on the U.S.A.

In *1937* the United States share in world exports of *war* material to Japan reads as follows: petroleum and products, 62.71 per cent; metal-working machinery, 69.53 per cent; scrap or old iron and steel, 88.01 per cent; copper, 95.18 per cent; aircraft and parts, 70.19 per cent; other iron and steel semimanufactures, 66.39 per cent; automobiles, parts, and accessories, 92.41 per cent; ferro-alloys, 79.53 per cent; metals and alloys, not elsewhere specified, 59.88 per cent.

In *1938* the United States share had generally increased: petroleum and products, 65.57 per cent; metal-working machinery, 67.09 per cent; scrap or old iron and steel, 90.39 per cent; copper, 90.89 per cent; aircraft and parts, 76.92 per cent; other iron and steel semimanufactures, 53.65 per cent; automobiles, parts, and accessories, 64.67 per cent; ferro-alloys, 82.71 per cent; metals and alloys, not elsewhere specified, 99.33 per cent.

Counting all items, not only those quoted above, Mr. Bisson calculates that the share of the United States in preparing Japan's war machine was *54.54 per cent* in 1937, and *56 per cent* in 1938. In fact, nearly 70 per cent of all United

[16] T. A. Bisson, "American Trade and Japanese Aggression," *Annals of the American Academy of Political and Social Science*, Sept., 1940, pp. 123-29.

States exports to Japan were classified as *"war materials."* They amounted to over $142,000,000 each year. The author is therefore wholly correct when he admits that "the scope of the United States' commercial relationship with Japan, both on the export and the import side, makes this country *a partner in Japanese aggression."* Or: "For nearly three years Japan has been engaged in an aggressive and destructive assault on China—with the overwhelming material support of the United States." [17] Those are sad truths indeed; but truths. They teach us the lesson that under no circumstances should blind or narrow property interests be allowed to run afoul of national interest.

In the case of Latin America, United States trade must not stand in the way of United States foreign policy; and —what is equally important—it must not stand in the way of Latin American democracy.

United States capital and trade, intelligently readjusted and if necessary officially guided, may yet become the most powerful allies of the democratic forces of this and the other Hemisphere.

[17] *Ibid.,* p. 128.

Part Three: EXTRA-*America*

CHAPTER XI

Monroe Faces Europe

BETWEEN Bolívar and Monroe there is a fundamental difference: a breach as wide as that between Don Quixote and Sancho Panza. The South American is by nature an incorrigible romantic, the North American a down-to-earth realist. The former thinks in terms of an entire continent, the latter's concern is in the legitimate, but necessarily narrow, interests of his own country.

Yet, idealistic as Bolívar's concept of Pan Americanism may have appeared in his time, it is today much nearer to us than Monroe's. By one of those paradoxes of history, Bolívar has become the realist. Practical as the Monroe Doctrine was at the time of its promulgation, the course of relations between the nations of North and South America has demonstrated that we have outgrown its obvious limitations. Under the leadership of Franklin D. Roosevelt, Pan Americanism is swiftly moving along lines traced by Bolívar and *not* by Monroe. A permanent international order, established on mutual obligations, was the essence of the great Liberator's prophetic vision. Monroe's plan, on the other hand, was concerned only with the security of the United States; that security, not unrealistically, resting upon its unchallenged supremacy over the Western Hemisphere. Contemporary Pan Americanism is becoming more and more a joint enterprise, seeking in a way to bring about the broad objectives of Monroe's policy with the realization that Monroe's implied isolationism is not adequate any more to meet the Axis threat to inter-American relations.

My purpose in analyzing the Monroe Doctrine [1] was exclusively to consider its effects on inter-American relations. But, because the famous Message of 1823 combined inextricably two distinct aspects of the international conduct of the United States, I cannot deal with its implications in the field of inter-American relations without also touching upon its significance in the field of European relations.

The United States began its life in stubborn isolationism; that is, except for the French Alliance of 1778, a fact too often forgotten.

No sooner had it gained independence than it became a thriving enterprise, steadily growing in territory, population, and wealth; expanding west and south, and again farther west and farther south; until, from the Great Lakes to the Rio Grande, from Atlantic to Pacific, it occupied the vast space in which move today some hundred and thirty million people responsible for the welfare of the strongest industrial commonwealth the world has ever known. In the course of its continental growth, the United States purchased territory, mostly from France; or wrested it by force, mostly from Mexico. And in so doing, it behaved no worse —but certainly *no better*—than any other imperialistic power under similar circumstances.

Besides, from 1867 (year of purchase of Alaska) to 1916 (purchase of the Virgin Islands) it built a colonial empire spreading over the Caribbean Sea, the Atlantic and the Pacific Ocean. Finally, at the same time, it engaged in the more or less prolonged military occupation of at least half a dozen smaller Latin American countries.

Yet, in spite of this national policy, decisively expansionist and imperialistic, the United States enveloped itself in a snug—and at the same time smug—isolationism, while insisting upon a policy of nonintervention on the part of European nations.

[1] See Chap. VII.

Isolationism is a policy whose roots go deep in American history. One year before independence, in 1775, Thomas Paine wrote: "Our plan is commerce, and that, well attended to, will secure us the peace and friendship of all Europe. . . . I challenge the warmest advocate for reconciliation to show a single advantage which this continent can reap by being connected with Great Britain. . . . But the injuries and disadvantages which we sustain by that connection are without number; and our duty to mankind at large, as well as to ourselves, instructs us to renounce the alliance; because any submission to, or dependence on, Great Britain, tends directly to involve this continent in European wars and quarrels, and set us at variance with nations who would otherwise seek our friendship, and against whom we have neither anger nor complaint. As Europe is our market for trade, we ought to form no partial connection with any part of it. It is the true interest of America to steer clear of European contentions, which she never can do, while, by her dependence on Britain, she is made the make-weight in the scale of British politics." [2] The Revolution was isolationist, yes. All wars of independence are isolationist movements *per se*. That is common sense.

Isolationism, however, survived Independence. John Adams was the arch isolationist. His was airtight isolationism. "The principle of foreign affairs which I then advocated," he wrote, ". . . was that we should make no treaties of Alliance with any European power; that we should consent to none but treaties of commerce; that we should separate ourselves, as far as possible and as long as possible, from all European politics and wars." [3] He went further, in 1781. He then suggested and expressed the hope that if the United States, disregarding his advice, should ever interfere in the

2 *The Great Works of Thomas Paine* (New York, 1866), p. 24.
3 *Works of John Adams,* ed. Charles Francis Adams (Boston, 1856), Vol. I, pp. 200-201.

broils of Europe, the powers of that continent would unite to fight that intervention. Said he: "It is obvious that all the powers of Europe will be continually manœuvring with us, to work us into their real or imaginary balance of power. They will all wish to make of us a make-weight candle, while they are weighing out their pounds. . . . But I think it ought to be our rule not to meddle; and that of all the powers of Europe, not to desire us, or perhaps, even to permit us, to interfere, if they can help it." [4] Here is *one* complete, consistent Monroeist in 1781, forty-two years before the doctrine! Most Monroeists, while insisting on the legitimacy of the doctrine in the Western Hemisphere, deny other continents the right of adopting a similar doctrine. At least John Adams was willing to grant to other continents the privileges he wanted for his own. Indeed, he was such a coherent isolationist that on one occasion he declared that it would "be the best thing we can do, to recall every Minister from Europe and send embassies only on special occasions." [5] That is quite clear. But the isolationist tradition does not spring from John Adams. Rather it rests on two other great names: Washington and Jefferson. It is therefore very important to know, with precision, the views of these famous leaders on this timely subject.

Were Washington and Jefferson "isolationists" in the strict sense of the word? Were they interpreted faithfully by the men who bitterly denounced the international policy of Franklin D. Roosevelt, on the ground of its being a dangerous departure from the traditional policy of the country? Would Washington and Jefferson—so often quoted by pre-Pearl Harbor noninterventionists—have joined the ranks of his "isolationist" opponents? My answer is: *Emphatically no!* Without the shadow of a doubt, *no!* In fact, if there is such a thing as logical reasoning, one may venture to predict,

[4] *Ibid.,* Vol. III, p. 316.
[5] *Ibid.,* Vol. VIII, p. 37.

without any great risk, that both the "father of his country" and the "author of the Declaration of Independence" would have enthusiastically endorsed President Roosevelt's policy of all-out aid to England and stanch opposition to Nazi imperialism.

One of the most frequently used arguments in favor of United States isolationism was the following extract from President George Washington's Farewell Address: "Europe has a set of primary interests, which to us have none, or a very remote relation. Hence she must be engaged in frequent controversies, the causes of which are essentially foreign to our concerns. Hence therefore it must be unwise in us to implicate ourselves by artificial ties in the ordinary vicissitudes of her politics, or the ordinary combinations and collisions of her friendships, or enmities. . . . Why forego the advantages of so peculiar a situation? Why quit our own to stand upon foreign ground? Why, by interweaving our destiny with that of any part of Europe, entangle our peace and prosperity in the toils of European ambition, rivalship, interest, humor, or caprice?"

Jefferson is the other great American most frequently quoted by isolationists in our time. Several examples, cited below, are typical of the justification for their position and their dependence upon Jefferson. In 1811, aware of the significance of the Wars of Independence then current in South America, Jefferson wrote: "But in whatever governments they will end, they will be American governments, no longer to be involved in the never ceasing broils of Europe. The European nations constitute a separate division of the globe; their localities make them a part of a distinct system; they have a set of interests of their own in which it is our business never to engage ourselves. America has a hemisphere to itself. It must have its separate system of interests which must not be subordinated to those of Europe. The insulated state in which Nature has placed the American continent, should so far avail that no spark of war kindled in the other quarters of the globe should be wafted across the wide oceans which separate us from them, and it will be so." [6]

In his Inaugural Address of March 4, 1801, Jefferson with the greatest of economy expressed what are commonly thought to be his isolationist views. At that time he said: "Peace, commerce, and honest friendship with all nations, entangling alliances with none."

It is the common view, and I believe a mistaken one, that Jefferson's isolationism and his doctrine of "the two spheres" excluded normal relations with Europe, other than commercial. From these expressions and George Washington's Farewell Address it is generally assumed that both men were unalterably opposed to a policy of intervention in European affairs. A more extensive reading of their works, plus an understanding of the events of that time, reveals that these statements were the expression of a wish, rather than the expression of a means to attain that goal.

Washington and Jefferson stood against permanent alliances and foreign entanglements. The former emphasized the "permanent"; the latter, the "foreign." But it is equally true that neither of these two enlightened patriots ever intended to commit their young country to *permanent isolationism*. For instance, in Washington's Farewell Address, in part quoted above, there is a most important intermediate paragraph—which traditional isolationists usually delete. It reads: "Our detached and distant situation invites and enables us to pursue a different course. If we remain one people under an efficient government, the period is not far off when we may defy material injury from external annoyance; when we may take such an attitude as will cause the neutrality we may any time resolve upon, to be scrupulously respected; when belligerent nations, under the impossibility of making acquisitions upon us, will not lightly hazard the

[6] Jefferson, *Works*, Vol. IX, p. 431.

of Europe to intermeddle with the affairs of our nations. It is to maintain our own principle, not to depart from it. And if, to facilitate this, we can effect a division in the body of the European powers, and draw over to our side its most powerful member, surely we should do it. But I am clearly of Mr. Canning's opinion, that it will prevent instead of provoking war. With Great Britain withdrawn from their scale and shifted into that of two continents, all Europe combined would not undertake such a war. For how would they propose to get at either enemy without superior fleets?" [7]

Comparable in importance only to Bolívar's hitherto un-published Memorandum of 1815—with which it has much ideological affinity—Jefferson's letter integrates, as does no other American document on the subject, the three domi-nant trends in its international policy: the isolationism of Washington, the noninterventionism of Monroe, and a cer-tain pragmatism concurrent throughout all American his-tory. In the light of present-day events the advocacy by Jeffer-son of the theory of Anglo-American interdependence in time of war appears, like much of his political thinking, to have been prescient. Franklin D. Roosevelt, in our time, has not only reaffirmed but, more important, put into action, Jefferson's policy.

Ex-President Madison's reply to Monroe's inquiry also favored a joint, Anglo-American statement and made the suggestion that the two countries not only issue a warning against intervention in the American Republics, but also in Spain and Greece. However, neither Monroe, Jefferson, nor Madison seem to have attached great importance to the fact that the proclamation should be made by the United States *alone,* and not jointly with Great Britain. It is to Secretary of State John Quincy Adams—generally pointed

[7] Quoted in John Holladay Latané, *From Isolation to Leadership* (New York: Doubleday, Page & Company, 1922), pp. 28-30.

out as the author of the historical Message—that the credit must go for Americanizing the Monroe Doctrine.

The President read his Message to Congress on December 2, 1823. What we call the Monroe Doctrine consists of two widely separated passages, comprising about two printed pages out of a total of thirteen.[8] Monroe alluded to discussions with Russia about its encroachment upon the northwest coast of the United States and proceeded to say: "The occasion has been judged proper for asserting . . . that the American continents, by the free and independent condition which they have assumed and maintain, are henceforth not to be considered as subjects for future colonization by any European powers." [9] Then after a seven-page interlude came the well-known passages which embody the essentials of the Doctrine: "The political system of the allied powers is essentially different . . . from that of America. . . . We owe it, therefore, to candor and to the amicable relations existing between the United States and those powers to declare that we should consider any attempt on their part to extend their system to any portion of this hemisphere as dangerous to our peace and safety. . . . With the existing colonies or dependencies of any European power we have not interfered and shall not interfere. But with the Governments who have declared their independence . . . we could not view any interposition for the purpose of oppressing them, or controlling in any other manner their destiny, by any European power in any other light than as the manifestation of an unfriendly disposition toward the United States." [10]

Truly, the occasion of Monroe's historical statement had been suggested by Great Britain; but whether or not Foreign Minister Canning had sent such a suggestion to Presi-

[8] Thomas A. Bailey, *Diplomatic History of the American People* (New York: F. S. Crofts & Co., 1941), pp. 185 ff.

[9] *Messages and Papers of the Presidents* (Washington, 1896), Vol. II, p. 209.

[10] *Messages and Papers of the Presidents* (Washington, 1896), Vol. II, pp. 218-19.

dent Monroe, through United States Minister Rush in London, and Secretary of State Adams in Washington, it is reasonable to assume that Monroe himself or any other American President would have, sooner or later, proclaimed a similar doctrine. It suited too well the interests of the United States. It was too embedded in American history, not to have been expressed by an astute American spokesman at some time during the life of the country. The fortunate thing for the United States is that, because of the tacit Anglo-American entente, and because of the unchallenged supremacy of the British fleet, the Monroe Doctrine, at the time of its proclamation, could not be lightly dismissed by any power. The second good thing for the United States was that after the proclamation of the doctrine, and for over a century, England remained the happy possessor of an unchallenged fleet. The third good thing for the United States was that British interests during that same period never inexorably clashed with those of America.

The interrelation between the Monroe Doctrine and the power of the British fleet cannot be overestimated. This fact has been fully recognized by many North American statesmen, beginning with John Quincy Adams, the very man credited with drafting the historical Message. "Safely sheltered behind Britain's 'stout wooden walls,' America could blow a 'republican blast' of defiance at all Europe," writes Bailey, summarizing Secretary Adams' stand on this point.[11] No one, however, has put it more clearly than Professor Latané: "Americans should not forget the fact that at any time during the past twenty years Great Britain could have settled all her outstanding difficulties with Germany by agreeing to sacrifice the Monroe Doctrine and give her rival a free hand in South America. In the face of such a combination our navy would have been of little avail." [12] In other words, Eng-

[11] *Op. cit.*, p. 184.
[12] Latané, *op. cit.*, p. 53.

land could have chosen to throw in her lot with Germany, thus nullifying the Monroe Doctrine at the expense of the United States.

But since the time the Monroe Doctrine was proclaimed, England has not changed her mind. Nor has the United States.

CHAPTER XII

Swastika Over the Acropolis

THE most powerful enemy of fascism is reason. As long as men are permitted to think freely, they will cling to democracy. Fascists know it.

Any attack against reason is a direct blow to democracy. That is why fascism attacks reason from all angles. It is no mere coincidence that so many eminent representatives of human intellect are ruthlessly persecuted. Einstein's name is in itself a whole indictment of fascism. There is no room in the same country for a Hitler and an Einstein. One or the other must leave. Einstein left because at the onset battles are won by brutal force. But reason ultimately prevails because no nation can live permanently without it.

Fascism is essentially *action*—a movement, not a philosophy. However, especially since their first spectacular triumph, fascism and nazism have tried to give their movements spiritual dignity and philosophical background. When doing so, they have always looked for support to doctrines and philosophies outspokenly anti-intellectualist: intuitionism, activism, vitalism, voluntarism, and even pragmatism. Nowhere have I found a single nazi or fascist "thinker" claiming to convince through logic alone. They know better. Not being able to use intelligent arguments, first they avoid them and secondly they systematically disparage reason, hoping to discredit the value of any reasonable conclusion. The springboard of fascism in any of its brands—whether *à la* Mussolini, *à la* Hitler, or *à la* Franco—is *psychological:* feeling, impulse of the lower type. The main ideological structure of democracy, on the contrary, is intellectual; democracy is logical. Fascism is fireworks, a maelstrom of instinct and passion. Intellectually, it is complete chaos. Democracy has a calm objective value. It is orderly and shows a sense of proportion. Democracy is a science. Fascism wants to be an art. In reality fascism is nothing but the art, exploited by a self-appointed "superman," of stirring up and using the masses in the pursuit of an esoteric Myth. Hitler or Mussolini—not to mention Franco—could have been equally successful as barkers, street peddlers, or county-fair magicians. Had these glamorous leaders been women, they would have been "strip teasers." I am serious when I say this. I mean that if they had to win men, they would choose to win them through sex rather than through anything else. Democracy is handicapped by its moral discipline. The difference between fascism and democracy is the difference between sex appeal and virtue. Those possessing the first seem to have an easier time, but their victory is always short-lived. Fascism, like prostitution, is the systematic exploitation of man's lower instincts.

There are still in this world a few people—of good faith, I assume—who are convinced that fascism and democracy may after all find a meeting ground. These are the people who believe in "appeasement" or "negotiated peace." Nothing could be more impossible. Democracy and fascism are like two trains moving in opposite directions, on the surface of a world infinitely flat. They cannot and will never meet. They are diametrically opposed, from whatever angle you wish to view them, economic or intellectual. Fascism means, in the first instance, the violent conquest of power by and for a handful of people who control the implements of production. Democracy, integral democracy, means the participation in government, through popular election, of a majority precisely determined to prevent that control by and for a few. Fascism is nothing but a ruthless adventure of an aggressive minority. Democracy is mainly the job of a peaceful majority. This is another of the apparent advantages of fascism. It is aggressive, it takes the initiative. Democracy waits and deliberates. It is no mere coincidence that fascism, whether of the Italian, German, or Spanish brand, was originally financed by a powerful combination of reactionary forces among which could always be found some notorious "big shot" of the financial world. The fact that among those "big shots" one or two have lately become alarmed at the misbehavior of their unruly protégé, Hitler, does not alter my statement.

Fascism is pessimistic. It rests on the assumption that the people are helpless. There is a hierarchy set up by nature, at the top of which sits one man, a leader. This omnipotent, glamorous, mystic creature sits at the top simply because he got there, and for no other reason. Hitler and Mussolini were self-appointed. (Franco of fascist Spain was pushed in by the two original Big Bullies.)

Democracy is optimistic. It assumes that men can take care of themselves. They are equally respectable and should be treated as such. Because there is a fair average of common sense among men, majority rule is considered to be the safest guide. The people *find* and *elect* their leader. The responsibility for the choice is theirs, and to them at all times the leader must give account.

Fascism is to the field of international relations what anarchism is to the field of individual relations. A fascist country behaves—I should say, misbehaves—in the concert of nations exactly as an anarchist would within a given nation. On one side, every nation for itself; on the other, every man for himself; both cases imply the survival of the fittest, without any intention to protect the weak. The latter is precisely the concern of democracy. In fascism, as in the world of gangsterism, the only sin is actual failure. As long as fascism wins battles, it keeps on going. Its tactics, however, did not grow directly from gangsterism. Syndicalism was the spring.

Mussolini acknowledges his deep debt of gratitude to syndicalism. From that dynamic movement he learned the technique of mass agitation. Mussolini tried syndicalism among the workers: it failed. He tried it against them: it succeeded. Philosophically speaking, anarchism, syndicalism, and fascism are one. People know a little about anarchism and each day more about fascism; but I think something should be said concerning syndicalism. When I say syndicalism, I have exclusively in mind the so-called "revolutionary" or "anarchist" brand, usually opposed to trade unionism or to "reformist," socialist syndicalism.

Trade unions are peaceful associations of workers, organized for the sole purpose of looking after their own economic interests. They are *neither political nor revolutionary*. Their purpose is limited. They recognize governmental authority and, on the whole, seem to be content with the prevailing economic system. With them the question is not "capitalism," or "class struggle," but rather harmony between capital and labor.

Unions belonging to reformist or political syndicalism present many of the features of trade unions, plus affiliation to a political party, usually moderate socialism of the Second International. These unions are definitely *political but not revolutionary*. Like the former they stand against violence, although they advocate strikes as a last resort. They believe in "class struggle," but they think that the wisest way to fight capitalism is through peaceful democratic means. Their general conduct is disciplined and outlined by the general policy of the party for which they stand, usually a labor, progressive, or socialist party.

The third type of unions—the anarchist kind—are *revolutionary but definitely not political*. More than that, they are *anti*political. They fight for the destruction of the state, of whatever kind it may be. According to them, society should be ruled not by a central political government, but by a plurality of loose economic units, the syndicates. They aim to replace government by a federation of independent unions. They advocate strikes, of course, not only as a last resort but as a *permanent* strategy; and they advocate violence as the only means to destroy the state. Mussolini was one of these "revolutionary socialists." On several occasions, he has acknowledged his debt of gratitude to Sorel, the doctrinaire of syndicalism, whom *Il Duce* calls "Master," and to whom he repeatedly has referred as the man to whom he owes the most in his revolutionary formation. Hitler was also in contact at one time with "revolutionary socialists."

Syndicalism contributed to fascism in several ways: first, by its violent *attacks on democracy;* secondly, by its emphasis on *violence;* thirdly, by its faith in *élites;* fourthly, by fomenting *division* in the ranks of organized labor; and fifthly, by *arousing public feeling* against labor.

The main objection to democracy was its *political* foundation. To an anarchist that is Sin Number One! To him, democracy is a costly bureaucratic institution invented and exploited by "intellectuals" and non-productive parasites called "politicians." You cannot fight democracy with words— it takes too long. Violence is the way. Strike! Strike constantly, to wreck the economic structure of the political state. The masterpiece of the famous doctrinaire of syndicalism, Georges Sorel, is significantly called *Reflections on Violence* (*Réflexions sur la violence*). People who do not believe in violence are cowards. There is no middle way. Intellectuals, politicians, law-abiding citizens and, in general, all democrats fall into that category. Only violent people should and will rule. Syndicalism, because of the constant practice of strikes, is a "School of Heroism." But even among workers (whom syndicalists call "producers" in opposition to the rest of the population, the "bourgeois") only a few, an aristocracy, are fit to make use of violence. These few, belonging to what syndicalism calls an "active minority" (*minorité agissante*), are the real leaders. They do not have to rely on a majority. Majorities are mediocre and passive. These revolutionary aristocrats—supermen of the Movement—will show the way during the battle; the masses will follow.

In Sorel, for instance, the socialist distinction between "capitalist" and "proletariat" has no Marxist meaning. This distinction, which is economic in the eyes of a socialist, becomes "moral" in the eyes of Sorel. For the latter, there are two kinds of people in this world: the "soft" and the "tough." The world belongs to the second. These are the "producers," the creators; the others, an inert population of bourgeois. If bourgeois—employers, big promoters—would become "tough," Sorel himself would have nothing but admiration for them. One can easily see how inspiring all this must have been to a young Mussolini or a young Hitler. But it is not all: syndicalism went further. Some of its most outstanding leaders became ardent advocates of the fascist forces in France, known then as "nationalists" (*à la* Barrès, or *à la* Maurras), and forerunners of the "king's henchmen" and other brands of contemporary French fascism. Some went so far as to move to Italy to act as advisers of Il Duce, and are now back in France collaborating with the Laval government. This is history, not interpretation.

Next, by inciting workers against trade unions, the labor movement, and all forms of political socialism, the anarcho-syndicalists actually divided and weakened the forces of organized labor.

Again, the invention of what Sorel called a Myth, an irrational legend to agitate mass feeling, was equally helpful to fascism. The Myth of syndicalism was *the* General Strike. The day it would happen, the whole nation would be paralyzed, and the state would have to surrender. Sorel himself recognized this to be a Myth, but a popular one loaded with emotion, a stirring appeal which could not fail to draw the mob. Sorel's strategical advice was thus twofold. First, find a Myth, a dazzling vision enveloped in a mystic halo. Then, crack the whip. The frenzied mob will follow.

Finally, because of its indiscriminate use of strikes, rash syndicalism aroused public feeling, first against *some* labor unions, then against *all* labor unions, and ultimately against *labor*. Law-abiding, God-fearing citizens, candid but indignant, became the unconscious tools of shrewd and powerful financial interests, only too happy to seize an opportunity to wave the banner of patriotism in their selfish, mercenary fight against labor.

So, the most precious contribution of syndicalism to fascism was its *tactics*. But, in the field of ideas, several other philosophies have also helped it by undermining reason, which is the stronghold of democracy and civilized society. Among such philosophies, I have mentioned intuitionism, vitalism, organicism, mobilism, nationalism, and to a great extent, pragmatism.

Sorel's master was Henri Bergson, the famous and brilliant theorist of intuition, also the idol of pragmatist William James. Growing syndicalism badly needed some sort of philosophical ground on which to stand. Sorel, and through him, Mussolini, clung desperately to Bergson's philosophy, hoping to find in it a spiritual justification for their revolutionary movements. Phrases like *"élan vital"* (vital force), *"national élan,"* or Hitler's *"Lebensraum"* (living space), often found in the contemporary lexicon of the Axis, are specific symptoms of Bergson's influence. When Bergson died, early in 1941, he was officially mourned by the fascist Vichy government. He was the first Jew to be offered exemption from a law forbidding Jews to hold educational posts in France, the exemption having been proffered, said the Vichy government, for his "literary and artistic services to the nation."

Bergson, however, declined the offer and in December, 1940, resigned as honorary professor of the Collège de France. The Minister of Education in Marshal Pétain's government, Jacques Chevalier, the most devoted and also the most famous of Bergson's disciples, declared upon the death of his "master and friend" that the philosopher was one of the "forerunners and builders of the reborn [sic] France."

No one has more carefully and more convincingly analyzed the influence of Bergson's philosophy on the anti-intellectual movements of Europe than Professor A. O. Lovejoy, one of the outstanding thinkers of America. He deals at some length with the subject in *Bergson and Romantic Evolutionism,*[1] *The Practical Tendencies of Bergsonism,*[2] and "Some Antecedents of the Philosophy of Bergson." [3]

I shall emphasize here only the fact that Bergson's philosophy offers the most impressive glorification of a vague, mystic intuition of life at the expense of the normal play of intelligence. For Bergson, there is only one reality: life, concrete, subjective, experienced life. Bergson's substance is psychological, not intellectual. He tried to prove, in some of the most alluring pages ever written in the French language, that intelligence is totally incapable of contacting life, although it may deal successfully with matter. The field of intelligence is space and nothing else. Intelligence deals efficiently only with matter, objects, geometry. It is appropriate to science. Science is dynamic but, unable to grasp life, it leads nowhere. The world of intuition is Time; not objective, mathematical time, but "concrete duration," psychological, subjective time. When, through that mysterious Bergsonian intuition, we actually feel the stream of duration, we establish contact with life. In other words, ultimate reality is psychological and definitely nonintellectual. As a matter

[1] Berkeley, Calif.: University of California Press, 1914.
[2] Johns Hopkins University.
[3] *Mind: A Quarterly Review of Psychology and Philosophy*, Vol. XXII, N.S., No. 88.

of fact, it is not even intelligible, nor does it have to be intelligent—all of which, in Bergson's mind, is a metaphysical asset. Not only intelligence but language, its most useful instrument, draws us away from life. That torrential blind force called life is unpredictable. Life acknowledges no determinism, it follows no prearranged plan. Sorel's syndicalism is referred to as the "Bergsonian Left Wing." It is a wing, but not a *left* one.

Vitalism emphasizes the hegemony of such blind force. If life is the only reality, it alone has all the rights. Nothing can stand in the way of the *"élan vital."* Try to stop it, and it will overrun you. If life follows any plan, we have no more chance to modify it than we have to prevent lightning from crossing the sky. The only thing to do is to follow that driving force. Hitler uses similar statements in *Mein Kampf,* only he calls "life" Nature. Vitalism is plain brutality, subtly glorified.

Organicism makes of every individual in society a helpless part of a gigantic body, an organism. The parts have no rights. Their only mission is to exist so that the organism may function. The organism is the State. The individual is nothing. In reality he does not exist, as an individual.

Since life is in perpetual motion, since there are no objective universal principles, *mobilism*—perpetual movement—becomes the law. This doctrine would be truly revolutionary if its aim were some scheme of radical organization; but mobilism has no definite goal. What matters is to keep on moving. The Swastika is a graphic symbol of such perpetual motion. Its very shape suggests movement. In what direction? The Leader, the aristocracy of Party initiates, will tell you. Your only task is to follow, to keep on moving. In such a blind rush, *heroism* is the only virtue. Heroes in war, Leaders in politics, Saints in religion, are the saviors of the masses. Never mind the principles. People do not follow principles. They follow individuals.

There is one steady trend in all these philosophies of force, and that is to strengthen *tradition*. Tradition, like a snowball, keeps on growing and rolling faster. Life is essentially traditionalist. Since you cannot go against tradition, you can never radically change society. To strengthen tradition is to work for nature, even if reason tells you otherwise.

Finally, all anti-intellectual philosophies welcome, of course, the philosophical dignity which *pragmatism* endeavors to bestow upon any movement that is successful. For a pragmatist, whatever works out is true. Success, not logical coherence, is the sole criterion of truth. Therefore, in this political philosophy, all successful conquerors are right. If they fail, they are wrong. Might is right. Victory alone makes truth.

The features that we have just emphasized are common to *all* philosophies that either have directly influenced fascist thinkers or can in one way or another justify fascism. They are not all found in a single philosophical system; but, I repeat, we can trace them all whenever exponents of fascism dare to give it a semblance of philosophical dignity.

Lastly, fascism and nazism (which is nothing but a German version of the former) present, together with *all* so-called "nationalist" movements, the following four general characteristics: first, they are against intellectualism; secondly, against democracy; thirdly, against "politicians"; and fourthly, against internationalism. We find definite proofs of this in the nazi Bible, *Mein Kampf*. This book will stand, in generations to come, as an appalling example of intellectual mediocrity and cynical shrewdness. I know of no more irrational book. Irrational, in the light of what I have already said; dangerous, because it appeals directly to prejudice and impulse. It is intended not to convince people but to arouse them.

Discussion is the instrument of democracy. But the moment people begin to discuss objectively, they must forego their personal feelings. The dialectic of objective reasoning leads to a logical, not necessarily a personal, conclusion. Discussion is therefore taboo in a fascist state.

The instrument of fascism and nazism is not discussion but *propaganda*. Play upon feeling! Warp the psychology of your audience! Never appeal to the intelligence of your listeners. Such is the advice given by Hitler. There are only a few intelligent people. Why bother with them? Propaganda must be *popular*. It must adapt its intellectual level to the receptive capacity of the least intelligent; that is, the most numerous. And Hitler goes further: he advises his followers to become less and less intellectual, as the size of the crowd increases. Since in times of struggle you must try to influence the whole nation, "you will never lower enough your intellectual level." "The receptive capacity of the masses is very limited and their intelligence is weak," we read in *Mein Kampf*. The people are too stupid to think, but fortunately they are never too weak to act. The good speaker is not the speaker who convinces but the one who stirs.

The leader must be fanatic and intolerant. Only fanatics can win. If you admit that your enemies may be right, you weaken your position. Only *you* are right. Herr Hitler claims that, along this line, we have much to learn from the tactics employed by the Catholic Church in its fight to propagate the faith. The Church, he says, never gives up a single syllable of its doctrines, even when they do not coincide with scientific truth. The strength of the Church is the intolerance of its dogma.

People who read *Mein Kampf* will learn also that Hitler, continuing on the subject of propaganda, advises his followers to speak in the evening, because then the listeners are more tired and therefore their intellectual resistance is weaker. The speaker must have no convictions of his own. He must guess the feelings of the audience and exploit them.

He receives from his listeners a continual orientation which allows him constantly to modify his speech. In that part of his book, Hitler unwillingly pays a sound compliment to Karl Marx and *Das Kapital.* "The book of Marx was not written for the masses but exclusively for intellectual leaders." But Karl Marx was a Jew, and in Hitler's eyes that settles him . . .

Not only must one speak at the end of the day, as mentioned above, but again one should copy the churches in utilizing the mystery of dim lights, candles, and incense. Thus, stir up not only the feelings but even the senses. Anything to handicap clear thinking. If this method does not work, then use sheer physical force to impose your argument.

Do not hesitate to eject from the audience any and every opponent. Those were the tactics followed by the Nazis when they started. Hitler mentions an incident in which members of the audience opposing his views were knocked out and expelled, under the direction of Parachutist Friend Hess, the "splendid Maurice," and other clowns of the nazi circus.

What has been said in this chapter is enough to show the intimate connection between irrationalism and fascism. The connection is so strong that the latter must rest on the former, just as surely as irrationalism leads to fascism. It is so obvious that such a scholar as Professor W. Y. Elliott writes that "the political products of the current revolt against rationalism are the most characteristic contributions of the period."[4] Another American professor of philosophy, explaining why the mob is susceptible to authoritarian fascism, describes in a colorful manner the psychological danger of nazi tactics. "There is always a great emotional release, a sliding off of the painful burden of personal responsibility, a great emotional uplift, an ecstasy in sinking one's

[4] Elliott, *The Pragmatic Revolt in Politics* (New York: The Macmillan Company, 1928), p. viii.

little, hesitating, doubting, painful self in the glorious welter of mass feeling, of getting into the current that carries one along effortlessly instead of trying to buffet against it when the band plays and the crowd marches in uniform. We see this phenomenon at conventions, parades of uniformed men, Shriners, Knights, Eagles, Elks, Moose; we see it running wild in mobs and even in religious gatherings, so that Christians fight at the Holy Sepulchre." [5]

The lesson that we have learned from fascism, and particularly from Mussolini and Hitler, is the technique of spectacular mass politics. If democracy wishes to meet triumphantly the challenge of such technique, it must expose the frauds of the magicians and throw light on all their tricks. Once a trick is explained, it loses its spell; and fortunately, in this case the tricks are so naïve that the task of exposing them becomes relatively facile.

A gangster may appear, at times, more exciting than an officer of the law. A gangster takes the initiative. He is reckless, even courageous. The officer who pursues him, at the risk of life, may lack appeal in the eyes of some people. He simply does his duty. People take his accomplishment as a matter of course. They are eager for thrills. But, on second thought, the chances are that they will boo the villain and cheer the hero. One cannot too long endure hysterical excitement. In the long run, reason prevails. It dissipates false values just as sunlight disperses darkness. The black-out of reason is always short-lived.

When the swastika was hoisted over the Acropolis, a philosophical sacrilege was consummated. The swastika is the flag of brutality; the Acropolis, the symbol of rationalism. Of the military triumphs of Hannibal, Attila, Genghis Khan, or even Napoleon, nothing remains save a feeling of horror. Of the intellectual contribution of Greek rationalism that

[5] Joseph A. Leighton, *Social Philosophies in Conflict* (New York: D. Appleton-Century Company, 1937), p. 6.

flourished under Pericles, the Olympian, five centuries before Christ, everything survives.

Swastika over the Acropolis is the symbol, the tragic symbol, of an unceasing struggle between beast and man, impulse and intelligence, might and truth. But no conqueror's boot is heavy enough to crush forever the classic spirit of Greece. There is no swastika large enough to hide forever the sun of reason that *was* the gift of Athens, *is* the hope of Democracy today, and *will be* the law of Mankind tomorrow. Centuries from now, only patient scholars will examine the forgotten pages of *Mein Kampf*. But, as long as men live, the best of them and in them will delight at the reading of Plato's Dialogues.

A single stone from the ruins of the Parthenon is more precious to mankind than all the dazzling monuments ever erected to the passing glory of any conqueror.

CHAPTER XIII

Meaning for Democracy

IF IT is true, as I firmly believe, that the strongest tie among the nations of America—North, Central, and South—is a common political belief, then any endeavor to clarify our concept of democracy will ultimately consolidate the whole structure of Pan Americanism.

Democracy is not a theory. It did not come out like a Mickey Mouse from the magic inkwell of a political scientist. It was not invented by scholars but created by the people. They made it with blood, sweat, and tears. It is their way of life. It was born and can only die, with them. The collective character of its origin is so manifest that no single man can claim to be the father of democracy, for the same reason that no individual is the father of truth. The life of democracy began when men first understood the dignity of labor. The slaves who rose against their masters, the serfs who rebelled against their lords, the bourgeois who challenged the aristocrats, the citizens who fought on the barricades, the workers on strike and in picket lines, the people who died fighting tyranny in the American, French, Mexican, and Russian revolutions, and more recently the millions who have fought barbarism on any of the world battlefields where Nippo-Nazi-Fascist hordes were halted: *they* made democracy. They fought and died for freedom and justice.

Also the countless victims of religious intolerance, the early Christians persecuted by pagan Roman emperors, as well as those murdered during centuries of terror by decision of the Holy Inquisition, and the victims of political persecutions, labor organizers, mobbed or lynched, and the martyrs of intellectual freedom hunted by Church and State because of their philosophical opinions: *they* also made Democracy. They struggled and died for freedom of thought. And Democracy means not only bread but freedom.

For some forty centuries of history, the struggle of man for democracy has been recorded. And whenever or wherever there have been masses of workers, voices for democracy must have been heard. Even those whose echo has not reached us were not lost, because they must have been heard by others. Whether the pariahs of India, the coolies of China, the slaves of Egypt and Greece, the proletarii of Rome, the serfs of the Middle Ages, the muzhiks of Russia, the peons of Latin America, or the share croppers of the United States: it is but one strenuous endless fight put up by the underdogs eager to find their place in the sun.

Freedom of speech, and of the press—the right to express our opinions in conversations in the streets, in speeches to gatherings and over the radio. Also freedom from unwarranted search and arrest—the right of any citizen to know the charges against him and to demand a speedy trial, so that he cannot be kept in jail merely because someone does not like him. These rights and the others in the historical Bill of Rights represent what is usually called "the American way of life." They are truly the United States' "heritage of freedom." They are also ours. We, of Latin America, have incorporated similar rights into most of our respective constitutions. Not only are these rights known to us, but we cherish them with like devotion. They are truly American, in the continental sense of the word. Like you, we of Latin America had to fight for them; and like you, we mean to keep them. For that reason, we stand ready to fight.

Life is perpetual motion; nothing remains static save death. Even our most essential possessions are constantly challenged by changing circumstances. If the daily enjoyment of our rights has rendered us so blind that we cannot see our shortcomings, or so soft that we have no courage to correct them, we deserve to lose all these essential rights.

Also let us remember that the problem of democracy is not geographical but historical; not local but universal. It acknowledges no frontiers. One either stands for democracy at home and abroad, or stands against it, also at home and abroad. The struggle today is between two diametrically opposed ways of life. The victory of one inexorably means the extinction of the other.

What has happened in Europe can happen anywhere—even in our America. As human beings, we are no worse and no better than any of the people now fighting in Europe. Under similar circumstances we should probably react alike. What matters, therefore, is not to think that we are miraculously different, but to take precautionary steps so that the circumstances that caused the debacle of democracy in Europe cannot develop among us.

Democracy failed in Europe, first, because only a few people received its benefits; and, secondly, because those who did actually enjoy those benefits did not want to pay the price.

Rights are precious, yes. Everybody loves them. Who would refuse personal advantages? But it is not enough to proclaim rights. We must at the same time provide a practical access to them. Rights have meaning only for people who actually can enjoy them. They become empty words to the people who have no access to them. If we want to preserve the Bill of Rights, we must endeavor to make these rights accessible to the greatest number of individuals. The larger the number of actual beneficiaries of democracy, the stronger democracy will stand.

Another point: when we say "democracy," most of the time we think exclusively of the Bill of Rights—that is to say, of personal advantages. Seldom do we have in mind the corresponding democratic duties.

The Declaration of the Rights of Man by the National Assembly of France had already asserted, "The exercise of the natural rights of every man has no other limits than those which are necessary to secure to every other man the free exercise of the same right" (Article IV). Commenting on this eighteenth century document which shaped the history of that period, Thomas Paine added: "While the Declaration of Rights was before the National Assembly, some of its members remarked, that if a Declaration of Rights was published, it should be accompanied by a Declaration of Duties. The observation discovered a mind that reflected, and it only erred by not reflecting far enough. *A Declaration of Rights is, by reciprocity, a Declaration of Duties also. Whatever is my right as a man, is also the right of another; and it becomes my duty to guarantee, as well as to possess.*" [1]

No political system can give you something for nothing. If it claims to do so, beware. It is either another Utopia or one more hoax. Rights can be summed up in this one word: liberty. The price of liberty is equality, economic justice. In a democracy, the constitution aims at reconciling the rights of the individual with the welfare of the community: liberty with equality. There lies the beauty but also the weakness of our type of democracy. Can those two, individual and society, harmonize their interests within a constitution?

So far, it is evident that the emphasis has been overwhelmingly placed on the easy side of democracy, the political one, the enjoyment of personal rights. It is time to shift that emphasis on the other side of democracy, the economic one, the side of social duties. The first could be called the human side of democracy; the second, the Christian one.

The more the benefits, the greater the obligations. When

[1] *The Living Thoughts of Tom Paine*, presented by John Dos Passos (New York: Longmans, Green & Co., 1940), p. 131.

we hear a selfish individualist shout like a spoiled kid, "I want my rights—I want my rights!" we should ask him point-blank: "What price are you paying for them? What have you done to deserve them?" To be born in a democratic country is not in itself sufficient merit to deserve for life the benefits of democracy. One does not inherit democracy, like a family name. One must prove worthy of it.

To be free! To think, speak, and pray as one pleases: that, in the mind of most people, is the meaning of Democracy. There is only one thing wrong with such widespread opinion: its excessive simplicity. Democracy means freedom, yes; but a certain kind of freedom. And it also means many other things; so many, in fact, that we find nowhere a comprehensive, and much less an exhaustive definition of it.

The word is ambiguous because it denotes a technique of government as well as a social ideal. Democracy is thus, to begin with, both a form and a content, a means and also an end. For example, one is a democrat if one believes in popular, representative government; or if one says that all men must share the common wealth; or, again, if one thinks that the workers are entitled to organize freely, bargain collectively, and strike.

Generally speaking, not only a discussion of democracy but any discussion of government leads up to these two fundamental questions: (a) *Who* governs? and (b) *For whom?* Monarchy, the republican form of government, and parliamentarism, are some answers to the first question; while despotism, plutocracy, and collectivism are, in the same manner, some answers to the second.

A democratic *form* of government, although a necessary condition, is not sufficient in itself to make of any nation a true democracy. It remains for the government democratically elected actually to work for the benefit of at least a majority of the citizens. On the other hand, neither an autocracy (government of *one* man) nor an aristocracy (government of a *few* men) that might claim to rule for the benefit of the collectivity, could properly be called a democracy. A true democracy must be so in form as well as in content. Both the means and the end must be democratic. Some people (the "liberals," for instance) seem to attach greater importance to the means—"formal" or "political" democracy; others (the "socialists," for instance) lay greater stress upon the ends —"social" or "economic" democracy. Plain orthodox democrats refuse to separate the one from the other. For them, only a democratic form of government can successfully carry out any kind of popular program.

When Abraham Lincoln in his famous Gettysburg address spoke of "government of the people, by the people, for the people," he coined a badly needed general definition of Democracy. In its conciseness, Lincoln's sentence finds only one rival: the French Revolution's "Liberty, Equality, Fraternity." These two maxims are, in reality, not rivals. They complement each other. "Government *of* the people, *by* the people, *for* the people" can be taken as a definition of democracy from the standpoint of the government; "Liberty, Equality, Fraternity," as a definition from the standpoint of the governed. Together they cover both the form and the content of democracy. Government *of* the people involves the principle of popular sovereignty; *by* the people, the technique of representative government; and *for* the people, the ideal advocated by a socially minded government. On the other hand, *Liberty, Equality,* and *Fraternity* stand as the essential benefits expected from that type of democratic government.

Government of the people deals with the problem of sovereignty. Government is power. Who gives that power? God, according to believers in absolute monarchy. For them, the "divine right of kings" is transmitted by law of heredity. Democracies oppose popular right to that so-called "divine right." They claim that power, political power, springs from and remains in the people. The people alone are sovereign. They delegate their inalienable sovereignty to a government which remains in power only as long as the people continue to support it, through popular suffrage. President Nicholas Murray Butler of Columbia University summarizes pertinently the popular feature of democratic government when he writes: "No government is democratic which does not spring from the people's will, and which is not answerable to the people in forms and ways that the people themselves have determined." [2]

Who are the people? Everybody in general and no one in particular. You and I and all our fellow citizens. And since your vote on election day counts only for one, like mine and everyone else's, it is generally claimed that, in a democracy, all men are considered equal. This is hotly contested by the enemies of democracy. They maintain that men are *not* equal; that they differ physically and intellectually; that there are and always will be among them fundamental differences; and that, therefore, one man's opinion cannot be so precious and cannot count the same as that of any other of his fellow citizens. Majority becomes here synonymous with mediocrity. It is not a quantity of men, a mere majority, which should rule; but men of quality, a natural élite. Assuming that, nothing prevents one from coming to the conclusion that in many cases the opinion of even *one* man, a "Leader"—*Duce* in Italian, *Führer* in German, *Caudillo* in Spanish—is far superior to that of the whole population put together. Never be the dupe of such criticism! On the surface, it looks correct; but it is misleading because it does not apply to the meaning of equality or majority rule as we understand them. The democratic statement that "all men are equal" does not imply that men are equal in physical strength, creative talent, or economic power, but simply that they are

[2] *True and False Democracy*, The Macmillan Company, New York, 1907, p. 36.

equal before the law. Political democracy deals exclusively with the legal equality of men; not with natural equality or any other. It gives all the citizens equal political rights. Of course that equality is not sufficient, but it is indispensable. Standing on practical, economic grounds, socialists may question the meaning and actual value of such an abstract equality; but even they wish to maintain it, once economic equality has been attained. Equality ultimately implies a faith in man; a faith in the possibilities of human nature. As John Dewey wrote: "Belief in the common man is a familiar article in the democratic creed. That belief is without basis and significance save as it means faith in the potentialities of human nature as that nature is exhibited in every human being, irrespective of race, color, sex, birth and family, of material or cultural wealth." And again: "The democratic faith in human equality is belief that every human being, independent of the quantity or range of his personal endowment, has the right to equal opportunity with every other person, for development of whatever gift he has. . . . Democracy is a way of personal life controlled not merely by faith in the capacity of human nature in general, but by faith in the capacity of human beings for intelligent judgment and action if proper conditions are furnished." [3]

Because it has faith in men, democracy is optimistic. It is mainly interested in the elements that bring men together, and it claims that, on important public issues, the chances are that men guided by plain common sense will agree. Fascism emphatically denies any kind of equality. This system, fundamentally pessimistic, is not concerned with similarities, but on the contrary tends to accentuate and exploit the differences that separate men. Democracy draws its strength from the good points of mankind; fascism, from the bad ones. The

[3] John Dewey, "Creative Democracy—the Task Before Us," *Washington Post*, Oct. 24, 1939. See also similar statement by Dewey in *John Dewey's Philosophy*, The Modern Library, New York, 1939, p. 402.

first stands on love and reason; the second, on hate and impulse.

When the citizens of a democracy do not agree, the opinion of the majority prevails. *Majority rule,* admitted by socialists, is also strongly decried by fascism. But majority rule, like equality, can also be properly defended if we understand what it actually means. In the very keen analysis written by Alexis de Tocqueville more than a hundred years ago, *Democracy in America,* this scholarly French aristocrat gives us a sound, practical argument in favor of majority rule. Says De Tocqueville: "Democratic laws generally tend to promote the welfare of the greatest possible number; for they emanate from a majority of the citizens, who are subject to error, *but who cannot have an interest opposed to their own advantage.* The laws of an aristocracy tend, on the contrary, to concentrate wealth and power in the hands of the minority, because an aristocracy, by its very nature, constitutes a minority. It may therefore be asserted, as a general proposition, that the purpose of a democracy in the conduct of its legislation, is useful to a greater number of citizens, than that of an aristocracy." He adds sarcastically, "This is, however, the sum total of its advantages." [4] But we can say that advantages like these would justify in themselves the system of democracy even if, as De Tocqueville and other critics have not failed to indicate, sometimes the men entrusted with the direction of public affairs and elected by the majority are not themselves superior in talent or otherwise. Sharing the same problems and feeling the same needs, these representatives cannot help reflecting the conditions of their constituents. What matters is not only personal capacity but also personal interest. Equality of political rights is a good thing because men do not vote only with their heads but also with their stomachs; and (a) one stomach deserves as much con-

[4] *Democracy in America,* transl. Henry Reeve (New York: George Dearborn & Co., 1838), pp. 218-19.

sideration as another, and (b) each stomach knows its own needs. Thus, not only does equality have an ethical *raison d'être;* it also stands on plain, common sense.

Government by the people implies a political principle, dealing mainly with the problem of representative government. Ideal democracy would be of the so-called "absolute" or "direct" type, which, as we know, the city state of Greece and to a certain extent the Roman republic and the republics of the Italian Renaissance practiced on a reduced scale. In those primitive types of democracy, the possession and the exercise of power were but one, for the simple reason that the number of citizens was extremely limited within the states; and that most of the few enjoying the privilege of citizenship resided in or near the political capital of the state. Those democracies failed when the state became larger and its problems became more and more technical and complex. Representative government then became indispensable. We must not feel sorry for the loss of the so-called "pure" democracies, because they were, in the best of cases, aristocratic and therefore inconsistent democracies. We must admit, however, that representative government created a new social danger: the "politician," who has been the target of attacks by all the enemies of democracy—anarchists, their affiliated syndicalists, and more recently, the fascists. You cannot have modern democracy without representatives; that is to say, without politicians. And, since "all politicians are crooked," according to the enemies of democracy, that system cannot be good. So runs the usual argument. Here again the criticism is not valid. Politicians are no better or worse than the citizens who elect them. Besides, the field of politics in a democracy is open to all the citizens. There are good and bad politicians, just as there are good and bad citizens. For the same reason that we believe in equality, popular suffrage, and majority rule, we remain optimistic concerning these representatives of the voters. De Tocqueville himself acknowledges that the interest of such popular representatives is identified and confounded with that of the majority of their fellow citizens. Says he: "They may frequently be faithless and frequently mistaken; but they will never systematically adopt a line of conduct opposed to the will of the majority; and it is impossible that they should give a dangerous or an exclusive tendency to the government." [5] Some representatives, once elected, may be tempted to yield to powerful pressure groups rather than to follow the popular aspiration of the voters, but dissatisfied and defrauded voters can at least remove their representatives in the next election, while they would not have the slightest chance to do so under a dictatorial form of government. Also, precisely because we deal in a democracy with a larger number of representatives, we take fewer chances of being helplessly ruled by a notorious scoundrel. Ideal democracy would be a government of *all* the citizens, by *all* the citizens. But since this cannot be, because of practical reasons, the government of a majority, by its freely elected representatives, readily seems more reasonable than the dictatorship of a man or that of a political aristocracy whose arbitrary policy is totally unpredictable and completely immune from any sort of popular check.

A parliamentary regime under a monarchy, as in England, is a partially democratic form of government. However, the republican system, because it is wholly integrated by representatives of the people, offers a more consistent type of democracy. This explains why, in the minds of many people and even in standard dictionaries, the words "republic" and "democracy" have the same signification. A republic is defined as a democratic form of government; but let us not forget that democracy is more than mere republican form. It means not only government of the people and by the people, but also *for* the people.

Government for the people, third and last part of Lincoln's

[5] *Ibid.,* p. 220.

definition, has become the criterion of a true democracy. It leads to the consideration of *collectivist* democracy, if we give the word "collectivist" its logical connotation—namely, the collectivity. When an autocrat governs for his own benefit, we call him a despot. When an aristocracy in power exercises that power for its own political benefit, we call it an oligarchy; and if it does so for its own economic interest, we call it a plutocracy. These designations take into consideration not the form of government but its content, its *purpose*. *Collectivist* or, if you prefer, *constitutional* democracy is a government of at least a majority, by elected representatives of the latter, and for the benefit of the collectivity: majority as well as minority. Our analysis of the major implications of Lincoln's historic sentence ends here. To analyze the *content* of democracy—political as well as economic—we have to look somewhere else. I suggested that, for that purpose, we consider the "Liberty, Equality, Fraternity" of the French Revolution. To analyze the benefits of democracy, we could find no better epigram.

Everyone loves Liberty; even dictators. The trouble with them is that they love it for themselves but deny it to others. *Liberty* is the fundamental aspiration of man. It is his essential characteristic. Men are men only when they are free. The whole process of history could be broadly defined as a world struggle to move from slavery to freedom. Any movement against freedom is therefore, as far as man is concerned, a sin against nature. To introduce more and more freedom into the world seems to be man's destiny.

The difficulty arises when we try to clarify our concept of freedom. Is freedom an absolute right? totally unrestricted by anything? Is it so precious that it can oppose and even deny equality? Liberty is associated with the individual; equality, with society. Liberty implies political rights; equality, economic duties. "Liberal" democrats lay stress on individual rights, while leftist democrats, or socialists, place their emphasis upon economic duties. The first consider that the best government is the least government. The others, on the contrary, render government responsible for everything that happens to society. The fight between liberty and equality, in our modern democracies, is only another phase of the fight between the individual and society since the dawn of history.

When speaking of democracy, most people have in mind *political* democracy, meaning an institution which insures civil freedom and the rights of the individual. The believers in this democracy principally consider the personal advantages—not the collective obligations—of democracy. For them, the role of the state becomes quite simple: the state is nothing, the individual everything. Here, the political business of the state is merely to maintain the existing economic order and to stay out of individual activities. The government becomes an indifferent umpire whose function, essentially negative, is to insure the free play of private initiative and guarantee the three well-known freedoms, of religion, thought, and speech.

Economic democracy can be defined, in general terms, as the reverse of that picture so dear to the right-wing, political democrats, to whom I have just referred. The economic, or left-wing, democrats lay definite stress on the collective benefits of democracy, rather than the personal advantages bestowed upon those who enjoy them under present economic conditions. For them the state becomes a dynamic agent, with a positive function to perform, actively concerned with the tangible welfare of the collectivity. Its principal aim is social justice, even at the temporary expense of personal rights and indivdual freedom.

Collectivist, or *constitutional,* democracy is more ambitious since it claims to benefit *all* the people, majority as well as minority. It is, I repeat, of the utmost importance that we all in America have a clear idea of constitutional democracy, because it is the *form* of government adopted in the United States as well as in all other nations of our continent. Popular suffrage, representative government, division of powers, and the system of checks and balances are the four pillars of that modern type of democracy. The terms are too well known to need more explanation. What is less clear is the *content,* the purpose of constitutional democracy.

It claims to harmonize both individual freedom and social justice. The result is a serious inner contradiction, an irritating conflict between two antagonistic forces within the same political framework. Right-wing democrats—especially the extreme type, the so-called "rugged individualists"—think at times, as orthodox anarchists would, that the world is made for them and for them alone. Whatever stands in the path of their personal initiative, even if socially justified, becomes to them abominable and even "unconstitutional." They keep on reminding the government that it should let them alone.

On the other hand, the left-wing or economic democrats, moving also within the framework of constitutional democracy, would rather sacrifice some individual rights when they stand in the way of popular demands. They, on the contrary, keep on reminding their government that it cannot sit still; that it has a social task to perform. Thus, between democrats of the right and democrats of the left—both supported by the *same* constitution—lies an abyss. Sometimes serious conflicts are avoided through open discussion, arbitration; in a word, through reason. Sometimes their solution is merely postponed. And again, at other times, violence breaks out and threatens, from either side, brutally to disrupt the complicated political structure of this all-embracing form of government.

The problem for all our democracies in America is then, ultimately, the following one: will a conciliatory type of democracy succeed in securing the normal life of society? If it fails, because of the intransigence of right-wing "political" democrats, as well as the impatience of left-wing "economic" democrats, then each one of the governments of our continent, as happened in Europe, will be faced soon or late with one of these two extreme alternatives: *fascism,* or *bolshevism* (not socialism). In other words, if democracy refuses to admit the socialistic implications which are inherent in it, then this recalcitrant patient will have to undergo a major surgical operation.

Last, but certainly not least, the French epigram enhances the value of *fraternity.* This word means more than "equality." Equality is a concept: it is objective; it involves an extrinsic relation among distinct, isolated individuals. Fraternity is a feeling. It is subjective, yet common to all. Equality comes from without; fraternity from within. Equals may remain indifferent to each other; brothers cannot. Fraternity means that all human beings, regardless of talent, power, sex, or race, not only consider themselves as *equal* but also feel *alike;* that they belong to their neighbors as these in turn belong to them. Equality gives the citizens dignity and requires of them mutual respect. Fraternity adds a certain warmth because it springs from love. It is the moral, Christian ground of democracy. Some hasty materialists may reject this "moral" ground on the assumption that political systems are nothing but economic superstructures. But you can always ask these intransigent doctrinaires: "Why then should economic injustice be eliminated?" And above all: "Why even those *not* affected personally by injustice, are at all interested in fighting against it?" The only answer is: Because it is fair. Thus, besides material and economic motives we find also a moral feeling. Socialists are not only logical but moral people. Those alone are without any moral feeling, those alone are complete materialists, who insist on closing their eyes, and on turning their backs to the evils of injustice. Those are the people who have no feeling of brotherhood among men.

In that respect, religion can become a most valuable auxiliary. Unfortunately it has not always been so. Too many "religious" people, and especially too many religious bodies, have systematically and selfishly ignored or opposed the traditional struggle of the underdogs to improve their living conditions. When the church opposes the fight for political and economic equality, it betrays its very essence and its noblest purpose. There is nothing in democracy that is irreconcilable with religion. On the contrary, true religion should be the moral ground of democracy. Few churchmen have understood it so well as the popular author of *The Soviet Power,* the Very Reverend Hewlett Johnson, Dean of Canterbury. His remarkable book is the best proof that even official Christendom is becoming more and more aware of the close affinity between the teachings of Christ and the economic tenets of integral democracy. If the two do not always coincide, it is because "our system lacks moral basis," as the Dean says; not that religion's purpose is any different from that of democracy. "To Him every man was of infinite worth and His goal for society was the creation of a community of all human beings, irrespective of color, sex, or race." [6] Little wonder that the eminent Dean laments a "fatal divergence between principles and practice of Christian people which is so damning to religion." [7] Nor can anyone dispute his statement that "the gap between Sunday, with its sermons on brotherhood, cooperation, seeking of others' good, and Monday, with its competitive rivalries, its veiled warfares, its concentration upon acquisition, its determination to build up one's own security, becomes so wide that many of the better men and women of today remain outside the churches altogether." [8] Those "better men and women" cannot be fooled. They

[6] Hewlett Johnson, *The Soviet Power* (New York: Modern Age Books, 1940), p. 41.

[7] *Ibid.,* p. xiii.

[8] *Ibid.*

know intuitively that true religion and true democracy are two manifestations of the same supreme Idea.

The ultimate meaning of democracy, like that of religion, is love. In 1938 Mussolini said: "We prefer to be feared rather than loved, and we care not if we are hated, because we have nothing but contempt for those that hate us." Hitler, Franco, or Japan's military leaders could very well undersign this shameful statement. That is the way of fascism. Democracy prefers to be loved. For that, if for no other reason, democracy will survive; because life itself would be destroyed if the forces of hate could permanently overcome the power of love. And democracy *is* love.

Only those intent upon beclouding the issue have vociferously claimed that socialism is the enemy of religion. But these are usually the same people who come out with the statement that fascism and socialism are but one thing—which would be equivalent to maintaining that capitalism and democracy are also one. Both contentions are false.

Nothing could be less alike, in fact more diametrically opposed, than socialism and fascism. On the other hand, there is no ground to proclaim the identity of capitalism and democracy. Truly enough, capitalism developed, after the industrial revolution, under democratic governments advocating economic liberalism. But, theoretically at least, nothing prevents us from conceiving a democratic form of government in which capitalism, as developed under liberal democracies, has ceased to exist. Capitalist democrats could at best try to prove that democracy and capitalism may work hand in hand, and that the one does not exclude the other. Socialists maintain that democracy—in the economic and not only in the political field—cannot tolerate unrestrained capitalism; and, since the two cannot live together, one of them must be thrown out. In order to save democracy they chose to throw out capitalism.

"To begin with," writes Walter Duranty,[9] "there is an absurd confusion in foreign minds between the genuine Socialism of the U.S.S.R. and the pseudo-Socialism, or more correctly War-Socialism, of Germany and Italy. Foreigners seem to think because Karl Marx demanded the possession and control of production and means of production for his Socialist State, that this was the beginning and end of Socialism. Theoretically, of course, it is true, but in practice the thing which distinguishes a real working Socialist system from a pseudo-Socialist system is the abolition of the power of money and the profit motive and of the possibility for any individual or group of individuals to gain surplus-value from the work of others. This and this alone is the true foundation of Socialism."

The people who insist on decrying socialism from the standpoint of democracy do not seem to be fully aware of democracy's meaning. But when, beyond that, some bluntly pretend that socialism and fascism are the same thing, they show alarming symptoms of intellectual blindness or, what is worse, of political perversity. It would be easier, although perhaps equally rash, to pretend that fascism and capitalism are also one.

The trouble with socialism, from an exclusively capitalistic viewpoint, is that it wants *too much* democracy. It wants democracy in business as well as politics; whereas fascism completely rejects the process of democracy in the fields both of politics and of business.

To be mistaken is only human; but deliberately to confuse other people's minds is criminal. The meaning of democracy is so clear that only those who refuse to see may keep on talking as if they did not understand.

[9] *I Write As I Please* (New York: Simon & Schuster, 1935), p. 338.

CHAPTER XIV

Our United Destiny

WERE it reasonable to simplify so grave an issue, one could say that, on the mighty stage of the Western Hemisphere, a drama is taking place. The first act—*Independence*—has already been played. The second—*Good Neighborliness*—is nearing its climax. The curtain will rise next on a third, dealing this time with the fate of *Inter-Americanism*. And, after an interlude which the gravity of the hour will undoubtedly cut short, our Hemisphere will have to play the final act in the organization of a civilized *World Order*. The analogy would be appropriate if it did not involve the risk of creating the dangerous illusion that we are mere spectators of, and not actors in, that drama. In the destiny of the Western Hemisphere, every man of America—North, Central, and South—plays a part.

Our first job was to secure freedom. It required years of hard fighting. We won, and that was the initial step in the direction of a common destiny. Freedom is the beginning of life. Only where we detect an evidence of initiative can we be sure that there is life: and initiative requires freedom. Not unlike the gods, we human beings are essentially creative —if not creators. The farmer who watches the growing of the seed he has planted, the dancer who traces in the air a fleeting yet immortal step, the scientist who discovers a formula that summarizes a universal law, the poet who finds the image that interprets his feeling, are happy because they create. And there is no creation without freedom.

Liberty has been so highly valued that some philosophers have seen in it the beginning and the end of all things. It has even been maintained that our mission is exclusively that of introducing freedom and indetermination into the world of matter. Let us not confuse the issue. Liberty is the foundation of life, but not the end. Unless it has a purpose, it remains incomplete. When allowed to ignore everything else, freedom for itself or for one's own sake leads to selfishness and anarchy. If we are to participate in a civilized community instead of living as happy savages, we must find means of coordinating and harmonizing the several individual freedoms. We are truly free only in so far as others are free. No real freedom can be irresponsible. Our neighbor's freedom is as precious as our own; unless we recognize it, our personal freedom is a liability to mankind. Let every member of a family, every continent of the earth, have the right to exercise its respective freedom without consideration for the freedom of others, and clashes will inevitably occur. From these clashes, only the strongest will emerge. The *survival of the fittest* has been called a Law of Nature. Perhaps it is; but even so it is not, it must not be, the Law of Man. Human law is natural law, *plus* man. Human law is an improvement on nature, or it is nothing. Yes, freedom is essential, but it is not enough.

We attained independence. But strong nations were left free to use their power, even in thwarting the freedom of weaker neighbors. Little wonder the century that followed independence was one of imperialism and deadly inter-American wars. It took years for us to understand that, in order to live decently, we needed something more than freedom. After becoming free, we had yet to become friends.

The second act corresponds to a longing for peace among good neighbors. The vision and the purity of Franklin Delano Roosevelt are, to a large extent, the main factors in this transition from freedom to friendship. The "Good Neighbor Policy," clearly stated and above all consistently maintained by the great American whose prominence can only be compared with that of Simón Bolívar, was the climax of this second act in the destiny of our Hemisphere. It succeeded, not only because Franklin D. Roosevelt was its brilliant star, but because it is a genuine expression of a popular feeling which can be found in the hearts of the great majority of United States citizens, regardless of their political affiliation. The Good Neighbor Policy is more than a government's pledge: it is a mandate from the people of the United States. To the skeptics who, north and south of the border, ask us *why* we believe in the Good Neighbor Policy, our answer is: "Because we believe in the American people." We have faith in America; and, since Franklin D. Roosevelt, this faith has not been broken.

The pages of history are crowded with glorious deeds of military leaders. But the example of a most powerful nation, spontaneously foregoing the advantages of its material might, in order to adopt a policy resting on the respect of the territorial, political, and economic integrity of twenty weaker neighbors—that example finds no parallel in history. The United States of America should not only be proud of the moral victory it has won, but be deeply satisfied with its practical results. The Good Neighbor Policy has won for the United States the esteem and cooperation of an entire Hemisphere. It does not require a retrospective prophet to see that, had such a policy as Yankee Imperialism or the Big Stick or Dollar Diplomacy inspired the conduct of the present Washington administration, there could not have been any demonstration of inter-American solidarity. Also, let us not forget, the Good Neighbor Policy was proclaimed in a year when the United States was in no international difficulty; when no one could reasonably foretell that, some ten years later, it would need the cooperation of Latin American countries, not only for Hemisphere protection but for its own safety.

Yes, this policy was needed and welcomed; but, just as independence was not sufficient, good neighborliness must not be the final act.

Inter-Americanism goes one step farther. It implies not only feelings, which are always somewhat vague, but specific commitments. It is a step in the direction of *inter*dependence. To be good neighbors is not enough. It could mean simply that we pledged ourselves to mind our own business and let our neighbors alone. Of course, even that was an improvement on the previous act. But Inter-Americanism wants more: it makes it impossible for any of us to ignore the fate of our neighbors. Still more: if something happens to these neighbors, it gives us specific instructions on what to do during the emergency. Inter-Americanism is thus a continental blow to disorderly laissez-faire internationalism. Rugged nationalism is as dead as "rugged individualism." Whether in the national or in the international field, human progress may be defined as the transition from the illusion of independence to the necessity of interdependence.

We are not alone. The world was not created for an individual, a nation, or a race. We share it in common, not only as free men and good neighbors but, in the Western Hemisphere at least, already as *partners* in a common undertaking. This undertaking is the democratization of a Hemisphere. Just as the aim of our domestic policy is the consolidation of a system that will allow as many people as possible to share the good things of life, so the aim of Hemisphere policy must be the consolidation of an inter-American democratic system that will assure our sister nations of the equal enjoyment of these good things. Thus, whether within or without our respective borders, the test of America lies in its ability to democratize life. Inter-Americanism is a joint enterprise, undertaken by partners with equal rights and mutual obligations—partners linked together by a pledge of loyalty. As such, Inter-Americanism becomes a continental training school in world organization. And this permits us, without making rash predictions, to foresee the act which must and will be the final one in the destiny of our Hemisphere.

This will be the act of America's international mission: the part that, as a united continent, it will play in the shaping of a world society. Contractual Inter-Americanism is an improvement on loose Good Neighborliness or mere Freedom. But we must have the courage to carry our experiment to its logical conclusion. Inter-Americanism leads to world organization. The history of America must not be circumscribed by geography. Precisely because it is a product of all races and all ideas, America has a greater obligation than any other continent to place itself entirely at the disposal of mankind. We of the Western Hemisphere have been the pioneers of cosmopolitanism and universality. We, more than any other continent, cannot escape this historic duty. Also, let us not fear that world-mindedness may diminish our national or continental characteristics. If we consider the structure of America, we can safely contend that, by being *world*-minded, we shall remain typically American.

That we are already determined to transform inter-Americanism into a more specific partnership for the cause of world democracy is made clear by such remarkable professions of faith as that of Vice President Henry A. Wallace, when he said in a recent memorable speech: "Those who write the peace must think of the whole world."

And, because this Hemisphere of ours already has demonstrated its capacity for thinking in world terms, we of the Americas fear not our coming rendezvous with Destiny.

Truly, too many people claim that any consideration of tomorrow must be proscribed until the fight is over and victory is won. I should be the last one to underestimate the positive value of action in the face of danger. I fully realize that the immediate aim of the war effort is and must be the actual defeat of our common enemy. But, on the other hand, I see no incompatibility between action for today and planning for tomorrow. On the contrary, it is evident that the best fighter is also he who knows best what he is fighting for. The clearer the issue, the more vigorous the fight. And today, one of the issues at stake is the establishment of a reasonable World Order.

Wars are like earthquakes, frightful, destructive. They create nothing; they add nothing to culture and civilization. However, because of their brutal impact upon life they awaken people to the necessity of consolidating peace, security, and happiness, at least for the future.

We are responsible for our present only in part. But we are wholly responsible for the future. We inherit conditions from the past, but *we* are the makers of tomorrow. Our children do not necessarily have to go through what we have lived. We must leave them a better world than we received; one in which, among other improvements, powerful but irresponsible nations can no more disturb the peace of others. And a necessary guarantee of international peace is international organization; not one brutally imposed upon the weak by the mighty, but an international order voluntarily adopted by all concerned.

We belong to mankind. We come and go, but mankind remains. Nations also belong to the world, for the same reason that individuals belong to the community. The general trend of progress goes from multiplicity to unity; from a plurality of selfish conflicting personal interests to a unity of purpose for the welfare of the collectivity; a unity in which, far from losing his originality, the individual finds a new source of enrichment. When we understand and love others we feel elated, not diminished.

Also, practical reasons move us to believe in union. Union is more efficient than isolationism. A union based on equal rights and mutual obligations is profitable to both the weak and the strong. To the weak it assures independence; to the strong, a healthful control. This control prevents the strong from succumbing to the temptation of abusing his power. And this is important because we have learned that no nation is big enough to achieve permanent prosperity through the ruthless disregard of the rights of its weaker neighbors. *Crime does not pay*, the popular North American saying, embodies a great truth, indeed.

In the light of all this, it may be said that the day has come when we must dedicate ourselves to the serious job of organizing the international life of our American Republics. To this task we are pledged by a common history. No other continent presents a more impressive record of labor in the field of international good will. America *is* the Continent of Confederation.

Long before the coming of the white man, we find this longing for union among the aboriginal American population: for instance, the Aztec Confederacy, and again, north of the Rio Grande, right after the Discovery, the Iroquois League of the Five Nations which spread its authority from the Hudson River to Lake Michigan and from the Potomac to the Ohio Rivers.

The same ideal prevailed among the English Colonies. No sooner had they been founded than, although unsuccessful, an attempt was made to unify Massachusetts Bay, New Plymouth, Connecticut, and New Haven in a confederation of the "United Colonies of New England." A century later the concept of union had broadened. In 1754 Benjamin Franklin's celebrated Albany Plan proposed a "General Government" over all the colonies. After Independence, first under the Articles of Confederation in 1778, then under the Federal Constitution of 1787, the same principles continued to take form.

Thus the United States of America offers the most successful example of the goodness of the spirit of confederation. Union is an American idea, American in the literal sense of the word. In the technique of Confederation no people have more historical experience.

In Latin America, Bolívar was the herald of confederation. For this idea he struggled, with sword and pen. Constitutions, Treaties of "Perpetual Union," plans for an all-American community were to him as familiar as battles. So deep was his conviction and so clear his vision that he is rightfully considered today not only as a pioneer of true Pan Americanism but also the pioneer of a League of Nations. Of all his endeavors in this direction, the Congress of Panama in 1826 remains the most spectacular. The Panama Congress may be cited as the early climax in the shaping of a united hemisphere. It is up to us to continue the job and to complete the building for which the great South American Liberator laid the foundation.

"Association," "Family," "League," "Union of American Republics": the designation matters little. The time is ripe for a modest *Permanent Committee of the United Nations of America.* This regional committee would itself be a section of a larger Assembly or *Committee of the United Nations of the World.* If the United States of America became a reality, there is no reason to reject the possibility that, perhaps sooner than we expect, the United Nations of America will also become a reality.

Our continental organization must not be conceived as competing with, or as opposed to, a world organization. On the contrary! We believe, in America, that by giving shape to the international life of our twenty-one republics, we are facilitating the higher task of organizing the international life of the world. Peace and order at home does not mean that we remain indifferent toward peace and order abroad. Just as there would be a Permanent Committee of United American Nations, there would also be similar Committees for the United Nations of Europe, Asia, and Africa.

The four Permanent Regional Committees—corresponding to America, Europe, Asia, and Africa, with continental capitals at easily accessible points—would periodically send a delegation of their representatives to a General Assembly of the "United Nations of the World" at Geneva. We must insist on the maintenance of regional—continental—groups of nations, because experience has taught us that a world organization is not apt to deal competently with all the intricate situations created in distant corners of the earth.

To a great extent, the apparent failure of the Geneva League of Nations can be attributed to its excessive jurisdiction. For instance, I think that a Regional Committee of Asiatic Nations could have dealt with the problem of the Japanese invasion of Manchuria more efficiently than did the League of Nations. For one thing, such a Regional Committee would have been in a better position to understand the problem and to find a practical solution. The same reason could apply to the case of Ethiopia, and all the others. Definitely, conflicts between American republics may be better understood by the other American nations. They should be the first to deal with such conflicts.

Again, this does not imply that we shall isolate ourselves from Europe or from any other continent. The world is a unit. Anything affecting one nation affects the others as well. But conflicts naturally are of more immediate concern to the nearest neighbors. Ultimately the World Assembly will deal with the case, but only after the Regional Committee has taken the first step.

The League of Nations did not fail nor is it dead. More than ever we realize its mission. We cannot conceive the world of today, much less the world of tomorrow, without the existence of the League or a similar body.

We of the Americas, by organizing our inter-American life, are contributing positively to the establishment of a democratic world government. We can offer to other continents a mass of historical experience, which was lacking to the intensely nationalistic makers of the first League of Nations.

The America of the "Good Neighbor Policy" is materializing the dream of Bolívar. Already it constitutes a powerful international force. This force must not be wasted. It will make itself felt, not only for the good of one hemisphere, but for the benefit of all mankind.

Union now? Yes, for the Americas! But not a selective union ruled by self-appointed leaders of democracy. An all-inclusive union, that will bring together in a regional pact all the nations of the Western Hemisphere so as to facilitate their contractual collaboration with the rest of the world. There is no reason why the set-up of a League of the Americas should not be drawn now. Victory is near. The beast has lost. Man rises, once more.

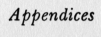

Appendices

Appendix A: Essential Figures

THE AMERICAN REPUBLICS

I. *Year of Independence*

1776	United States
1804	Haiti
1811	Paraguay, Venezuela
1816	Argentina
1818	Chile
1819	Colombia

1821	Mexico
	Central America (Costa Rica,
	   El Salvador, Guatemala,
	   Honduras, Nicaragua)
	Dominican Republic

1822	Brazil, Ecuador
1824	Peru
1825	Bolivia, Uruguay
1898	Cuba
1903	Panama

II. *Area*

Square miles

1.	United States	3,738,395	12. Uruguay	72,153
2.	Brazil	3,286,170	13. Nicaragua	57,143
3.	Argentina	1,079,965	14. Guatemala	48,290
4.	Mexico	758,258	15. Honduras	46,332
5.	Peru	504,300 *	16. Cuba	44,164
6.	Colombia	439,828	17. Panama	34,169
7.	Bolivia	419,470	18. Costa Rica	23,000
8.	Venezuela	352,170	19. Dominican Republic	19,325
9.	Chile	286,396	20. El Salvador	13,176
10.	Paraguay	169,266	21. Haiti	10,700
11.	Ecuador	99,170 *		

* Approximate (after 1942 settlement).

248

III. *Population*

1. United States	133,886,372 *	12. Haiti	3,000,000
2. Brazil	45,002,176	13. Ecuador	2,921,688
3. Mexico	19,848,322	14. Uruguay	2,122,628
4. Argentina	13,129,723	15. El Salvador	1,744,535
5. Colombia	8,701,816	16. Dominican Republic	1,655,779
6. Peru	6,762,881	17. Nicaragua	1,133,572
7. Chile	4,677,089	18. Honduras	1,038,061
8. Cuba	4,227,597	19. Paraguay	1,000,000
9. Venezuela	3,491,159	20. Costa Rica	639,197
10. Bolivia	3,457,000	21. Panama	573,351
11. Guatemala	3,284,269		

IV. *Capitals, with Population*

1. Buenos Aires	(Argentina)	2,345,221
2. Río de Janeiro	(Brazil)	1,896,998
3. México D. F.	(Mexico)	1,229,576
4. Santiago	(Chile)	829,830
5. Montevideo	(Uruguay)	703,518
6. Washington	(United States)	663,153
7. Habana	(Cuba)	568,913
8. Lima	(Peru)	450,000
9. Bogotá	(Colombia)	330,312
10. La Paz	(Bolivia)	250,000
11. Quito	(Ecuador)	215,921
12. Caracas	(Venezuela)	203,342
13. Guatemala City	(Guatemala)	166,456
14. Port-au-Prince	(Haiti)	125,000
15. Asunción	(Paraguay)	104,819
16. San Salvador	(El Salvador)	102,316
17. Panamá	(Panama)	82,827
18. San José	(Costa Rica)	78,883
19. Ciudad Trujillo	(Dominican Republic)	71,297
20. Managua	(Nicaragua)	70,000
21. Tegucigalpa	(Honduras)	40,000

V. *Density of Population*
Per square mile

1. Haiti	280.4	12. Nicaragua	19.8
2. El Salvador	132.4	13. Panama	16.8
3. Cuba	95.7	14. Chile	16.3
4. Dominican Republic	85.7	15. Peru	14.0 †
5. Guatemala	68.0	16. Brazil	13.7
6. United States	35.8	17. Argentina	12.2
7. Uruguay	29.4	18. Ecuador	10.0 †
8. Costa Rica	27.8	19. Venezuela	9.9
9. Mexico	26.2	20. Bolivia	8.2
10. Honduras	22.4	21. Paraguay	5.9
11. Colombia	19.8		

* Exclusive of Philippine Islands and military and naval services abroad.
† Approximate.

VI. *Foreign Trade, 1939*

(In thousands of U.S. dollars)

Imports		Exports	
1. United States	$2,276,099	1. United States	$3,123,343
2. Argentina	312,088	2. Argentina	393,293
3. Brazil	296,127	3. Brazil	333,674
4. Mexico	121,597	4. Venezuela	298,871
5. Cuba	105,862	5. Mexico	176,569
6. Colombia	104,819	6. Cuba	147,676
7. Venezuela	102,324	7. Chile	138,368
8. Chile	84,655	8. Colombia	101,169
9. Peru	48,088	9. Peru	71,707
10. Uruguay	32,649	10. Uruguay	50,632
11. Bolivia	25,754	11. Bolivia	34,613
12. Panama	20,464	12. Dominican Republic	18,643
13. Costa Rica	16,885	13. Guatemala	16,985
14. Guatemala	15,296	14. El Salvador	12,740
15. Dominican Republic	11,592	15. Ecuador	11,533
16. Ecuador	10,202	16. Honduras	9,867
17. Honduras	9,703	17. Paraguay	9,825
18. El Salvador	8,850	18. Costa Rica	9,086
19. Haiti	8,181	19. Nicaragua	8,301
20. Paraguay	7,822	20. Haiti	7,268
21. Nicaragua	6,365	21. Panama *	6,826

* Includes reexports.

(Source: *Latin American Foreign Trade, A General Survey,* The Pan American Union, Washington, D.., 1942.)

Appendix B: Essential Books

A FEW OF THE MANY BOOKS PUBLISHED IN ENGLISH ON THE GENERAL SUBJECT OF INTER-AMERICAN RELATIONS.

Aikman, D., *The All-American Front*. New York: Doubleday, 1940. 344 pp.

Álvarez, A., *The Monroe Doctrine*. New York: Oxford University Press, 1924. 537 pp.

Beals, C., *Pan America*. Boston: Houghton, 1940. 545 pp.

Bolton, H. E., *History of the Americas: A Syllabus with Maps*. Boston: Ginn, new ed., 1935. 365 pp.

Chapman, C. E., *Hispanic America, Colonial and Republican*. New York: Macmillan, 1937–38. 2 vols. in 1, 405 + 463 pp.

Childs, Marquis W., and Stone, William T., *Toward a Dynamic America: The Challenge of a Changing World*. New York: Foreign Policy Association, Headline Books, 1941. 95 pp.

Duggan, Stephen, *The Two Americas: An Interpretation*. New York: Scribner, 1934. 277 pp.

Fernández Artucio, H., *Nazi Underground in South America*. New York: Farrar, 1942. 311 pp.

Foreman, C., *and* Raushenbush, J. B., *Total Defense*. New York: Doubleday, 1940. 256 leaves.

Frank, Waldo, *America Hispana: A Portrait and a Prospect*. New York: Scribner, 1931. 388 pp.

Goetz, D., *Neighbors to the South*. New York: Harcourt, 1941. 302 pp.

Gunther, J., *Inside Latin America*. New York: Harper, 1941. 498 pp.

Haring, C. H., *South America Looks at the United States*. New York: Macmillan, 1928. 243 pp.

Herring, H., *Good Neighbors*. New Haven: Yale University Press, 1941. 381 pp.

Hull, C., *Addresses and Statements . . . in Connection with His Trip to South America, 1933–1934, to Attend the Seventh International Conference.* Washington: Government Printing Office, 1935. 103 pp.

Inman, S. G., *Latin America: Its Place in World Life.* Chicago: Willett, 1937. 462 pp.

Inter-American Statistical Year Book, 1940. (In 4 languages.) New York: Macmillan, 1940. 612 pp.

James, P. E., *Latin America.* New York: Lothrop, 1942. 908 pp.

Kirkpatrick, F. A., *Latin America: A Brief History.* New York: Macmillan, 1939. 456 pp.

Latané, J. H., *A History of American Foreign Policy,* rev. and enl. by D. W. Wainhouse. New York: Doubleday, 1934. 862 pp.

Lockey, J. B., *Pan Americanism: Its Beginnings.* New York: Macmillan, 1926. 504 pp.

McCulloch, J. I. B., *A Challenge to the Americas.* New York: Foreign Policy Association, Headline Books, 1940. 64 pp.

Moore, D. R., *History of Latin America,* New York: Prentice, 1938. 826 pp.

Nerval, Gaston, *Autopsy of the Monroe Doctrine.* New York: Macmillan, 1934. 357 pp.

Perkins, D., *Hands Off: A History of the Monroe Doctrine.* Boston: Little, 1941. 455 pp.

Raushenbush, J., *Look at Latin America.* New York: Foreign Policy Association, Headline Books, 1940. 64 pp.

Rippy, J. F., *Historic Evolution of Latin America.* Crofts, 2nd ed., 1942. 582 pp.

—— *Latin America in World Politics.* New York: Crofts, 3rd ed., 1940. 303 pp.

Schurz, W. L., *Latin America: A Descriptive Survey.* New York: Dutton, 1941. 378 pp.

Statistical Activities of the American Nations, 1940. Washington: Inter-American Statistical Institute, 1941. 842 pp.

Tannenbaum, F., *Whither Latin America?* New York: Crowell, 1934. 185 pp.

Tomlinson, E., *New Roads to Riches in the Other Americas.* New York: Scribner, 1939. 438 pp.

United States Tariff Commission, *Latin America As a Source of Strategic and Other Essential Materials.* Washington: Government Printing Office, 1941. 397 pp.

Webster, H., *History of Latin America*. Boston: Heath, 3rd ed., 1941. 326 pp.

Wertenbaker, C., *A New Doctrine for the Americas*. New York: Viking, 1941. 211 pp.

Whitaker, A. P., *The United States and the Independence of Latin America, 1800–1830*. Baltimore: Johns Hopkins Press, 1941. 632 pp.

Whitaker, J. T., *Americas to the South*. New York: Macmillan, 1940. 300 pp.

Wilgus, A. C., *The Development of Hispanic America*. New York: Farrar, 1941. 941 pp.

—— and d'Eça, R., *Outline-History of Latin America*. New York: Barnes, rev. and enl. ed., 1941. 410 pp.

Williams, M. W., *The People and Politics of Latin America*. Boston: Ginn, new ed., 1938. 888 pp.

Ybarra, T. R., *America Faces South*. New York: Dodd, 1939. 321 pp.

Index

Adams, Charles Francis, quoted, 195
Adams, John, Isolationist views, 195-196
Adams, John Quincy, opinion on Pan Americanism, 93; invitation to Congress of Panama, 105; message to Congress (Mar. 15, 1826), 106; 115, 201
Alberdi, Juan Bautista, 36
Alvear, Carlos María de, 91, 97
America, North and South, 3; Anglo-Saxon and Latin, 3, 6; Eastern and Western, 4; Atlantic and Pacific, 4; Pan America, 4; Greater America, 4; a continent, 14; a history, 15; pre-Columbian civilizations, 16; settlers and conquistadores, 17; liberty, independence, freedom, 17-20; a culture, 20; a voice, 22; voices of America, 23, 24; opulent and indigent, 51; an American standard of life, 85-86; destiny of, 237; international mission of, 241
American men, Latin American conception of, 38-39
American Republics, international life of, 243
American way of life. See United States
American women, Latin American conception of, 39-40
Amlie, Rep. Thomas, quoted on distribution of wealth in U.S., 53-54; 65
Anderson, Richard C., U.S. Delegate, Congress of Panama, 105
Anderson, Wilhelm, quoted, 60
Appeasement, 206
Arbitration, adopted at Congress of Panama, 109; First Pan American Conference, 139; pecuniary claims, 141

Arciniegas, Germán, quoted on American Continent, 5
Argentina, white population, 7; 12, 27, 36, 37; land ownership, 76; wages, purchasing power, 79-82; illiteracy, 84; alliance with Chile, 92; with Colombia, 97; not represented at Congress of Panama, 108; appeal to Monroe Doctrine, 117; estranged from U.S. policy, 159; Anti-War Pact, 159; 160; attitude on Hemisphere war policy at Rio, 169; exports to U.S., 178-179; to Europe, 179; national revenue sources, 180; trade with other Latin American countries, 183
Argentine Anti-War Pact, 159
Art, Latin American, 36
Arthur, Chester A., succeeded Garfield as President, 132; attitude on Pan American Congress, 132-135
Artigas, José, 92
Asunción Silva, José, 36
Avila Camacho, Manuel, 22; quoted on condemnation of aggressors, 24

Bailey, Dr. Charles A., 75
Bailey, Thomas A., 154 n., 202 n.
Baker, Ray Stannard, quoted, 153
Batres y Montúfar, José de, 36
Bayard, Thomas Francis, Sec. of State, quoted, 124; invitations to Pan American Conference, 136; 137
Bello, Andrés, 36
Bergson, Henri, 22; his philosophy, 211-213
Berle, A. A., Jr., Assistant Sec. of State, 55; quoted on Latin American economic development, 173
Bilbao, Francisco, 8
Bill of Rights, 220, 221
Bisson, T. A., quoted, 188